D1252318

The
Economic
System

H. ROBERT HELLER

University of Hawaii

The Economic System

The Macmillan Company, New York
Collier-Macmillan Limited, London

HB
171.5
. H3924

Copyright © 1972, H. Robert Heller
Printed in the United States of America

All rights reserved. No part of this book may be reproduced or transmitted in any form or by any means,
electronic or mechanical, including photocopying, re-
cording, or any information storage and retrieval system,
without permission in writing from the Publisher.

330
H477

The Macmillan Company
866 Third Avenue
New York, New York 10022

Collier-Macmillan Canada, Ltd.
Toronto, Ontario

Library of Congress catalog card number: 72-163232
First Printing

to Ente

APR 3 1972

Preface

This book provides the student with a basic tool kit for the analysis of economic problems. Leaving aside institutional, historical, and descriptive detail, the emphasis is on analysis. The tools of economic analysis, often scattered and fragmented throughout voluminous textbooks, are presented in a succinct, clear, and comprehensive fashion. In the first half, the text studies the basic components of the economic system from a microeconomic viewpoint. In the second half, the interactions among these components and the aggregate implications of economic behavior are developed.

The Economic System may be used alone in a brief introductory course or be supplemented by a wide variety of outside readings that deepen the student's understanding of the analysis presented. In the modern ever-changing economy, new problems present themselves on a day-to-day and month-to-month basis. This book presents tools of analysis that are useful in attacking these current problems, and carefully selected outside readings offer maximum flexibility to adapt courses in principles of economics to changing challenges. *The Economic System* presents an analytical core around which a comprehensive course may be built.

The book benefited greatly from the detailed comments and suggestions of Professor Conrad P. Caligaris, of Northeastern University, as well as those of several generations of principles-of-economics students. I am grateful for all the suggestions received.

H. R. H.
Honolulu

Brief Contents

Contents

Contents

Contents

16

*The economic
system* 271

1

The economic problem

Science is the systematized knowledge of nature. It encompasses all of man's knowledge of the universe, derived by observation, study, and experimentation. To bring some order into the mass of accumulated knowledge, we generally distinguish between the physical sciences, the life sciences, and the social sciences. Further subgroupings are employed within these broad categories; in the social sciences we distinguish political science, sociology, psychology, and economics. Economics concentrates on three main areas of human endeavor: production, exchange, and consumption. It studies how limited resources are used for the production of commodities that are want-satisfying, how our resources are distributed, and how transactions are conducted.

The other social sciences probe different aspects of human behavior. Psychology studies the reasons why people behave as they do, sociology concentrates on man's interactions with other persons, political science involves the study of man's political behavior, and so on. Hence economics encompasses only a small fraction of the social sciences. It is a small subsystem, dealing with the economic behavior of people.

Systems and subsystems

Each one of the sciences creates its own system: a simplified model of the world, which its practitioners study. Once scientists have built such a system, they can analyze its working, study its component parts, and thereby derive an understanding of that area of our environment.

A system can be described as an arrangement of related components that form an organic whole. Each component of a system stands in a functional relationship to other components of the system. This functional relationship between any two components need not be a direct one, but may involve many complex linkages.

The analysis of a system involves several distinct tasks. First, we must gain an understanding of the component parts. How are the components made up? What is their basic mode of action? What are their characteristics? In physics we may study the structure of atoms, in chemistry molecules, in forestry trees, and in economics households and firms.

Second, we must analyze the functional relationships between the component parts of the system. Does one component influence other components? If so, how? And by how much? Again, in physics we study the interaction of different atoms, in chemistry complex organic structures, and in economics the interaction between households, firms, labor unions, and governments.

Third, we may look at the operation of the system as a whole. How does everything fit together? Is it a viable system? Is it stable? Will it tend to grow? The economist analyzes the manifestations of individual economic actions on the aggregate whole: inflation, unemployment, booms, and depressions are all phenomena that are the result of actions taken by individual economic units, but they manifest themselves as aggregate phenomena.

The study of the economy as one system involves many closely interconnected parts. To tackle this task all at once would surpass the abilities of the most diligent student. Hence it is necessary to further divide the economy into various subsystems. These subsystems can then be studied in detail and we can arrive at an understanding of their operation. But each time we isolate some component of the economic system for study, we are bound to neglect some interrelationships of this component to the rest of the economy. There is no easy way out of this dilemma. Either we look at one tree only and forget for a while about its relationship to the surrounding forest, or we look at the forest as one system without focusing direct attention on the component parts. Clearly, both approaches are legitimate endeavors and may be pursued fruitfully. In this book we will look both at individual economic units such as households, firms, and governments, and at the operation of the economic system as a whole.

The economist's endeavor, then, is to analyze and describe the economic systems. In this task it is often convenient to build theoretical models that are abstract generalizations of the "real" world. We deal in abstractions from reality because we must leave out much unnecessary detail. We try to isolate the important and essential features of economic behavior. By doing this, we necessarily simplify the complex observed relationship into a manageable package. Of course, the danger of leaving out an essential ingredient of economic behavior is always present, and we must guard against too high a level of abstraction. Economic analysis abstracts from or takes as given the philosophical, political, sociological, and psychological pressures and conditions that affect decisions and behavior.

Economic models are also generalizations, in that we attempt to fit one model to a large number of real world situations. By generalizing, we have to accept the possibility that certain exceptions to prevalent behavior patterns are not well represented in our model. Because economics, as a social science, deals with changing and diverse human behavior patterns, our generalizations may not be applicable to every situation at every moment in time. In other words, our models are subject to error. Good economic models, of course, are less error-prone than bad ones. And the careful economist may make a statement as to the reliability of his model. He might say that a certain model was found to give a correct representation of behavior in ninety-five out of one hundred cases or use some similar measure of reliability. But many generalizations in economics must be regarded as broad tendencies within some set of often unspecified conditions and institutions.

Economic models and economic policy

The process of developing and testing an economic model may be long and cumbersome. Seldom are models the result of a sudden brainstorm or even a dream. In most cases, the construction and the testing of a model involve hard work and long hours. But independent of how easy or difficult it may be to specify a model, its complete development always involves two crucial steps: one, the construction of an *economic theory*, and two, the *testing* or verification of the validity of that theory. A valid model, then, is a theory that has been successfully subjected to empirical testing. Such validated theories are useful to the economist because they enable us to explain economic phenomena and the consequences of policy changes. They may help us to find an answer to the question Why? We might wonder why some people cannot find employment, why inflation reduces the purchasing power of the dollar, or why the price of our favorite pizza has gone up. Economic models try to get at the underlying causes, help us to determine ultimate reasons, and enable us to take appropriate remedial action.

This brings us to the second function of economic models, namely to predict the consequences of changes in some economic variables on other variables. This predictive function of economics is important if we want to assess the effects of a change in the tax laws, the amount of money in circulation, or a strike, on other variables, such as inflation, unemployment, or the price of our pizza. If we are not able to predict accurately, we are unable to influence economic events in the desired fashion. Consequently, economists would be of little use to the politician, the president of a company, or a labor leader.

These people are concerned with the making of *economic policy:* the influencing of economic events by deliberately taken actions. Naturally, the making of economic policy involves choosing among various alternative outcomes. These possible outcomes can be analyzed with the help of our models. It is the task of the policy maker to choose from among the various outcomes the one that is the most desirable. This involves the application of value judgments as to the desirability of the alternatives open to us. In general, this is not the realm of the economist, whose task is analysis. Of course, some economists have involved themselves in economic policy making by suggestions or direct participation in the policy-making process. But like all humans they have different values and their policy recommendations necessarily differ depending on their own preferences. In this book we will be concerned mainly with economic analysis: with the development of economic models that can help us to explain economic problems and phenomena. As a start, it may be useful to survey some of the basic economic problems that we encounter.

Some central economic problems: scarcity and choice

Ever since the bygone days of the Garden of Eden, man has had to face the problem of scarcity. Presumably, in Paradise everything was available to Adam and Eve in great abundance. All conceivable commodities—except the proverbial apple, of course—were free to Adam and Eve and scarcity was an unknown experience.

Unfortunately, Paradise is no longer with us, and we have to contend with life in our world with its limited resources. That these resources are very limited indeed is borne out by the fact that the per capita income in India in 1970 was a mere 50 rupees a month—and there are 7.50 rupees to the dollar! In the United States per capita income amounts to approximately $400 per month, and most people would gladly see an increase in their income, so that they would be able to have command over more resources.

Of course, scarcity is a relative concept, and there are two basic ways by which we can try to reduce the gap between our wants on the one hand and the limited amount of resources available for the satisfaction of these wants on the other. One way is to convince ourselves and our fellow men that we really don't want all those things. By reducing our wants to a pair of sandals and a daily bowl of rice, we would probably be able to satisfy everybody's desires with the resources now at our disposal. This is the approach of the Indian guru, who succeeds in placing mind over matter. But for most people this approach leaves something to be desired. Hence the other approach, namely, to increase production of as many of the want-satisfying commodities as our resources and technological know-how will permit, becomes of central importance to society.

Economics, then, analyzes how people—both individually and collectively—choose to employ scarce resources to satisfy their wants in the most effective manner.

Scarce goods and free goods

Most goods are *scarce* in the sense that people would consume more of them if they were available for free, i.e., if they would not have to give up something else in order to obtain the good. It does not matter whether we purchase the good from somebody else or produce it ourselves. In both instances we have to give up something if we want to have the good. In the first case it is the money we must pay, thereby forgoing the opportunity to buy something else; in the second case it is the effort and resources that go into the production of the good. When purchasing or when producing something, we forgo the opportunity to obtain another good. It is these forgone opportunities, the other things that we have to sacrifice, that make the good scarce to us. Even when we ourselves produce something we incur opportunity costs because we have to give up leisure time. Time itself is scarce, and to use some of our time for a certain task means that we have to forgo the opportunity of doing something else during that time.

But note that scarcity is a relative concept. Only if there are not enough goods of a certain nature to satisfy everybody's desires, do we talk about the existence of scarcity.

There exist some goods in this world that are available in such abundance that they are *free goods*. If we want to obtain some of these free goods, we do not have to give up something else. Free goods are ours for the asking. Their basic characteristic is that they are available in greater quantity than people wish to obtain them. Ocean water is a good example. The available quantity of salty ocean water is greater than the amount people may want to use, hence it is free. This used to be true of clean river water, too. But with our great population upsurge we find that clean drinking water has become scarce and that we have to pay for its use. Water is no longer a free good.

Given a growing population with its ever-increasing demands, more and more goods that used to be free become scarce. It used to be true that the air we breathed was clean and pure. But with growing industrialization, more and more waste products are emitted into the atmosphere, and the result is a deterioration of the quality of air. The day may arrive when we have to pay for clean air as, indeed, we must already in places where air is relatively scarce: oxygen tanks allow us to survive on top of Mount Everest, at the bottom of the Pacific Ocean, and on the surface of the moon. In these places the oxygen required for survival is greater than the available supply—air is a scarce good in those locations.

The production possibility curve

A simple economic concept, the production possibility curve, serves well to illustrate the problems of scarcity and choice. In Figure 1-1

Figure 1-1

The production possibility curve *The production possibility curve shows the maximum combinations of different commodities that can be produced with our limited resources and given technological knowledge.*

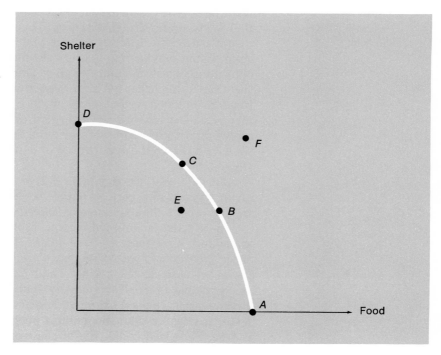

we measure amounts of food along the horizontal axis and shelter along the vertical axis. If we were to devote all our available resources to the production of food, we could, for instance, reach point *A* in the diagram. At *A* we are producing no housing at all, but we have lots of food. Alternatively, we might put all resources into housing and produce no food at all, reaching point *D* on the vertical axis. Clearly, it is also possible to produce a combination of the two commodities. Thus we might allocate some resources to food production and some resources to housing construction, and attain commodity combination *B*, or, alternatively, *C*. The line showing all conceivable commodity combinations that we are able to produce—given our limited resources and our technological know-how—goes through the points *A*, *B*, *C*, and *D*. Because this line shows the maximum commodity combinations that we are able to produce, it is called the *production possibility curve*.

To produce at a point *below* the production possibility curve, such as *E*, would mean either not using all resources or not using them efficiently. Commodity combinations that are located *outside* the production possibility curve, like point *F*, are not attainable given our limited resources and technical know-how.

The production possibility curve shows that because of the scarcity of resources at our disposal, the commodities food and shelter are also scarce. We are not able to obtain *any* desired commodity combination, such as *F*, because of this scarcity. Instead, we are limited to commodity combinations on the production possibility curve, such as *A*, *B*, *C*, or *D*. Which one of these commodity combinations we prefer is a matter of *choice*. A person who lives in sunny Hawaii may elect a combination that gives him relatively more food than shelter, such as represented by point *B*. Someone living in Alaska may opt for relatively more shelter and less food because he has to face a much more hostile climate. Hence he might elect combination *C*. Because we are limited in our choices by the production possibility curve, which reflects the scarcity of the commodities, we have to give up some of one commodity in order to obtain more of the other: we have to make sacrifices, we have to make choices.

Choice makers

Choices are made by various people or groups of people, and it may be instructive to take a brief look at some of the major classes of decision makers, the groups that do the actual choosing.

The most elementary type of choice is made by the individual.

The individual person decides whether he wishes to have mushrooms or anchovies on his pizza, whether he is going to work or to the beach. Nobody else needs to be affected by his choice, and he will generally make a decision that will permit him to maximize his own satisfaction or utility.

Life starts to become a bit more complex when we look at a group of individuals, like a family, clan, or tribe. There are certain decisions that a family can make only as a unit. If it does not do so, it ceases to exist as a family, as we know it. For instance, a decision has to be made about the appropriate residence. If the husband wants to live in an apartment and the wife wishes to live in a house, a compromise has to be worked out—unless the husband deserts his wife and moves to the apartment without her. Similarly, if she wishes to have a baby and he does not, there is no way in which both wishes can be fulfilled at the same time within that family unit.

The basic unit of production is the firm. In a firm a group of people join together in the production process whereby resources are transformed into commodities. Firms have to make decisions regarding the production of a new product, the employment of more workers, and the payment of a dividend to the stockholders.

We can conceive of larger groupings composed of either persons or firms, such as labor unions and industries, which make collective choices regarding union wage contracts, working hours, and holiday periods.

All the different choice agents that have been discussed so far belong to the *private* sector of the economy. Individuals, households, firms, unions, and industries are—at least in the American economy—composed of and run by private citizens. But not all choices are made in the private sector of the economy.

Governmental units, at various levels, do make collective choices for the people who are subject to their jurisdiction. Municipalities decide on the construction of new roads, the establishment of new hospitals and schools, and other matters of concern to the residents of the community. The state deals with problems that transcend the interests of one community or are too large to be handled by one city alone. Flood control and irrigation systems that affect a large area, highway networks, and universities all may require resources that are beyond the capacity of a single city. The federal government has a still broader charge; national defense is one vast area in which decisions have to be made on a federal level. Another is the organization of coinage and currency problems. It would be neither practical nor feasible to have separate armies maintained, trained, and commanded by each state in the Union. To have a different currency in each and every state would not only be confusing, but would effectively make each state into a separate economic entity.

The economic system

Finally, let us give a brief outline of the economic system which we will develop more fully in the following chapters. An economic system is composed of various component units: the United States economy comprises slightly over 200 million persons, 12 million firms, the federal government, 50 state governments, 3,000 counties, and 35,000 municipalities and townships. In addition, there are innumerable foreign economic units to be dealt with.

In our simplified model we will deal with four corresponding sectors: households, firms, governmental units, and the foreign sector. When analyzing each sector, we may adopt a *micro*economic or a *macro*economic view. In microeconomics we focus attention on the decisions and actions of *individual* economic units. In macroeconomics we deal with the *aggregate* manifestations of the behavior of the individual units.

The conceptual scheme of Figure 1-2 may be useful in clarifying the relationship between the various parts. The columns show the four sectors, and the two rows indicate the level of analysis: the

Figure 1-2

The economic system   *The vertical columns show the various sectors of the economy, while the rows depict the level of analysis.*

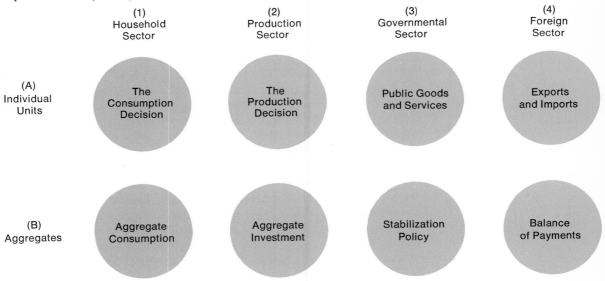

individual economic unit or the collective behavior of all units in a particular sector.

The eight resulting classifications correspond to the division of this book. We will start with an analysis of the consumption decision of the household, proceed to the production decision of the firm, turn to the analysis of governmental decision making regarding individual projects, and close out the first half of the book by considering the export and import decisions made by domestic and foreign economic units. After having considered the individual decisions, we will follow the same sequence with respect to the aggregate implications of the individual decision. We will look at total consumption by households, aggregate investment by firms, the macroeconomic implications of government spending and taxation, and, finally, the balance of international payments.

The basic sequence followed by analyzing the four sectors first from an individual and then from an aggregate viewpoint is arbitrary, of course. We might as well have started with the aggregate behavior patterns and then focused attention on the individual units. (In Figure 1-2, we might have interchanged the rows A and B.) Or we might have analyzed each sector from both a micro- and a macroeconomic viewpoint before proceeding to the next sector. (In terms of Figure 1-2, we would have considered first Column 1, then Column 2, and so on.) The important thing is that we gain an understanding of each one of the economic units comprising the economic system as well as of their interactions with each other.

Markets, edicts, and traditions

There are various ways in which individual economic units can interact with one another. Three basic ways may be described as the market system, the administered system, and the traditional system.

In a *market system* individual economic units are free to interact among each other in the market place. It is possible to buy commodities from other economic units or sell commodities to them. In a market, transactions may take place via barter or money exchange. In a barter economy, real goods such as automobiles, shoes, and pizzas are traded against each other. Obviously, finding somebody who wants to trade my old car in exchange for a sailboat may not always be an easy task. Hence, the introduction of money as a medium of exchange eases transactions considerably. In the modern market economy, goods and services are bought or sold for money.

An alternative to the market system is administrative control by some agency over all transactions. This agency will issue edicts or commands as to how much of each good and service should be produced, exchanged, and consumed by each economic unit. Central planning may be one way of administering such an economy. The central plan, drawn up by the government, shows the amounts of each commodity produced by the various firms and allocated to different households for consumption. This is an example of complete planning of production, consumption, and exchange for the whole economy. A variant of this complete central planning involving households and firms is practiced in many Eastern European countries, where the government exercises virtually complete control over production, but leaves consumers free to choose which commodities they wish to buy. Of course, the drawing up of such a plan, which specifies not only the precise quantities of each and every product to be produced, but also the prices at which these commodities are to be sold to consumers, is a monumental task. One mistake made by an administrator may lead to large surpluses or shortages of certain commodities.

In a traditional society, production and consumption patterns are governed by tradition: every person's place within the economic system is fixed by parentage, religion, and custom. Transactions take place on the basis of tradition, too. People belonging to a certain group or caste may have an obligation to care for other persons, provide them with food and shelter, care for their health, and provide for their education. Clearly, in a system where every decision is made on the basis of tradition alone, progress may be difficult to achieve. A stagnant society may result.

The modern American economy may best be described as a *mixed economy:* some decisions are made in the market place, some by administrative edict, and some by tradition. Within family units, for instance, tradition governs a large part of the interactions between the family members. Within the federal government, administrative control determines the relations between the various agencies and offices. Markets in which goods and services can be bought and sold dominate the economic interactions between different households, firms, and governmental units. Hence we will have to take a closer look at the functioning of the market as the link between different economic units. This is the task of the next chapter.

Summary

□ The economic system describes and analyzes that part of human behavior which is concerned with *production,* *exchange,* and *con-*

sumption. Among the social sciences it is a subsystem that deals with the economic actions and interactions of people. The social sciences themselves represent a subsystem of science as a whole, whose area of concern—as compared with the physical sciences and the life sciences—is the behavior of man.

□ The economic system can be further divided into component parts such as households, firms, and governmental units. We will study the behavior of the various economic units and analyse their interactions.

□ In studying the behavior of individual economic units, their interactions, and the economic system as a whole, it is often convenient to employ *models,* which represent abstract generalizations of reality.

□ In constructing an economic model, we have to follow a two-step sequence: first, we have to construct a *theory* that will yield useful predictions about economic behavior, and, second, we have to *test* the validity of the theory by empirical verification.

□ The basic problem of economics is *scarcity:* if there were enough resources to produce all goods and services in abundance, we would not have to economize.

□ Given the problem of scarcity, economic units are forced to choose between various alternatives open to them. The decision makers will act in a way that maximizes the welfare of the economic unit.

□ Markets are one institution through which individual economic units interact with one another. Alternatives are provided by economic systems where all transactions are governed by administrative rules or plans, and by traditional systems, where economic actions are determined by custom and historical precedent. While administrative edicts and traditions determine some economic behavior patterns in the American economy, the dominant type of interaction between economic units is through the market.

2

The market

The economic system is made up of various component parts: house-holds, firms, governments, and the foreign sector. Obviously, there has to be some mechanism that links the individual economic units and allows the components to interact with each other. If there were no linkage between the components, we could not consider them as part of the same system. Only the fact that interaction does take place between them allows us to see the economic system as one coherent whole.

In a market system all the individual units are left free to make their own decisions regarding their interactions with other units. The market serves as the institution through which different economic units transact with each other. To analyze the nature and function of the market is the main purpose of this chapter.

Market dimensions

Markets function as the links between economic units. It is through markets that the units that comprise the economic system interact. Whenever somebody wants to sell or buy something, that is, if he wants to engage in a transaction with other economic units, he will do so in the market.

Of course, we must guard against the notion that a market has to be in one central place, where all buyers and sellers of a commodity meet. In fact, some such markets are in existence, like the weekly food markets in small towns where farmers truck their vegetables on Saturdays and the townspeople turn out to do their weekly shop-ping. One step removed from this direct participation of buyers and sellers are markets where the buying and selling is accomplished with the aid of brokers. The stock market is an excellent example of this. The actual buyers and sellers of stocks are represented by their respective brokers, who do the trading on the floor of the exchange. But in many markets no formal meeting place exists at all. All that is required to give a person instant access to a multitude of buyers and sellers in today's world is a telephone. For instance, all foreign exchange transactions are accomplished via telephone and teletype. The buyers and sellers may be continents apart. Yet we can speak of one integrated market for foreign exchange because all buyers and sellers can interact with each other.

What, then, distinguishes one market from the next? Can we separate markets, or does there exist just one gigantic market for all commodities? There are several criteria that we might use to delineate individual markets: (1) the homogeneity of the product, (2) transportation costs, and (3) costs of information and communication. Let us look at each one of these in turn.

By homogeneity of the product we mean the extent to which one unit is like another unit bought or sold. There are degrees to which items traded are similar to each other. All food is not alike. Nor are all cereals. But how about wheat? For an expert it is easy to distinguish different types of wheat. In order to facilitate buying and selling, wheat is classified according to certain criteria. Within each classification the wheat is reasonably homogeneous. Perfect homogeneity is achieved when buyers do not care whether they receive one batch or another. Perfect substitutability of one item for another is a practical test for homogeneity. Obviously, the more homogeneous the product, the more we are justified in looking at the market for this product as one unified whole. But for practical purposes it is often convenient to lump together in one market items that are not perfectly homogeneous. Most of us would say that we are in the market for a used automobile when we are interested in buying an old car. But is there only one market for used cars? Or is there a separate market for 1968 Mustangs, 1969 Mustangs, and 1970 Mustangs? For most people a green Mustang is a close substitute for a blue Mustang—but for some people it is not. In general, however, we are justified in treating reasonably homogeneous products as being traded in the same market.

Transportation costs play an important role. The more valuable a product in relation to its transport costs, the greater the market. Nobody would think of trucking ordinary bricks from Chile to Minnesota. The cost of transportation would be much too high compared to the value of the bricks. Hence the market for bricks is a local or at best a regional market. On the other hand, the market for gold bricks is truly world-wide. Here the value is very high in relation to costs of transportation, and hence it pays to ship gold over large distances in response to even relatively small price differentials.

Finally, costs of information and communication limit the extent of the market. For a housewife going on a shopping trip it generally does not pay to visit two dozen different supermarkets just to find out where she can get the best price for the one loaf of bread she intends to buy. However, there are many ways in which she can reduce the information costs. She might look at the advertisements in the local paper or call up different supermarkets and ask about the price. But would it be worth her while to spend 10 cents on a paper when the price of bread ranges between 27 and 32 cents? Certainly not, because the information cost (10 cents) added to the price of the cheaper loaf (27 cents) would put her total cost at 37 cents—a nickel more than the expensive loaf of bread. For certain transactions the costs of information may be extremely high. The housing market offers a good example. To learn about all available houses in a town you just moved to is extremely time-consuming and expensive. Hence, you are willing to pay a broker for his services in helping you to find a suitable residence.

To rigidly separate one market from another one is an exceedingly difficult task. But it is not necessary to draw strict lines separating each and every market. The precise delineations of the market we are interested in may change from situation to situation and year to year. Sometimes it may be necessary to take a rather broad view of the market; at others we may focus on a narrow group of economic transactions and the specific market where these take place. There is no uniform rule that can be applied to all situations, and that is one reason why economics constantly offers new challenges even to the seasoned practitioner.

Markets for inputs and outputs

Let us trace some of the interactions between economic units that take place in the market. We may start out with a farm, which produces wheat. The *output*, as the product produced is often called, is brought by the farmer to the market and sold there for cash. The farmer acts as a supplier of wheat. The buyer of the wheat may be a mill operator, who uses the wheat as an *input* into his production process: the production of flour. Along with labor, milling equipment, buildings, and storage facilities wheat is one of the ingredients used in the milling of flour, which in turn is the output of the mill. The flour is sold in the flour market to a baker, who uses it as an input into his production of bread, which is his output. The bread may be bought by a worker, who works on the farm where the wheat originated. The cycle is closed as illustrated in Figure 2-1.

This simplified framework of four individual economic units, linked by four markets, may be described as a rudimentary subsystem of the economy. Of course, much more complicated processes of interaction between economic units do occur, but the example may help to illustrate some of the principles of a market economy. (1) Most every economic unit participates both as a buyer and a seller of economic goods in the market: the baker buys flour and sells bread.

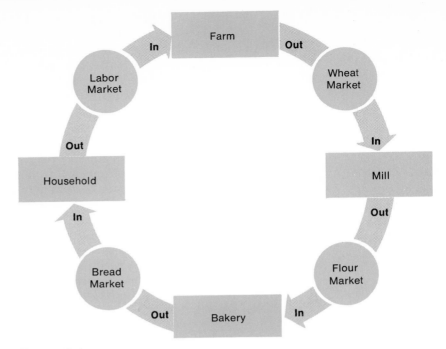

Figure 2-1

The circular flow *Outputs produced by one economic unit are used as inputs by other economic units. We may depict the economy as one gigantic circular flow chart.*

(2) Each commodity constitutes both an output of one economic unit and an input to another economic unit: flour is the output of the mill and an input into the bakery. (3) Each market links buyers and sellers of a product: farmers act as sellers in the wheat market and millers act as buyers in the same market.

There is no simple starting point at which the chain of economic transactions can be broken, where we can start to analyze the economic interactions taking place. Any beginning will be arbitrary. In this book we will start with individual consumers as buyers of goods and services and then analyze the behavior of firms as sellers in various market settings.

Demand

We generally observe that buyers will buy a larger quantity of a commodity if its price is lowered. The lower price will entice con-

Figure 2-2

The demand curve *The demand curve shows the quantity demanded by buyers at various prices. It refers to a given time period.*

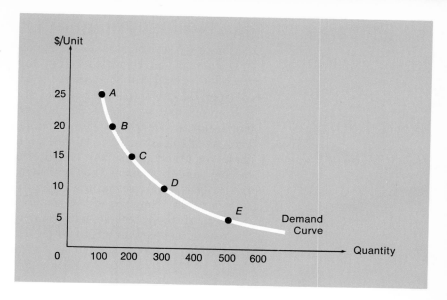

Table 2-1 Demand schedule

	Price per unit	Quantity demanded
A	$25.00	100
B	20.00	140
C	15.00	200
D	10.00	300
E	5.00	500

sumers to use more of the commodity, and it will also attract new buyers. Hence the quantity of a commodity demanded will vary inversely with its price. The relationship between price and quantity demanded is tabulated in a *demand schedule* or shown graphically by a *demand curve.*

Table 2-1 shows a hypothetical demand schedule for shoes. At a price of $25 per pair of shoes, 100 pairs will be sold per day in the relevant market area—say, a medium-sized town. If the price were to drop to $20, the quantity demanded would increase to 140 pairs. As the price continues to drop, still more people will turn out to buy shoes, and at a price of $5 a total of 500 pairs of shoes per day will be sold.

The data of Table 2-1 are also shown in Figure 2-2, where we show the demand curve for shoes by the residents of the town. Note that the demand curve always refers to a certain time period: here, a day. If we were to draw a demand curve showing the demand for shoes for a whole week, it would obviously be located farther out to the right.

There are several reasons for the basic downward-sloping pattern of the demand curve, which we can observe. For one, at a lower price more individuals will be attracted to buy the commodity; as the price of shoes falls, even people who did not buy them at the high prices will go out and buy some. Second, individual buyers might buy an extra pair at the lower price. This happens for two reasons. First, because of the lower price of shoes, individual buyers will substitute them for other goods they would otherwise be buying. Instead of buying sandals or boots they will switch to shoes. This is the *substitution effect*. And second, the buyers feel a little richer as the price of shoes falls. They spend less money on each pair bought. It is the same as if their income had gone up by an equivalent amount. Therefore, people can afford to buy a bit more. This is the *income effect* which is brought about by the fall in price.

Supply

The quantities of a product that sellers are willing to supply at various prices in the market make up the supply schedule. If shoemakers can get a higher price for their product, they will work longer hours, pay their employees overtime wages, and perhaps try to buy out the businessman who has his shop next door, so that the shoe factory may be enlarged. All this entails higher costs of production, and hence the quantity supplied will increase only if a higher price is offered as an incentive to the producer.

There is one possible exception to the general rule of an upward-sloping supply curve: this is the case of decreasing-cost industries. In decreasing-cost industries technology is such that additional units can be produced at lower and lower cost. But eventually costs are likely to turn upward and again bring about a supply curve that slopes upward to the right.

A supply schedule for our hypothetical shoe industry is given in Table 2-2, and the corresponding supply curve is depicted in Figure 2-3.

Equilibrium

We are now in a position to show how the market determines the equilibrium price and the quantity traded. If there are a very large

Figure 2-3

The supply curve *The supply curve shows the quantities of a commodity that will be supplied at different prices.*

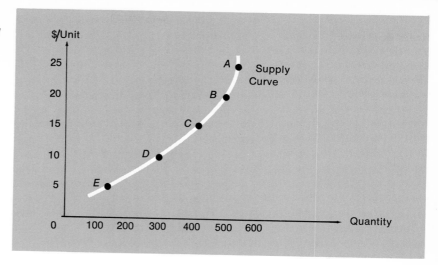

Table 2-2 *Supply schedule*

	Price per unit	Quantity supplied
A	$25.00	540
B	20.00	500
C	15.00	420
D	10.00	300
E	5.00	140

number of buyers and sellers in the market, so that no one person has a substantial share of the market for himself, all the market participants are price takers. Price takers have no control over the market price. Any quantity bought or sold by one individual does not have a large enough influence to affect the market as a whole—the price is a given magnitude to the individual buyer or seller.

Looking at the supply and demand curves that are reproduced as Figure 2-4 or Table 2-3 we see that the quantity supplied exceeds the quantity demanded at every price *above* $10.00. At any price above $10.00, there will be a surplus on the market. Sellers are willing to sell more shoes than buyers are willing to buy. Of course, the sellers are not willing to hold on to the unsold shoes forever. Eventually, some sellers will lower their prices in order to sell the additional pairs. At a price of $10.00, all the shoes that sellers want to sell will be bought up by buyers. If the price were to drop *below* $10.00, shortages would appear. Buyers would want to buy more shoes than sellers

Figure 2-4

Market equilibrium *The supply and demand curves in a market determine the equilibrium price at which the commodity will be traded. At the equilibrium price the amount that sellers are willing to sell is equal to the quantity that buyers demand.*

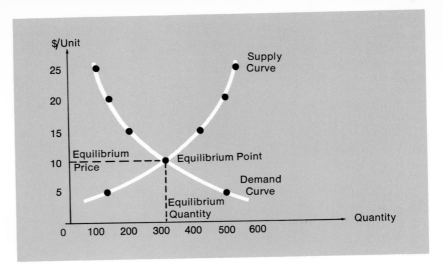

Table 2-3

Price per unit	Quantity demanded	Quantity supplied	Surplus or shortage	Pressure on price
$25.00	100	540	440 surplus	Down
20.00	140	500	360 surplus	Down
15.00	200	420	220 surplus	Down
10.00	300	300	Equilibrium	None
5.00	500	140	360 shortage	Up

would be willing to sell. Hence an upward pressure on price would exist.

Only at the price of $10.00 per pair of shoes do the quantities that sellers are willing to sell match with the quantities that buyers are willing to buy. Hence no shortages or surpluses exist—the market is cleared, and there is no further pressure for the price to change: we have found the *equilibrium price* for the market.

Disturbances to equilibrium

Equilibrium, once achieved, will tend to persist if no outside disturbances arise. We can distinguish disturbances having their origin on the supply side from those having their origin on the demand side.

Disturbances originating on the supply side will result in a shift of the whole supply schedule. For instance, if a new cost-saving device is introduced, if new firms enter the industry, or if the supply of resources used in the production of the good is increased—in all these cases we will find that sellers of the product taken together will want to sell a larger quantity than previously at the old price. Alternatively, they want to sell the same old quantity at a lower price. Graphically, this may be shown by a rightward (or downward) shift of the whole supply curve. Similarly, in the table we note an increase of the quantities supplied at each and every price.

As a result of the increase in supply, the old equilibrium point E is no longer at the intersection of the demand curve and the new supply curve S'. Given the new supply curve, a surplus exists at the old equilibrium price—because of the increased supply. Hence the price will tend to fall until a new equilibrium is reached at point E'. At the new equilibrium point, the quantity traded will be larger. This is shown in Figure 2-5, where the price falls from P_0 to P_1 and the quantity traded increases from Q_0 to Q_1 in response to the supply shift.

A shift in demand works in a similar fashion. Figure 2-6 shows an increase in demand: the demand curve shifts to the right or upward. Now a larger quantity is demanded at each and every price. This might have come about because people's incomes have increased,

Figure 2-5

A shift of the supply curve *A rightward (or downward) shift of the supply curve will lead to a new market equilibrium at a lower price and a larger quantity traded.*

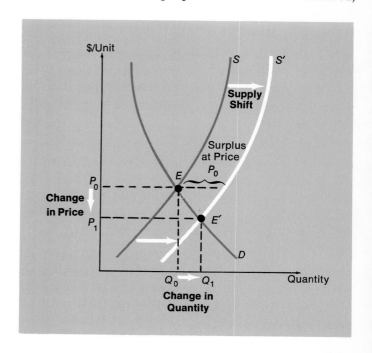

Figure 2-6

A shift of the demand curve *A rightward (or upward) shift of the demand curve will lead to a higher equilibrium price and an increase in the trade volume.*

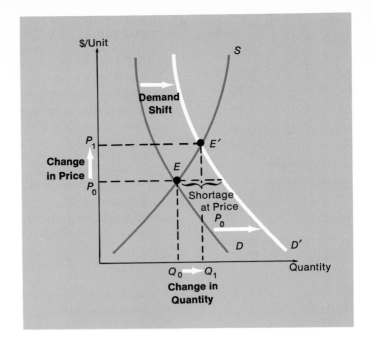

because there had been an increase in the price of some commodity that people used to purchase instead of this one, because more people have moved into the market area, or simply because tastes have changed. The result is that a new equilibrium E' will be established at the intersection of the supply curve and the new demand curve. The consequence is an increase in the price from P_0 to P_1, and an increase in the trade volume from Q_0 to Q_1.

Price controls

Sometimes we find that a governmental agency will attempt to control prices. Most frequently, the government tries to fix prices in a pattern that is different from the one that would prevail under free market conditions, but is judged desirable on other grounds.

Consider, for instance, what happens if the government legislates a maximum price that can be charged for apartment rental as illustrated by Figure 2-7. If the price ceiling established by law is at or above the prevailing market price, nothing at all will happen. The market will still allocate resources as before, and prices will be established, such that the quantity demanded and the quantity supplied will be equated. If, however, the legal maximum that landlords can charge or buyers can pay is *lower* than the free market price, shortages are likely to develop. What is a shortage? A *shortage* is simply an unsatisfied excess demand at the going price. The difference between the quantity demanded and the quantity supplied shows the excess demand that appears at the fixed maximum price. Those people who are lucky enough to get one of the cheap apartments certainly get a bargain, but the ones who are not as lucky will get no housing at all.

Is there a way out of the dilemma? One possibility is to try to shift the supply curve to the right. By increasing the supply of apartments available, competition between landlords will bring the rental price down. Note, too, that the imposition of a rent ceiling may actually *decrease* the number of apartments that will be available. This comes about because at the low rental rates, landlords will not only build no new apartments but will let their old ones deteriorate until eventually they will have to be torn down. Because apartment rental rates are so low, landlords will invest their money in more lucrative ventures, such as office buildings.

Similarly, minimum-price legislation is likely to lead to *surpluses* as shown by Figure 2-8. One area where minimum prices are frequently established is the labor market. The federal government has decreed by law that nobody employed in interstate commerce can

Figure 2-7

A maximum price regulation *A maximum price regulation is likely to lead to a shortage of the commodity at the regulated price. A shortage occurs when the quantity demanded exceeds the quantity supplied at the regulated price.*

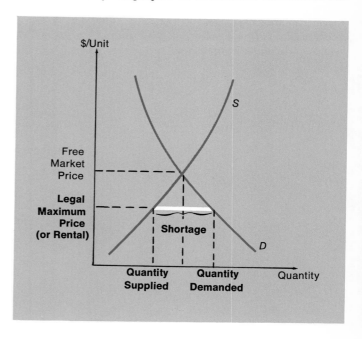

be hired at a wage of less than $1.80 per hour. Of course, if the law is required at all, it must be because the free market wage for many workers would be below this amount. By establishing a legal minimum, the government places an effective floor under the wage. At that wage the quantity of people willing to work is greater than the number of people hired by employers. Anybody who is not well trained enough to be able to produce an amount of output that will make it worthwhile for an employer to hire him at the minimum wage will go begging for a job—he will be unemployed. Price floors tend to do the exact opposite from price ceilings: they tend to create a surplus at the legal minimum wage or price.

Again, the way out of the dilemma consists in shifting the whole curves in such a way that the higher wage rate may be achieved. For instance, by increasing the demand for workers, the equilibrium wage rate increases, and *at the same time* the number of workers employed goes up too.

The key to the long-run solution of the problem of prices deemed too high or too low on social grounds lies not in interfering with the price system by legislative fiat prices, but in introducing programs designed to bring about the desired changes in market conditions. Interference with the free market in the form of price controls is

Figure 2-8

A minimum price regulation *A legally established minimum price is likely to lead to a surplus at that price.*

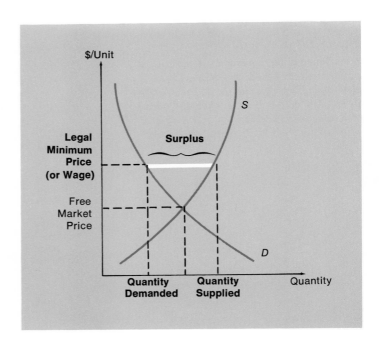

likely to lead to the creation of shortages or surpluses at the legally fixed prices rather than to a solution of the problem of resource allocation.

Summary

☐ Markets form the links between the individual units comprising the economy. It is through markets that households, firms, and governmental units interact by the exchange of economic goods and services.

☐ The size of the market is limited by the homogeneity of the product, as well as by the costs of transportation, information, and communication. There are generally no clearly defined delineations to any market. The appropriate definition of a market may depend on the aim of the analysis.

☐ In a market buyers purchase commodities for consumption purposes or as inputs into a production process. Sellers offer their products or outputs for sale. Note that any one commodity is both an input (from the buyer's viewpoint) and an output (from the seller's viewpoint).

☐ The *demand curve* shows the quantities of a commodity that buyers are willing to purchase at all conceivable prices. The demand curve slopes downward to the right, because at lower prices people will substitute the commodity for others whose price has remained unchanged. Also, they will realize a gain in spending power, caused by the lower price, which is comparable to an equivalent increase in income.

☐ The *supply curve* shows the quantities of a commodity that will be supplied at various prices. It slopes upward to the right because at higher prices producers are able to pay higher wages to their workers, purchase new machines, or increase the amount of land utilized, and therefore produce a larger quantity.

☐ The *equilibrium price* in the market is determined by the intersection of the aggregate supply and demand curve for all market participants. At the equilibrium price the quantity supplied equals the quantity demanded and hence there are no surpluses or shortages that would exercise any further pressure on the market price.

□ Disturbances to equilibrium may originate on the demand or the supply side. An increase in demand (shift of the demand curve) will increase the price and the quantity of the goods traded; an increase in supply (shift of the supply curve) will lower the price and increase the quantity traded.

□ Administrative interferences with the market mechanism may take the form of minimum prices or maximum prices. Minimum prices tend to create excess supplies (surpluses) of the price-regulated commodity; maximum prices lead to excess demand (shortages) of the goods or services subject to regulation.

3

The consumer

In 1970, a total of 204,835,000 persons lived in the United States, and all of them were consumers of goods and services. In this chapter we will analyse how consumption decisions are made.

Clearly, not all of the more than 204 million persons are decision makers in the full meaning of the term, because this figure includes babies and infants, inmates in penal institutions, persons in mental hospitals, and others whose decision-making power is limited in some way or other. Furthermore, many individuals are grouped in households, and their individual weight in any collective decision made may vary widely. Given our social system, households play an exceedingly important role in consumer decision making. If a household does not come up with one decision, but two mutually conflicting ones, that household may cease to exist as a unit. If the husband wants to live in New York and the wife in Hawaii, both cannot have their wish come true without breaking up the household as a unit. We will assume for simplicity's sake that the household decision maker accurately reflects the wishes of all the household members.

Each decision that a consumer makes is accompanied by certain benefits and costs. The benefits associated with a decision increase the consumer's welfare. They contribute to his satisfaction or utility. But these benefits can be attained only by incurring certain costs. Alternatives have to be forgone; other desirable things sacrificed. These are the opportunity costs that have to be borne. Often we simply pay a certain amount of money for a commodity. This money represents an acquisition cost to the consumer—not so much because the money paid has some inherent value, but because he forgoes the opportunity of buying other want-satisfying goods with the money.

We will develop a theory of how consumers make their decisions. Furthermore, we will investigate how behavior patterns are likely to change if consumers are faced with varying circumstances regarding prices, incomes, and tastes. To explain people's behavior, we have to construct a theory that will help us to explain the *goals* of their behavior. This will lead us—at least for a brief excursion—into the field of psychology, but we will try to restrict ourselves at all times to the economic implications of consumer behavior.

Goals of consumer behavior

The first question that has to be answered is very broad indeed. What are the goals of a person's behavior? What are the objectives he tries to reach? Some answers come to mind readily: we are all interested in survival, we desire food and shelter, we want to be loved and respected, and so on. In more general terms, we are interested in increasing our welfare, our satisfaction, or—to use a more technical term—our utility. It seems reasonable, therefore, to assume that people act in a way that is designed to maximize their utility or satisfaction.

This, then, is the goal of consumer behavior. Of course, we must be careful to define utility or satisfaction in terms broad enough to include *all* items that will yield utility to us. Thus we not only gain utility by having more pizza, more beer, more clothes, and so on, but also by going to concerts and museums, by receiving proper medical care, and by seeing the people whom we care for made better off.

But, clearly, we cannot have all the goods and services that contribute to our well-being. Our resources are not unlimited. It follows that we are constrained in our choices by the resources available to us. Given his available resources, such as his income, inherited wealth, donations received, and the like, the consumer will attempt to maximize his welfare or utility.

In technical terms, we face a *constrained maximization problem.* We have to take the resource constraint into consideration when making our consumption decisions. The consumption decision, then, involves the choosing from the hundreds of thousands of commodities available to us those that will yield us the greatest possible satisfaction.

Utility

Having specified the ultimate goal of the consumer, namely, welfare maximization, we have to investigate what kind of behavior pattern on the part of individuals will permit a person to achieve this goal. The first step is to find out how the amount of a commodity consumed is related to the benefits derived from it.

Imagine that your uncle takes you for your birthday to your favorite pizza house. He will foot the bill, and all you have to do is eat. Being a pizza-lover, you get quite a bit of satisfaction out of eating your first pizza. You order a second one. It still tastes great, and your total happiness increases. But you also notice that the second pizza is not quite as satisfying to you as the very first one, when you were really hungry and ready to eat. You might even order a third one, but while your total satisfaction still increases, the additional satisfaction gained from the third pizza is probably minimal. Finally, your uncle offers you a fourth pizza. This time, you might be indifferent about having it or not. Eating the fourth pizza would add nothing more to your satisfaction: you have had all the pizza you desire for the time being. If he were to offer you even a fifth one, you might actually experience a certain amount of discomfort, of *dis*utility, from consuming it, because it would make you feel too full and perhaps even sick. Thus you would turn down his friendly offer.

We have observed that up to the fourth pizza your total satisfaction actually increased. When eating the fourth pizza, your satisfaction did not change, and for the fifth one, total utility declined. This is shown in Figure 3-1, where we show the quantity of pizza consumed along the horizontal axis and the corresponding total utility gained on the vertical axis.

We have to take a careful look at the increases in total utility that you experience as you consume additional pizzas. The additional benefits derived from each additional pizza are called by economists the *marginal utility* of a pizza, where the term *marginal* refers to the extra utility gained by consuming just one additional pizza. We observe that the additions to total utility in Table 3-1 become smaller and smaller—and eventually negative. Consequently, marginal utility declines as more pizzas are consumed by you. This is shown in Figure 3-2, where we graph the downward-sloping marginal utility curve, corresponding to the total utility curve in Figure 3-1.

A careful look at the marginal utility schedule will reveal the point at which it would be rational to stop accepting the free pizzas offered to you. You will maximize your satisfaction by consuming only pizzas that yield a *positive* marginal utility to you and not eat any that would make you worse off. Thus you definitely will accept pizzas one, two, and three; you will turn down pizza number five; and you will be indifferent with respect to having or not having the fourth pizza. We may conclude that, offered a free good, you will maximize your satisfaction by consuming it up to the point at which its marginal utility to you reaches zero.

The demand curve

But birthdays are infrequent events in life, and generous uncles may be even rarer. Most of the time, we will find that we will have to

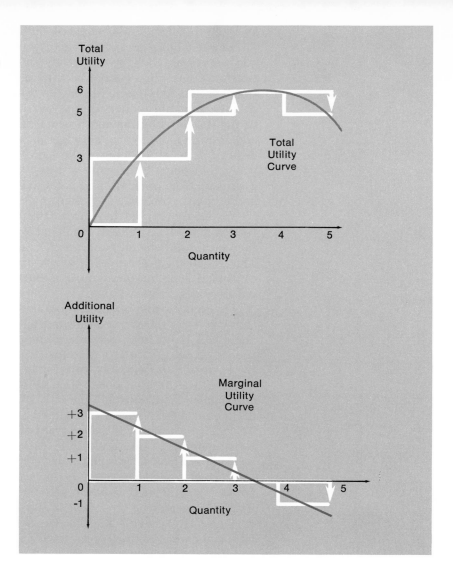

Figure 3-1

The total utility curve *The total utility curve shows the total amount of satisfaction received from consuming the quantity indicated.*

Figure 3-2

The marginal utility curve *The marginal utility curve shows the addition to total satisfaction derived from consuming the last unit of the commodity.*

Table 3-1

Quantity	Total utility		Marginal utility
0	0		
1	3	>	+3
2	5	>	+2
3	6	>	+1
4	6	>	0
5	5	>	−1

pay a price for the commodities we wish to consume: every pizza shop has its price list. Because you have to pay for pizzas, you will probably consume fewer than if they were free. In fact, the higher the price of pizza, the fewer you are likely to buy.

How does this relationship evolve from the principle of diminishing marginal utility discussed earlier? We said that it is the goal of the consumer to maximize his satisfaction. He can increase his satisfaction each time he purchases a commodity for which the *additional utility* (*MU*) is greater than the *additional cost* (*MC*) involved. Hence, if $MU > MC$, a purchase of that good or service will increase our total utility. Conversely, if the additional utility gained is smaller than the cost involved, $MU < MC$, it would be unwise to buy the good.

You will stop buying additional units when you have reached a point at which the marginal utility (*MU*) derived from the commodity is just equal to the marginal cost (*MC*) incurred. Because there is a natural tendency for a consumer to purchase the quantity at which this condition is fulfilled, it is often referred to as his *equilibrium point*. At equilibrium $MU = MC$.

We have discussed already the marginal utility curve shown in Figure 3-2. We must now turn to the marginal costs of purchasing additional pizzas. If you are able to purchase the pizzas at the price quoted on the menu, the additional cost (*MC*) of each pizza to you is simply its price (*P*). If the price is constant, price and marginal costs are identical.

The utility-maximizing consumer will purchase the quantity of pizzas at which the $MU = MC (= P)$ condition is fulfilled. If one dollar is defined also as the "unit" of utility, the task of converting the subjective marginal utility curve of Figure 3-2 into an objective demand curve is easy.

In Figure 3-3 we show again the marginal utility schedule. Now let us change the price of pizza and observe the consumer's behavior. If the price is $3.00, he will purchase one pizza, because $MU = MC$ ($= P$) at that quantity. If the price is changed to $2.00, the consumer will buy two pizzas; at a price of $1.00, he will order three pizzas. We have obtained now a relationship between price and quantity demanded—a demand curve. This objective relationship can be derived from the underlying marginal utility curve by allowing the consumer to maximize his own satisfaction at various alternative prices and by observing his purchasing behavior. What used to be the marginal utility curve of Figure 3-2 now becomes the demand curve of Figure 3-3. The demand curve shows the quantity of a commodity that the consumer will purchase—given a certain price. He makes this purchase decision with the goal of utility maximization

Figure 3-3

The demand curve *The demand curve can be derived from the marginal utility curve by confronting the consumer with various prices and observing the quantity he will actually purchase.*

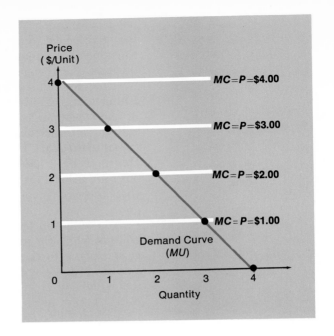

Table 3-2 *Demand schedule*

Price	Quantity demanded
$0.00	4 units
1.00	3 units
2.00	2 units
3.00	1 unit
4.00	0 units

in mind, observing the $MU = MC$ rule which tells him when he purchases the optimal quantity of a commodity.

Naturally, the principle elaborated here applies to each and every commodity. That is, the consumer will be in equilibrium when the price (or marginal cost) of each commodity is equal to the marginal utility he obtains from it:

$$P_a = MU_a; P_b = MU_b; P_c = MU_c; \cdots; P_z = MU_z.$$

By dividing the equation for each good by the price of that good, we can set the left-hand sides of each equation equal to one, and therefore equal to each other:

$$\frac{P_a}{P_a} = \frac{MU_a}{P_a}; \frac{P_b}{P_b} = \frac{MU_b}{P_b}; \frac{P_c}{P_c} = \frac{MU_c}{P_c}; \cdots; \frac{P_z}{P_z} = \frac{MU_z}{P_z}.$$

If the left-hand sides are equal to each other, the right-hand sides must be equal to each other too. Hence we arrive at the rule giving us the optimal allocation pattern of our expenditures among various goods and services:

$$\frac{MU_a}{P_a} = \frac{MU_b}{P_b} = \frac{MU_c}{P_c} = \cdots = \frac{MU_z}{P_z}.$$

The rule says that the rational consumer will purchase each commodity until the *ratio* of additional utility obtained to the price paid is equal for each commodity. Or, which amounts to the same thing, that the marginal utility derived from each dollar spent should be the same for every commodity.

Shifts in demand

The demand curve derived above is drawn up under the assumption that all other things remain constant. If other variables are permitted to change, then the demand curve might be affected by that change too. Obviously, some variables are more important than others in affecting the demand curve. Here we will look at three important factors that might affect the demand curve: income, prices of other commodities, and tastes. This is by no means an exhaustive list of all the possible factors, but it includes some of the most important effects.

Income changes Let us say that you have a pretty fair notion about the shape of your demand curve for pizza, represented by the demand curve *DD* in Figure 3-4. Now assume that your income increases. Having more money, you will probably spend more too. And part of that additional spending may be devoted to increased pizza purchases. As a result, the whole demand curve *DD* will shift over to the right, and the new demand curve D'D' now shows how many pizzas you are going to purchase with your higher income at each and every price.

While it is true that normally an increase in income will result in an increase (or rightward shift) in demand, the opposite is possible too. Consider this example. As a student on a very limited budget, you have a certain demand curve for Honda motorcycles. After graduation, your income increases. What happens to your demand for Hondas? Probably it will go down, as you now can afford a Mustang. With your income increase, your demand for Mustangs increases, while your demand for Hondas decreases. After a few years and several promotions, your demand for Mustangs might decline and the demand for Oldsmobiles go up. After you become a million-aire, the demand for Oldsmobiles may decrease and the demand for Rolls Royces go up. Similar observations might apply to other com-modities: you switch from Coca-Cola to beer to a cheap Scotch to Johnny Walker Black Label; or from a dormitory to your own apart-ment to a house and perhaps to a mansion with a swimming pool.

Table 3-3

Price	Quantity demanded before shift	Quantity demanded after shift
$1.00	3 units	5 units
2.00	2 units	4 units
3.00	1 unit	3 units

Figure 3-4

A shift in demand *The demand curve will shift to the right if consumers will want to purchase a higher quantity of the commodity at each and every price. This might be the result of an income increase.*

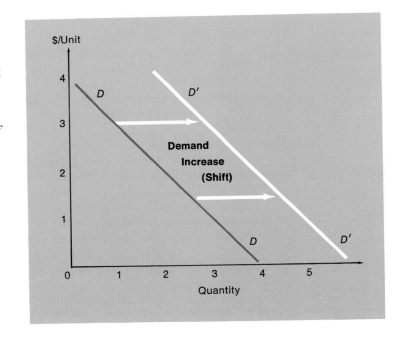

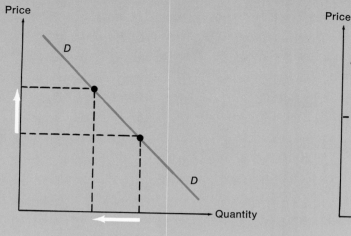

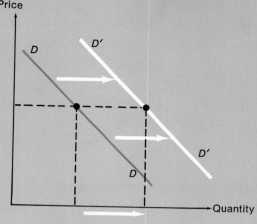

Figure 3-5a

The demand for automobiles

A price increase for automobiles (left diagram) will lead to a rightward shift or increase in the demand for motorcycles (right diagram), because they can serve as a substitute for the higher-priced automobiles.

Figure 3-5b

The demand for motorcycles
(a substitute for automobiles)

The point is that the demand for many goods will initially increase with income increases but eventually decrease. The decrease in demand (or leftward shift of the demand curve) need not occur for quite a range in incomes, but chances are that eventually it will happen.

Change in price of related commodities We mentioned that an increase in the price of automobiles will decrease the quantity of automobiles demanded. But it also might affect the quantity of motorcycles that people wish to purchase. As the price of automobiles increases (see Figure 3-5), the quantity demanded will decrease. But people still have to get around, and as a result some people will substitute other modes of transportation for the now too expensive automobile. For instance, they might buy motorcycles, whose demand curve will shift to the right (increase) as a result of the increased price of autos. Other substitutes, like the demand for bus, train, and airplane rides and perhaps even shoes—some people might take to walking—would be affected in a similar manner.

As the price of a commodity increases, people will move along the demand curve for that commodity and purchase less; but the whole demand curve for substitute commodities will shift to the right: people will buy more of the substitute at each and every price.

The reverse holds true for commodities that are used in conjunction with those goods that experience the price increase. Commodities

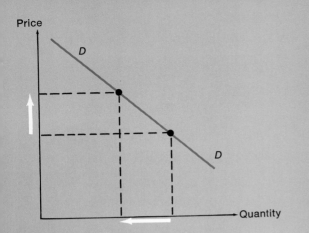

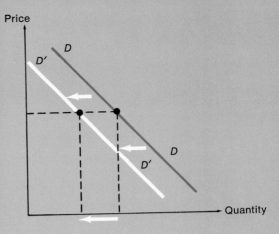

Figure 3-6a

The demand for automobiles

An increase in the price of automobiles will lead to a reduction of the number of automobiles purchased (left diagram) and a downward shift of the entire demand curve for automobile tires— a complementary good (right diagram).

Figure 3-6b

The demand for automobile tires
(a complementary good to automobiles)

that tend to be consumed together are called *complementary goods*. Automobiles and tires, tea and lemon, gin and tonic are examples. In Figure 3-6 we illustrate this case by an increase in the price of automobiles, and in the right-hand portion of the diagram we show how the demand for automobile tires decreases: as people buy fewer cars, they will also buy fewer tires. Thus an increase in the price of a commodity will result in a decrease (shift to the left) of the demand for complementary commodities.

Obviously, a third possibility exists: the price of one commodity may in no measurable way affect the demand for other commodities. That is the case with independent commodities, like tea leaves and ballpoint pens. There is no reason to expect that a change in the price of tea leaves will affect the demand for pens, because the commodities neither serve as substitutes nor can they be considered complements to each other.

Changes in tastes Changes in tastes is a broad catch-all phrase, which serves to explain changes in demand that might occur. In the late sixties, the demand for miniskirts increased rapidly, as tastes of people changed away from knee-length skirts. At the same time the demand for full-length dresses decreased. The reverse happened in the early seventies. Fashion is one area where we can observe the rapid effect of changing tastes. In other areas the changes may be more subtle or take a longer time, but the effects of changing tastes can nevertheless be felt. The effects are obvious: the demand for a product that has become fashionable will increase, shifting the demand curve to the right, while the demand for a product that has fallen out of favor will decrease, shifting the demand curve to the left.

As a final word, let us remind ourselves that only the change in the price of a commodity will result in a movement *along* the demand curve. A change in any other variable, be it income, the price of a substitute or complementary commodity, tastes, or anything else, will result in a *shift* of the whole demand curve.

Market demand

For many purposes it is necessary to determine the aggregate demand curve for a commodity in a certain market area. A newspaper publisher might want to find out how many papers he is able to sell if he charges a certain price, Christmas-tree salesmen want to get a rough idea of how many trees they can sell at the price they intend to charge, and so on. To derive the demand curve for a market area from our individual demand curves two essentials are required: (1) We must know how large the market area is—that is, whether we are operating in a limited local market, a regional market, or even a national market. (2) We must determine the shape of the demand curves of the individuals in the relevant market area.

In the previous chapter we stated that the size of the market area is limited by costs of transportation, communication, and information. Taking all these factors into account, we are able to delineate the relevant market area for the commodity in question.

Let us assume that we have succeeded in identifying the relevant market area. If we want to find out exactly what the demand curve for our product looks like, we have to add up the demand curves for all the individuals in this market area. That is, we have to add up the quantities demanded at each and every price by all the consumers in the market. Figure 3-7 and Table 3-4 shows the demand for pizza by Mr. Hilton and Mr. Smith. At a price of $1.00 per pizza, Hilton will purchase four and Smith will buy five pizzas. If the relevant market area consists of only these two persons, then the total quantity of pizza demanded at the price of $1.00 will be nine. In other words, in the graph we have to sum *horizontally* the quantities of pizza demanded by each individual to arrive at the market demand.

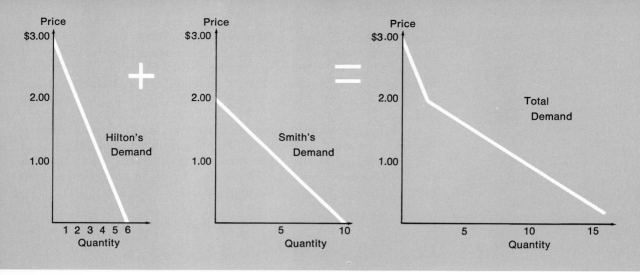

Figure 3-7

The market demand curve *A market demand curve is obtained by adding the quantities demanded by the various individuals at each and every price.*

Table 3-4

Price	Quantity demanded by Hilton	Quantity demanded by Smith	Total quantity demanded
$3.00	0	0	0
2.50	1	0	1.0
2.00	2	0	2.0
1.50	3	2.5	5.5
1.00	4	5.0	9.0
.50	5	7.5	12.5

In practice, it may be more convenient to try to estimate the market demand curve for a product directly, rather than going through the cumbersome procedure of obtaining the demand curve for each individual person and then summing them all up. This may be done by using questionnaires or interviews in market surveys or by relying upon data from past sales and making predictions as to the likely sales volume concommitant to a change in price.

Elasticity

Businessmen are interested in the total amount of money that people are willing to spend on a product at various prices. A producer contemplating a price change will want to get a fair idea about what will happen to his total cash receipts after the price change. Will his revenue go up, stay constant, or perhaps even go down? His decision to change the price will depend in large part on the answer to this question.

We know by now that a fall in price will be accompanied by an increase in the quantity demanded. But for some products the quantity demanded may increase very much and for other products very little. Thus we have to develop a measure of the responsiveness of consumers to price changes. This measure is called the *elasticity of demand*. The elasticity coefficient has a wide range of applications both in economic analysis and policy formulation.

The elasticity of a demand curve is defined by the formula:

$$e = \frac{\text{percentage change in quantity demanded}}{\text{percentage change in price}} = \frac{\dfrac{\Delta Q}{Q}}{\dfrac{\Delta P}{P}}.$$

To calculate the elasticity coefficient, we have to determine four numbers: the change in quantity, ΔQ, the quantity, Q, the change in price, ΔP, and the price, P.

An elasticity coefficient absolutely greater than one indicates that the percentage change in quantity demanded is greater than the percentage change in price. A lowering of the price will lead to a strong increase in quantity demanded and therefore an increase in total revenue. The response of consumers is said to be *elastic*, in that case. On the other hand, an elasticity coefficient smaller than one shows that total revenue will decrease as a result of a lowering of the price. The demand is called *inelastic*.

Let us illustrate by the use of an example. In Table 3-5 we show the prices and quantities demanded that are graphed in Figure 3-8. For a change in price from $5.00 to $4.00, we experience an increase in the quantity demanded from 10 units to 15 units. The elasticity formula (using midpoints for the prices and quantities) yields an elasticity coefficient of 1.8 (see Table 3-5), which is well above unity, and thus demand is elastic in the price range between $4.00 and $5.00.

However, having calculated the elasticity in that price range, we

Figure 3-8

The elasticity of demand
The elasticity of demand is a measure of the responsiveness of the quantity demanded to price changes. It is defined as the percentage change in quantity over the percentage change in price: $e = (\Delta Q/Q)/(\Delta P/P)$.

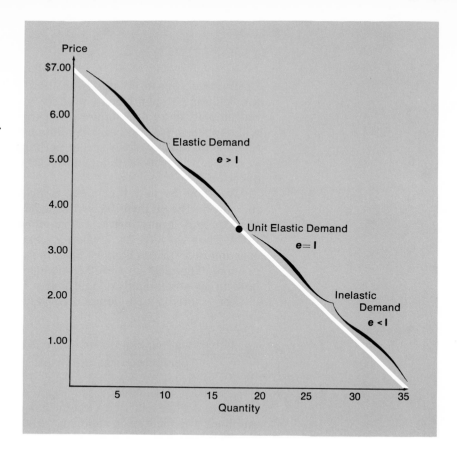

Table 3-5

Price	Quantity demanded	Total revenue	Elasticity (in range using midpoints)	
$7.00	0	$ 0.00	} $e = 13.00$	
6.00	5	30.00	} $e = 3.67$	Elastic demand
5.00	10	50.00	} $e = 1.80$	($TR\uparrow$ if $P\downarrow$)
4.00	15	60.00	} $e = 1.00$	Unit elastic demand
3.00	20	60.00	} $e = .56$	(TR unchanged if $P\downarrow$)
2.00	25	50.00	} $e = .27$	Inelastic demand
1.00	30	30.00	} $e = .08$	($TR\downarrow$ if $P\downarrow$)
0.00	35	0.00		

cannot say anything about the elasticity of the demand curve in other price ranges. For instance, in the region between $2.00 and $1.00, the elasticity coefficient is .27, and demand is inelastic. We must be careful not to attempt to guess at the elasticity of a demand curve. Except in a few limiting cases it is not possible to determine the elasticity by mere visual inspection of a graph. Instead, we will have to calculate the relevant coefficients each and every time.

There is a way to determine quickly whether a demand curve is elastic or inelastic without having to go through the cumbersome procedure of calculating the elasticity coefficient. This abbreviated procedure involves the comparison of the total amount spent by consumers *before* and *after* the price change. The total revenue received from the sale of the product is easily calculated by multiplying the price times the quantity sold. Price times quantity gives total revenue. If, subsequent to a *fall* in price total revenue falls, too, we can conclude that in that region the demand curve is *inelastic*. (The small increase in the quantity sold is not enough to make up for the revenue lost by lowering the price.) If revenue *increases* after a price decrease, then demand responds in an *elastic* fashion.

Limiting cases

Three limiting cases not only deepen our understanding of the elasticity concept but are also useful in much of the economic analysis to follow. These are the elasticities of infinity, unity, and zero. An *infinitely* (or perfectly) *elastic demand* curve is represented by a horizontal straight line (Figure 3-9). It shows that at that price *any* quantity will be demanded—i.e., a seller can sell all he wishes without affecting price. Because there is no price change, we will have to divide by zero when calculating the elasticity coefficient—which therefore will approach infinity.

A *unit elastic demand* curve shows a relationship where the loss in revenue from a price fall is exactly matched by an equal gain in revenue from the rise in quantity sold. Thus revenue stays constant all along the demand curve, which is described by a rectangular hyperbola. A unit elastic demand curve is shown in Figure 3-10.

Finally, a demand curve with an elasticity of zero—called a *perfectly inelastic demand* curve—is shown by a vertical straight line (Figure 3-11). No matter what the price, the quantity demanded remains constant. The elasticity coefficient in this case is zero.

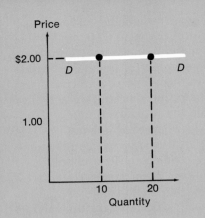

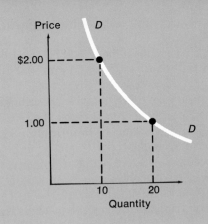

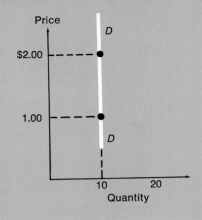

Figure 3-9

Infinitely elastic demand *Buyers are willing to buy any quantity at the going price.*

$$e = \frac{\frac{\Delta Q}{Q}}{\frac{\Delta P}{P}} = \frac{\frac{Q_1 - Q_2}{Q(\text{midpoint})}}{\frac{P_1 - P_2}{P(\text{midpoint})}}$$

$$= \frac{\frac{10}{15}}{\frac{0}{2.00}} = \infty$$

Figure 3-10

Unit elastic demand *A price fall is accompanied by a proportional increase in the quantity demanded.*

$$e = \frac{\frac{10}{15}}{\frac{1.00}{1.50}} = 1$$

Summary

Figure 3-11

Zero elastic demand *The quantity demanded is independent of price.*

$$e = \frac{\frac{0}{10}}{\frac{1.00}{1.50}} = 0$$

□ Consumption decisions are made by households. While a household may be composed of several members, there is one decision maker, who is responsible for the consumption decisions made.

□ The goal of the decision maker is to maximize the welfare of the economic unit. For the household this means the maximization of utility, satisfaction, or net benefits.

□ With each economic action we can associate certain costs and benefits. Costs incurred reduce the welfare of the unit, while benefits (utility) obtained increase welfare.

□ The rational decision maker will allocate his resources in such a way that costs and benefits (utility) are equal to each other for the last unit purchased: $MC = MU$.

□ For the consumer who faces given market prices, this means that he will demand the quantity at which the price of the product (his cost) is just equal to the marginal utility he can derive from the purchase of the last unit: $MU = MC = $ Price.

□ For many commodities, the optimal allocation rule says that the marginal utility obtained from the purchase of the last unit of each commodity should be proportional to its price:

$$\frac{MU_a}{P_a} = \frac{MU_b}{P_b} = \frac{MU_c}{P_c} = \cdots = \frac{MU_z}{P_z}.$$

□ Shifts of the whole demand curve occur when a variable other than the price of the commodity changes, such as the income of the household, the prices of other commodities, or tastes.

□ By adding the various quantities that individual consumers demand at each and every price, we are able to obtain a market demand curve for the product in a given market area.

□ *Elasticity* is an important measure of responsiveness of quantity purchased to price changes. It is defined as the percentage change in quantity divided by the percentage in price:

$$e = \frac{\Delta Q/Q}{\Delta P/P}.$$

The larger the elasticity coefficient, the greater the increase in quantity purchased after a fall in prices.

4

Production
and cost

The firm is the basic unit of production within the economic system. It is linked to other economic units in two main roles: it functions as a *buyer of inputs* required for the firm's operations, and it acts as a *seller of outputs* produced by the firm. The transformation of the various inputs into a product or an output that can be sold is called the production process. But before we can analyze in detail the firm's interaction with other economic units we must ask ourselves some basic questions about the goals pursued by the firm. Only if we have a clear understanding of the goal of the firm's actions, will we be able to analyze the actions the firm takes vis-à-vis other economic units.

Goals

There is somebody in each firm who has ultimate authority over the firm's actions: the decision maker. He may be the owner of the firm, the chairman of the board of directors, or somebody else. The only thing that is important is that he represents the ultimate authority responsible for the firm's actions. Just as a household ceases to exist as one economic unit if more than one person assumes the role of ultimate decision maker, a firm will no longer be one economic unit if two decision makers issue conflicting orders to the firm's employees.

If we are interested in analyzing the decisions undertaken by the decision maker, we have to seek out first of all the goal that the decision maker is trying to achieve. We will have to find an answer to this question if we want to be able to analyze and predict how a firm will react in response to various changes in its economic environment. Once the goal is defined, all other actions can be assessed in terms of this yardstick. All we have to do is seek out the course of action—among the alternative possibilities—that will bring the firm closest to its ultimate goal.

The ultimate goal of the firm is to *maximize its profits*. Of course, the firm must do so within the existing legal, social, and economic framework in which it is operating. This framework may impose certain constraints on the firm's actions: there are laws that prevent firms from utilizing child labor, from having women work over a certain number of hours per day, and from having them lift heavy loads. Laws require firms to install safety devices, to accept union representation in collective bargaining, to pay certain minimum wages, and the like. Not every constraint imposed upon a firm is in the form of a law. There may be social customs, which prevent people from opening their shops on Sundays, from changing their prices constantly, or from charging different prices to different customers. Sometimes a firm may find it profitable to refrain from "cashing in" on a short-run opportunity to make additional profits. If the firm were to grab every possible opportunity, some old customers might get upset and take their business elsewhere. Hence it might be in the interest of long-run profit maximization *not* to seize every short-run opportunity. But everything else being equal, the firm would always like to make more money, and make higher profits.

Profits are defined as the difference between the firm's revenues and its costs of production. Revenues are simply the receipts obtained from the sale of the firm's products. Costs are incurred because resources—which do have alternative uses—are used in the production process. While a more complete discussion of costs will follow later in the chapter, we should point out now that economic costs of production do not only include explicit monetary costs but also implicit costs that are incurred by the use of resources for which no monetary payments have to be made.

Profit maximization by the firm is a goal analogous to the goal of utility maximization by the consumer. One major difference exists. Profits can easily be measured in dollars and cents, and can thereby provide an objective yardstick by which we can evaluate the performance of a firm. Utility defies to some extent precise quantification. These problems of quantification are not as serious in the theory of the firm, where we are dealing with dollars and cents.

Why do firms exist?

The next question we have to tackle is the reason for the existence of firms. Rather than carrying on production in firms as we know them, we could have alternative systems of producing the commodities demanded by consumers. For instance, we could imagine a system where individuals produce commodities without ever employing anybody else. Rather than producing one whole automobile, there would be persons who would produce only wheels. Others would produce only windshield glass, taillights, or door latches. There might be a person who assembled engines, and who purchased all the required parts from other individuals. And eventually, there might be a person who would assemble the car from all the individual parts bought by him. While such a process is definitely possible, and may perhaps even be followed by specialty-car fans who want to build their own car from scratch, it is a very time-consuming and costly procedure to follow when building an automobile.

Rather than purchasing all the various inputs required for the car, it may be much more efficient to have the whole production process take place in one firm, thereby eliminating market transactions that would require an especially great amount of information and time. Information costs and time costs of purchasing every item in the market may be very high and therefore it may be a lot more efficient to build the required parts within the firm and to eliminate most direct market transactions.

A firm, then, is basically a production unit *within which* market transactions are eliminated in order to save on the costs associated with such transactions.

Obviously, the elimination of the market and its replacement by dealings with other economic units may not be an unmixed blessing. By going out into the market for the purchase of our inputs, we make sure that we will obtain the resources from the cheapest possible source. By substituting production within the firm for purchases from outside sources, this check on efficiency is lost. We may not be able to get very precise information about the cost of producing a specific item ourselves. In the market, where dollar and cent values are attached to individual items, we immediately know the precise cost of a resource or other input to us.

We should always keep in mind that there are both advantages and disadvantages associated with the use of the market and the by-passing of market transactions by substituting intrafirm transformations. Thus there are instances where we find both the use of the market and the circumvention of the market side by side in the same industry. In the petroleum industry there are certain large firms that do their own prospecting, own their own oilfields, do the drilling, transport the crude oil in company ships, refine the oil, and finally sell it in company-owned gas stations. In such vertically integrated industries, the market is eliminated to a very large extent. Compare this to the alternative, where an independent prospector does the exploring, somebody else does the drilling, the well operator sells his crude oil to a refinery, the oil is transported in chartered ships, and it is sold by independent gas stations. Here we find a market transaction at virtually every major step in the production process. At every step transaction and information costs are incurred. But we also make sure that we are able to utilize the cheapest possible source of our materials.

In a firm, once the inputs required for the production process are purchased or hired, it is up to the entrepreneur to combine these inputs in the most efficient manner. Workers, raw materials, and other productive resources can be combined according to his wishes. Obviously, the success—or failure—of the firm will depend largely on the skill and talent of the entrepreneur in combining the various factors of production to produce commodities in the most efficient manner possible.

The production function

In the production process the firm combines various inputs to produce different outputs. This *technological* relationship between inputs and outputs is called *the production function*. The production function occupies an extremely important place in the theory of the firm.

For simplicity's sake, let us assume that we have to deal only with one variable input and one variable output. All other parameters are assumed to be constant. We may consider the production function of a farm and assume that labor is the only variable input and wheat the only variable output. In other words, the acreage, the farm buildings, the tractors, and all other equipment used to produce wheat are held constant, and we will observe what happens to wheat output as successively more and more workers are hired.

Note that the production function is a purely technological relationship, where physical units of labor input are related to physical units of output, in this case, tons of wheat. In Table 4-1 we give a hypothetical production function for the farm, and we graph the data contained in the table in Figure 4-1. Along the horizontal axis we measure the number of workers employed and on the vertical axis the tons of wheat produced during a given time period. The production function shows the maximum amount of wheat that can be produced by the number of workers indicated.

One worker alone can produce one third of a ton of wheat. Two workers can produce a whole ton, three workers 2.4 tons and so on. Typically, the production function exhibits the slight **S**-shape indicated in Figure 4-1. We may distinguish two zones of the production function: a region of increasing slope, and a region of decreasing slope. In the area of increasing slope, each additional person employed increases the output by more than the previous person. The first person produces 0.3 tons of wheat, the second person 0.7 tons, the third 1.4 tons, and the fourth worker 1.6 tons. This phenomenon is

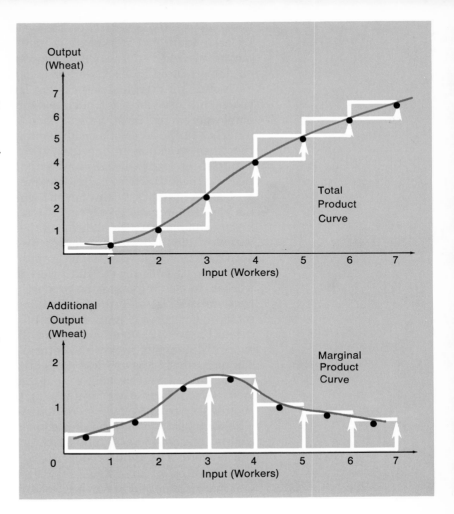

Figure 4-1

The total product curve *The total product curve—or production function—shows the relationship between physical units of inputs (graphed along the horizontal axis) and physical units of outputs (along the vertical axis).*

Figure 4-2

The marginal product curve *The marginal product curve shows the additional output produced by the last unit of input added.*

Table 4-1

Input units	Total output units		Additional output units	
0	0			
1	0.3	>	0.3	Increasing marginal returns
2	1.0	>	0.7	Increasing marginal returns
3	2.4	>	1.4	Increasing marginal returns
4	4.0	>	1.6	Increasing marginal returns
5	5.0	>	1.0	Decreasing marginal returns
6	5.8	>	0.8	Decreasing marginal returns
7	6.4	>	0.6	Decreasing marginal returns

due to *increasing returns*. Because we talk about the output produced by each additional worker, it is more accurately called *increasing marginal returns*. The curve showing the marginal (additional) output produced by each worker is depicted in Figure 4-2.

Increasing marginal returns are largely due to specialization of the inputs used in the production process. If only one worker is employed on the farm, he will have to perform a large variety of different tasks. As soon as additional workers are hired, each one of them can specialize in one task, save time spent in moving about and getting ready for each new activity, and increase his efficiency in doing the job because he becomes more competent with experience.

But there comes a point beyond which further specialization does not yield greater and greater additional returns. This point is reached in our example after the addition of the fourth worker. The additional output of the fifth worker is lower: he adds only 1.0 tons to the total output. After that, additional output per worker diminishes even further to 0.8 tons for the sixth worker and 0.6 tons for the seventh worker. In this region of the production function (between 4 and 7 workers) *diminishing marginal returns* prevail. The steepness of the total product curve (Figure 4-1) diminishes and the marginal product curve (Figure 4-2) slopes downward. The basic reason for the existence of diminishing marginal returns to labor is that each worker has successively less and less units of the *other* inputs to work with: there is only so much land, so many machines, and so much equipment. Given these other fixed inputs, the additional output that can be produced when we add more units of labor becomes less and less.

Eventually, we may reach a point at which further additions of laborers will not increase total output at all; i.e., their marginal output will be zero. The total product curve would be horizontal and the marginal product curve would show a zero output. It may even happen that marginal output of further workers is negative: they get in each other's way, start to trample down the wheat, and so on. Obviously, no firm would ever want to operate in the range of the production function where marginal returns are negative.

While the production function for most commodities has the general shape outlined here, its precise shape will vary greatly from commodity to commodity. The range of increasing returns may be very long, and prevail for all practically relevant output levels. Also, we often find a stretch of constant returns in between the increasing and decreasing returns segments. But, eventually, production functions will exhibit diminishing returns.

Economic costs

The production function provides us with the technological information underlying the production process. It relates physical inputs and physical outputs. It is now necessary to say something about production costs. But before we talk about the cost of production, we must make clear what we mean by costs.

The economic costs of doing one thing, e.g., producing wheat, are the alternatives that have to be forgone in order to produce the wheat. For instance, we have to forgo the production of corn, tomatoes, or barley. The alternatives forgone or the opportunities sacrificed constitute the true economic cost of engaging in an activity: economists speak of *opportunity costs* in this context.

It is generally quite simple and straightforward to determine the economic cost of using a resource, if a monetary payment has to be made for its use. In that case, the costs are *explicit:* the amount is stated in dollars and cents.

But quite often no direct payment is required for the use of a certain resource. In this case we have to estimate the *implicit* costs of using the resources. An estimation of the implicit cost of using an economic resource involves an appraisal of all the alternative uses to which this resource could have been put. The best possible alternative use constitutes the true cost of using the resource.

Let us elaborate a bit. If you work on your own farm, you generally do not pay yourself explicitly a salary. Instead, you take whatever is left over after accounting for all other costs. But what is the economic cost of your working on the farm? It all depends. It depends on the alternatives that you forgo by working on the farm. If the best outside job you could have held is being a storeclerk for $5,000 per year, this amount is your implicit cost of working on the farm. But if you hold an M.D. degree, your alternatives forgone might well be $20,000 or more per year, hence this amount would be your implicit cost of working on the farm.

All economic costs are opportunity costs and depend on the alternatives forgone. In case of money payments, the opportunity costs are explicitly stated. If no monetary payments are involved, we have to estimate the implicit costs by calculating the value of the best alternative sacrificed.

The total cost function

Having defined what we mean by costs, we can proceed with the derivation of the cost function for the firm. Let us return to the example of the farm, which uses labor as an input and produces wheat. We know the physical relationship between inputs and outputs as summarized in the production function. One additional piece of information is required to calculate the cost function for the farm: the wage that each worker receives. Let us assume that it is $10.00. We will also assume that labor is the only relevant cost of production for the time being. This will make our initial example a bit easier. Other inputs are introduced in the next section.

When graphing a cost function, it is customary to show the costs on the vertical axis and the output levels on the horizontal axis. Hence we have to reverse the axes from our production function diagram. Also, each *physical* unit of labor input has to be multiplied by the *costs* involved in using this input: the wage we have to pay each worker. Two workers at $10.00 each cost $20.00. It takes two workers to produce one ton of wheat output, hence the cost of the first ton of wheat is $20.00. It costs $28.00 to produce 2 tons, $33.00 for 3 tons, and so on. The data are presented in Table 4-2 and are shown in Figure 4-3.

We note that the cost function exhibits first a decreasing slope (rightward curvature) and then an increasing slope (leftward curvature). This is the precise opposite of the production function, whose mirror image the cost function is. Obviously, the reasons for the curvature of both curves are the same: at first increasing returns lower the costs of producing additional units because of the cost savings resulting from specialization. After that, costs increase more and more rapidly because of the prevailing decreasing returns to our variable input labor. Each additional worker has less and less of the other inputs to work with. In addition, costs of coordination between the workers may go up and cause the cost function to rise at an ever faster pace.

Fixed and variable costs

In the last section we assumed that labor is the only input required in the production of wheat. Obviously, this is a gross simplification. Other factors of production play a role: the land used to grow the

Figure 4-3

The total cost curve *The total cost curve shows the dollar cost (explicit plus implicit costs) of production along the vertical axis and the output quantity on the horizontal axis.*

Table 4-2

Output	Total cost
0	$ 0.00
1	20.00
2	28.00
3	33.00
4	40.00
5	50.00
6	64.00
7	84.00

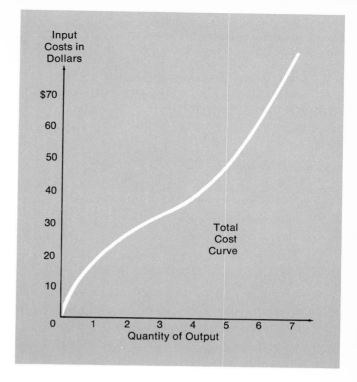

wheat, the fertilizer used, the seed grains, the machinery and other equipment used by the workers, and so on. These other costs have to be accounted for, too.

As a general rule, not all inputs can be adjusted instantly. Some inputs are fixed for a certain time period. We may have signed a five-year lease for the land, may have to pay a fixed amount of taxes, and the like. Fixed inputs do *not* vary with the rate of output.

Economists distinguish two different periods: the *long-run*, in which all inputs are variable, and the *short-run*, where some inputs are fixed. In the long-run period, all costs are variable; in the short-run some costs are variable, while others are fixed. Figure 4-4 depicts a total cost curve, which is decomposed into a variable cost curve, showing all costs that vary with the rate of output, and a fixed cost curve, showing the costs that remain constant. The vertical addition of fixed and variable costs shows the total costs of producing a certain quantity of output—resulting in the white total cost curve of Figure 4-4. The corresponding data are presented in Table 4-3.

Figure 4-4

Fixed and variable costs *In the short run, some factors of production cannot be changed, and we may therefore distinguish between fixed costs—which are independent of the rate of output—and variable costs—which depend on the output level.*

Table 4-3

Output	Variable costs	Fixed costs	Total costs
0	$ 0	$10.00	$10.00
1	10.00	10.00	20.00
2	18.00	10.00	28.00
3	23.00	10.00	33.00
4	30.00	10.00	40.00
5	40.00	10.00	50.00
6	54.00	10.00	64.00
7	74.00	10.00	84.00

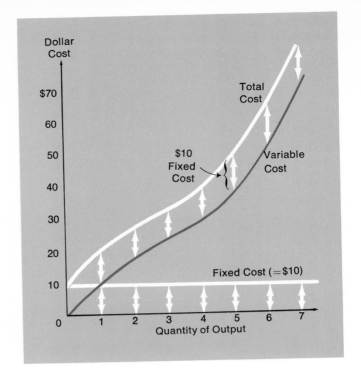

Table 4-4

Quantity	Average cost	Total cost	Marginal cost
0		0	
			$20.00
1	$20.00	$20.00	
			8.00
2	14.00	28.00	
			5.00
3	11.00	33.00	
			7.00
4	10.00	40.00	
			10.00
5	10.00	50.00	
			14.00
6	10.67	64.00	
			20.00
7	12.00	84.00	

Average and marginal costs

Two other cost concepts are frequently used and are highly important in the derivation of the supply curve and in establishing criteria for expansion or contraction of the whole industry. These are average and marginal costs.

Average cost can be calculated by dividing total cost of production by the quantity produced: $AC = TC/Q$. This is done in Table 4-4 and graphed in Figures 4-5 and 4-6.

Figure 4-5

The total cost curve

Average costs are obtained by dividing the total costs by the quantity produced. Marginal costs are the incremental costs of expanding output by one unit and are shown as the white boxes.

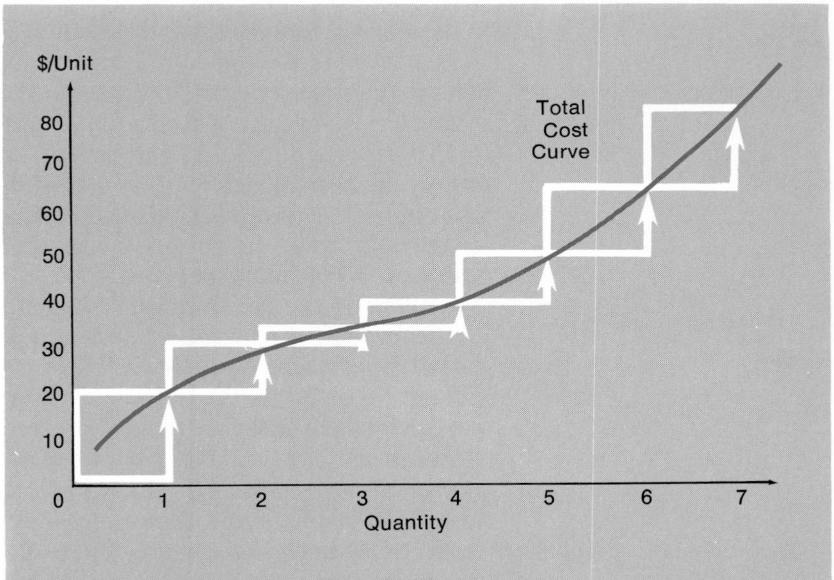

Figure 4-6

Average costs and marginal costs

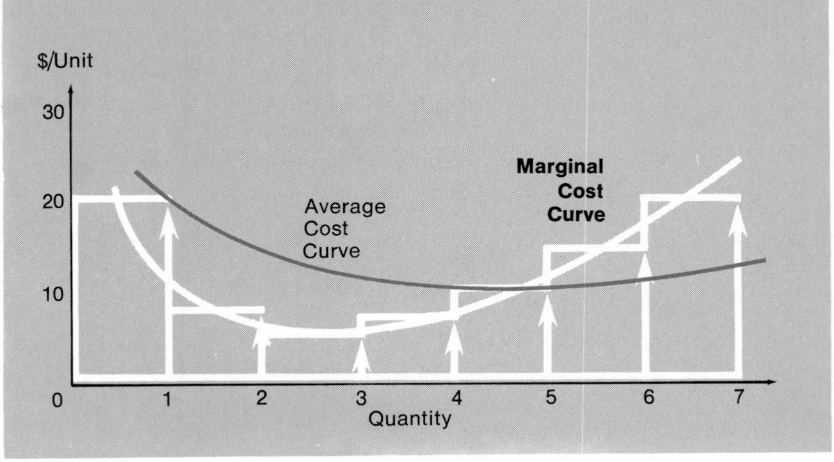

Marginal costs are the additional cost of producing one more unit of output. They are the increments by which total costs increase as output is expanded by one unit. For instance, the total cost of producing 4 tons of wheat is $40.00 and the total cost of 5 tons is $50.00. Hence the additional, or marginal, cost of producing the fifth ton is $10.00. Marginal cost curves are generally **U**-shaped. The reason is found in the mathematical relationship between total and marginal costs. If the total cost curve decreases in steepness, marginal costs decrease; if the total cost curve increases in steepness, the marginal costs rise too. Hence decreasing marginal costs are due mainly to increasing specialization, while increasing marginal costs are caused by diminishing returns to factors, as well as increased costs of information and coordination in production.

Because average cost and marginal cost curves look so very similar, it is all the more important to distinguish carefully between the two. The average cost curve shows *per unit* production cost; the marginal cost curve shows the cost of producing the *last additional* unit alone.

There is a simple geometric relationship between average and marginal costs, which may be noted. When marginal costs are *below* average cost—that is, the cost of producing an additional unit is less than the average cost of producing the previous units—average cost will fall. When marginal cost is *above* average cost, the higher cost of producing the additional unit will pull the average up—the average cost curve rises. This can be seen in Figure 4-6, where marginal cost is below average cost for the first 4 tons—resulting in a falling average cost curve. At output levels greater than 5 tons, marginal cost exceeds average cost and therefore the average cost curve rises. Because of this relationship between average and marginal costs, the marginal cost curve will always cut the average cost curve at the minimum point of the average cost curve.

Because marginal costs refer to the *increase* in total costs when one more unit of output is produced, the value for the marginal costs has to be graphed at the *midpoint of the interval* between two units. For instance, if the total cost of producing one ton of wheat is $20.00, and of two tons is $28.00, then the marginal cost of the second ton is $8.00 and should be graphed in the middle of the interval between 1 and 2 tons on the horizontal axis.

Summary

□ The *goal* of the firm is to obtain the largest possible *profits*. Profits are the difference between a firm's *costs* and the *revenues* it obtains by selling its products.

□ The *production function* gives us the technological relationship between *physical* units of *inputs* and physical units of *outputs*.

□ Typically, we at first experience *increasing marginal returns* when more inputs are added. This is due to increased specialization made possible by the larger scale of operations. But eventually, *diminishing marginal returns* set in because each additional input has less and less of the other inputs to work with. Also, costs of coordination between the inputs—the managerial effort—may increase.

□ Economic costs are *opportunity costs*. They represent *alternatives forgone*. Costs may involve *explicit* monetary payments for the use of the inputs, or they may involve *implicit* opportunity costs. Implicit costs are incurred when no monetary payments are made. They can be estimated by considering the value of the best alternative forgone.

□ The total cost curve can be obtained from the total product curve by replacing the physical units of inputs used in the production process by their opportunity costs in terms of dollars.

□ In the *long run,* all factors of production and therefore all costs are *variable*. The *short run* is defined as a period during which some inputs are *fixed* and cannot be altered. Hence there are fixed costs of production in the short run. Fixed cost plus variable cost equals total cost.

□ *Average costs* of production are the total costs divided by the quantity of output. They are the unit cost of production.

□ *Marginal costs* are the additional cost incurred by producing just *one* more unit of output. They are the *change in total cost* when output is expanded by one unit. Typically, marginal costs first decrease because of the savings from increased specialization, and then increase as a result of the diminishing marginal returns of a variable input that has to work with a fixed amount of other inputs.

5

The competitive firm

In the two previous chapters we analyzed the structure of the basic decision-making units of the economic system: households and firms. Households buy goods and services for consumption, and firms sell their products in the market place.

Market structure

The markets in which buyers and sellers trade vary greatly in their structure, and different market structures not only influence the behavior of buyers and sellers in the market but also lead to different prices and trade volumes. In this and the following chapters we will analyze the effect of different market structures on the behavior patterns of buyers and sellers.

Market structures differ from each other in slight gradations. They cover a spectrum that ranges from an industry where there are so many firms that each one supplies only a small proportion of the goods traded, to the case of only one firm, which constitutes the industry.

Economists find it convenient to distinguish between four basic patterns of market structure: pure competition, monopolistic competition, oligopoly, and pure monopoly. Of course, these basic types can serve only as approximations to the fine gradations that may be found in actual markets, but they provide us with some basic reference points that will be useful in the analysis of the different behavior patterns found in various industries. All "impure" market structures, like monopolistic competition, oligopoly, and monopoly are often referred to collectively as *imperfect competition.*

When talking about market structure, we must be careful to remember that there are always two sides to every market: the buyer's side and the seller's side. Different market structures may exist on each side of the market. For instance, we may find that the seller is a monopolist, but that there are many buyers who compete against each other. Our classification scheme applies to either the buyer's or the seller's side of the market as illustrated in Figure 5-1.

In a *purely competitive* market situation, we find a large number of sellers (or buyers) of a standardized product. That is, every firm

Figure 5-1

Market structure *The struc- ture of a market is deter- mined by the conditions of competition on both the buyer's and seller's side.*

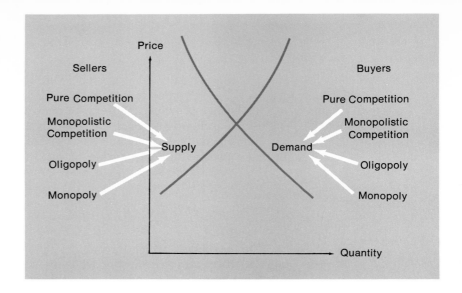

produces identical items, which are readily substituted for each other. Further, entry into the industry is easy. Anybody who wants to produce this product can do so, and there are no prohibitive amounts of capital required to start a firm. Firms are always free to discon- tinue production and leave the industry. One of the consequences of these characteristics is that each individual firm has no control over the price of the product. Each producer is too small to influence the price—even if that firm were to withdraw from production com- pletely.

A reasonably good example for a purely competitive market is farming, where there are many producers of standardized products, and no barriers to entry into the farming industry. The individual farmer is a price taker, who has no control over the price at which he can sell his product. On the other hand, a purely competitive firm can sell any quantity it wishes to sell at the going market price.

In *monopolistic competition,* each firm has some slight control over the market price. This is due to the assumption that while there are still a considerable number of sellers (or buyers) competing in the market, the product sold is slightly differentiated. Good examples are provided by the retail trade and the restaurant business, where we generally find a large number of sellers competing with each other— but the products are not perfectly identical. While all restaurants serve food, they will differ in the quality of the food, in the service provided, and in the pleasantness of the surroundings—all factors that differentiate one restaurant's product from that of another. A

Table 5-1 Characteristics of basic market structures

	Number of firms	Product differentiation	Entry and exit conditions	Firm's control over price	Example
Pure competition	Many	Standardized products	Easy	None (price-takers)	Agriculture
Imperfect competition					
□ monopolistic competition	Considerable	Differentiated product	Relatively easy	Slight	Retail trade, restaurants
□ oligopoly	Few	Standardized or differentiated	Difficult	Considerable	Automobiles, steel
□ pure monopoly	One	Unique product, no close substitutes	Effectively blocked	Strong	Public utilities

consequence of the product differentiation is that each seller has some slight control over the market price. The price of a pizza may differ from restaurant to restaurant, but not by very much.

In an *oligopoly* situation, we have only a few sellers (or buyers) in the market. Generally, these are fairly large firms, and there may be legal or financial barriers to entry into the industry: for instance, the firms may own patents for the production of their specialties, or the large sums of capital required to start a new firm may effectively bar newcomers from entry into the industry. Products may be standardized, as in the steel industry, or they may be differentiated, as in the automobile industry. Each firm in the industry has considerable influence over the price of the product it sells, and if the firms manage to make an agreement as to market shares, prices charged, or output to be produced, price control may be very strong.

Finally, in a *monopoly* situation, there is—by definition—only one firm in the industry. This monopolist is the sole producer of the product, and no close substitutes exist. Consequently, the monopolist has a very strong influence on the price charged. His position is generally protected by either legal or financial barriers to entry into the industry. Of course, if other firms were to succeed in entering, the monopoly would be destroyed, and the industry might develop into an oligopoly. Most public utilities like electricity, gas, and water companies enjoy local monopolies. The post office has a national monopoly on the carrying of mail. The characteristics of the various market structures are summarized in Table 5-1.

Profit maximization by the competitive firm

In this chapter we will analyze the behavior of the firm in a purely competitive market environment. The most important aspect of the firm's position in a purely competitive market is that the firm is a *price taker*—it has no control over the price that it can obtain for its product. The price is determined in the market by the interaction of a large number of buyers and sellers, and it is a given parameter for the firm.

In the last chapter we argued that the goal of the firm's behavior is the maximization of profits. Profits are the difference between a firm's revenues obtained by the sale of its output and the costs incurred by using the inputs required for production. Let us remind ourselves that costs include not only the explicit money costs paid out, but also the implicit opportunity costs of using other factors. Because a normal return to the funds invested as well as an appropriate charge for the manager's and/or owner's efforts is included in the firm's costs, our definition of profit used here differs from the one usually employed by businessmen. Businessmen consider as profits the difference between their dollar revenues and their dollar costs, that is, their explicit monetary costs. Profits—in their language—include the returns earned on the capital invested and the returns earned as a result of the efforts of the entrepreneur. But we consider that amount which these factors of production could have earned somewhere else as *opportunity costs* or implicit nonmonetary costs.

By using our more comprehensive cost concept, the actual profit figures arrived at are smaller than the ones usually quoted by businessmen. Only if we earn a return above and beyond the explicit and implicit costs of production do we speak of earning a profit in the economists' sense. To earn a profit, then, means that we are doing better than we could have possibly done anywhere else with all our resources. Profits, in the economists' language, are an *additional* amount earned above and beyond the normal return to all inputs. A firm that makes no profits at all according to our definition is still doing fine and has no incentive to go out of business. It is earning as much of a return on its resources as could be earned anywhere else.

The firm can determine its best profit position in one of two ways: (1) it may compare its total costs and total revenues from the sale of its product and choose to operate at that output level at which total revenues exceed total costs by the largest possible margin, or (2) it may adopt a marginal approach and determine up to which output level further production is adding to its profits. That is, up to which output level the additional revenues exceed the additional costs. Let us look at each approach in turn.

The total revenue–total cost approach

Total profit is the difference between total revenue and total cost of production. The total cost curve for the firm was derived in the previous chapter, and it is reproduced in Figure 5-2. Total revenue depends on the market price and the number of units sold. Let us assume that the market price is $17.00 per ton of wheat. That is, the total revenue obtained by selling 1 ton is $17.00, by selling 2 tons $34.00, and so on. The relevant data are presented in Table 5-2. The firm that maximizes profits will produce at an output level of 6 tons. At this output level the firm obtains $102.00 revenue and incurs $64.00 costs, leaving a profit of $38.00. Production of only 5 tons lowers profits to $35.00 and production of 7 tons results in only $35.00 profit. Hence, 6 tons is optimal from the profit viewpoint.

The marginal revenue = marginal cost approach

Using a marginal approach, the firm will produce more output as long as each *additional* unit brings more revenue than it costs to produce. That is, the firm's output will expand as long as marginal revenues are greater than marginal costs. If marginal revenues are smaller than marginal costs, the firm will not produce this unit because it would diminish its profits by doing so. Output will be cut back. At a point at which marginal costs (MC) are just equal to marginal revenues (MR), the firm has neither an incentive to expand nor one to contract. The firm has found its profit maximizing equilibrium output when $MC = MR$.

Let us remind ourselves that we are dealing with a firm that operates in a purely competitive market environment: it is a price taker. The price of $17.00 that the firm obtains for each ton of wheat is also its marginal revenue, that is, the revenue obtained by selling each additional ton. Hence, for a price taker, the $MC = MR$ rule might be expanded to give the profit-maximizing output level as

Figure 5-2

Costs, revenues, and profits
Total profits are the difference between total revenues and total costs. Costs include both explicit and implicit cost elements.

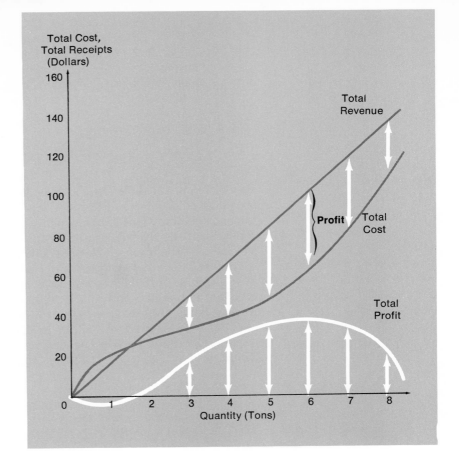

Table 5-2

Output	Total revenue	Total cost	Profit
0	$ 0.00	$ 0.00	$ 0.00
1	17.00	20.00	−3.00
2	34.00	28.00	6.00
3	51.00	33.00	18.00
4	68.00	40.00	28.00
5	85.00	50.00	35.00
6	102.00	64.00	38.00
7	119.00	84.00	35.00
8	136.00	112.00	24.00

Figure 5-3

Marginal costs and revenues
A firm will find it advantageous (from the profit viewpoint) to expand production as long as the additional revenues are greater than the additional costs incurred. The optimal output level is reached where MC = MR.

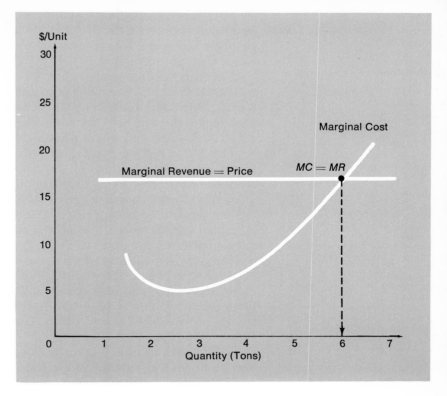

Table 5-3

Output	Total revenue	Marginal revenue		Marginal cost		Total cost
0	$ 0.00			$20.00	<	$ 0.00
1	17.00	> $17.00		8.00	<	20.00
2	34.00	> 17.00		5.00	<	28.00
3	51.00	> 17.00	MR > MC	7.00	<	33.00
4	68.00	> 17.00		10.00	<	40.00
5	85.00	> 17.00		14.00	<	50.00
6	102.00	> 17.00	MR = MC	20.00	<	64.00
7	119.00	> 17.00		28.00	<	84.00
8	136.00	> 17.00	MR < MC		<	112.00

occurring when *MC = MR = Price*. But note that this latter result will hold true only for the case of pure competition, where we have a constant price at which the firm's output can be sold and where price therefore is identical with marginal revenue. Using this rule, the optimal output level in Figure 5-3 is 6 tons.

Note that the marginal cost and revenue data refer to *increments* in output, and hence the *MC* and *MR* data shown in Table 5-3 and graphed in Figure 5-3 refer to the midpoints of the intervals for which they are calculated.

For output levels smaller than 6 tons, $MR > MC$, and the firm will find it profitable to expand output. For output levels greater than 6 tons, $MR < MC$, indicating that it is not profitable to produce in that range: the firm will cut back. The optimal output is 6 tons, at which $MC = MR$ and where profits are maximized.

The $MC = MR$ approach also provides a direct answer to the question about the nature of the firm's supply curve. The supply schedule of a firm shows the quantity that the firm is willing to supply at each and every possible price. Table 5-3 and Figure 5-3 provide the answer. If the market price is $20.00, the firm will supply 6.5 tons, as at that output level $MC = MR$. If the market price is $10.00, the firm supplies 4.5 tons, and so on.

The competitive firm, which is faced with a given market price, needs only to equate the market price (which is equal to *MR*) with its own marginal cost of production. The *MC* curve shows the marginal costs, and hence the profit-maximizing output level is shown by the firm's marginal cost curve. The *marginal cost curve* is the *supply curve* for the perfectly competitive firm.

One important qualification needs to be made, however. There may be prices at which the firm cannot even cover its variable costs of production. The mechanistic equating of $MC = MR$ to find the firm's optimal output level leads to loss minimization instead of profit maximization in this case. We have, therefore, to be careful to state the side condition that the firm's revenues must be at least large enough to cover its variable cost of production. Fixed costs are there in any case—irrespective of whether and how much the firm produces. But variable costs are incurred only if the firm actually produces some output. Hence, if the firm cannot cover at least its variable costs of production, it will shut down.

The industry supply curve

In Chapter 2 we indicated that the aggregate supply curve for the whole industry is nothing more than a horizontal addition of the individual firm's supply curves. All we have to do is add the quantities supplied by each firm at every possible price and we obtain the aggregate supply curve for the industry. Of course, this process assumes that the number of firms in the industry is known. By holding the number of firms in the industry constant, we have es-

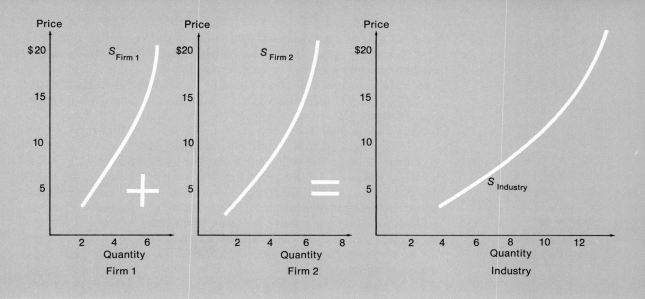

Figure 5-4

The industry supply curve *The industry short-run supply curve is obtained by adding the quantities supplied by the various firms at each and every market price.*

Table 5-4

Price	Output firm 1	Output firm 2	Industry output
$ 5.00	2.5	2.5	5.0
10.00	4.5	4.5	9.0
15.00	5.7	5.7	11.4
20.00	6.5	6.5	13.0

sentially a short-run situation. We derive the industry supply curve for a given number of firms in Figure 5-4 and Table 5-4.

To determine whether other firms will be attracted into the industry (or whether there are firms that will want to leave the industry) we will have to look at total profits. If the firms in the industry make profits, this offers an attraction for other firms to enter the industry. Hence we must look at the amount of profits made by individual firms before we can say anything about firms entering or leaving the industry.

Profit determination

So far, we have determined the output level at which the firm's profits will be maximized. But we still don't know how large the firm's profits actually are. This is our next task. To determine total profits we have to know about total revenues and total costs. We may derive total profits directly from Table 5-2. Alternatively, total revenues can be calculated by multiplying price (average revenue) times the quantity sold. Table 5-5 gives the total amount of revenue obtained at different output levels. Total costs are obtained by multiplying average costs times output. Of course, the difference between total revenues and total costs will give us our total profits figure. At the optimal output of 6 tons of wheat, total profit is equal to $38.00.

Graphically, profits can be obtained in Figure 5-5 as the difference between the *area ABEO* (price times quantity) showing total revenues, and the area *CDEO* (average cost times quantity) showing total costs. The crosshatched area *ABDC* shows the total profits of the firm.

But let us keep in mind that there is no reason why total profits should be positive in all cases. If, for instance, the market price were to fall to $8.00, the optimum output level for the firm would be 4 tons, according to our $MC = MR$ rule. But at that output level, average costs are $10.00, and hence greater than average revenues, which are equal to our price of $8.00. As a result, the firm will make a per unit loss of $2.00 or a total *loss* of $8.00 (total revenue of $32.00 minus total costs of $40.00).

The long run

Profits not only serve as an important signaling device telling the individual firm how much to produce; they also serve as a signal to other firms to enter or to leave the industry. If we assume that all firms within a given industry have the same production function, all firms will have identical cost curves. Hence, if one firm makes profits, all firms make profits. Let us remind ourselves what we mean by profits. They are the difference between total revenues and costs, where costs include not only the explicit monetary costs of production but also the implicit opportunity costs of employing nonremunerated inputs. Whenever a firm makes a profit, according to our definition, it earns more than all the inputs together could have earned in their best alternate use. The existence of profits is therefore a signaling device that indicates that in this industry returns are higher than in other industries. Obviously, this will attract new firms into the industry—all of them in search of higher returns.

Additional firms will enter the industry as long as positive profits offer an incentive to do so. But as the new firms enter, they will *shift* the *aggregate* supply curve for the whole industry to the right, because we have to add the supply curves for the new firms to those of firms already in the industry. Let us return to our initial example, which is illustrated by Figure 5-6 and Table 5-6. If the market price for wheat is $17.00 per ton, each firm produces 6 tons and makes $38.00 profit. Let us assume that there are 1,000 firms in the industry. As new firms enter, the aggregate supply curve for the industry shifts

Figure 5-5

Profits *A firm will maximize its profits by producing the output at which MC = MR. The total profits are given by the difference between total revenues (AR × Q) and total costs (AC × Q). Total profits are shown by the shaded area.*

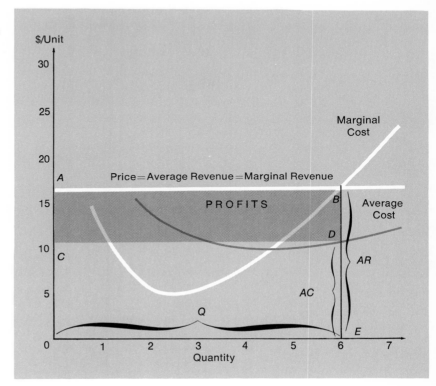

Table 5-5

Quantity	Average cost	Total cost		Marginal cost	Marginal revenue		Total revenue	Price-average revenue	Total profit
0	$ 0.00	$ 0.00					$ 0.00	$ 0.00	$ 0.00
1	20.00	20.00	>	$20.00	$17.00	<	17.00	17.00	−3.00
2	14.00	28.00	>	8.00	17.00	<	34.00	17.00	6.00
3	11.00	33.00	>	5.00	17.00	<	51.00	17.00	18.00
4	10.00	40.00	>	7.00	17.00	<	68.00	17.00	28.00
5	10.00	50.00	>	10.00	17.00	<	85.00	17.00	35.00
6	10.67	64.00	>	14.00	17.00	<	102.00	17.00	38.00
7	12.00	84.00	>	20.00	17.00	<	119.00	17.00	35.00
8	14.00	112.00	>	28.00	17.00	<	136.00	17.00	24.00

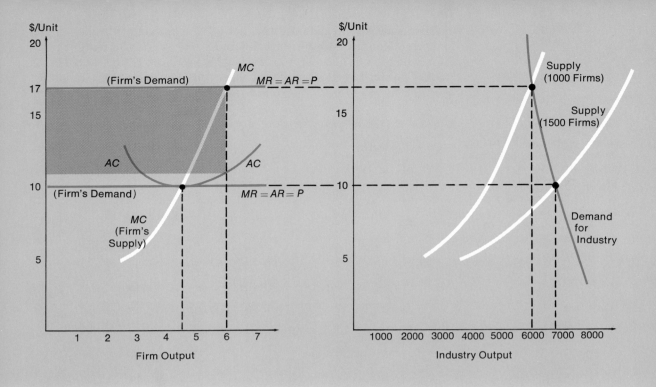

Figure 5-6

The firm and the industry

If individual firms earn profits, this serves as a signal for other firms to enter the industry. As the industry expands, the aggregate supply curve for the whole industry shifts to the right.

Table 5-6

Price	Quantity supplied by 1 firm	Quantity supplied by 1,000 firms	Quantity supplied by 1,500 firms	Quantity demanded
$ 9.00	4.2	4200	6300	6850
10.00	4.5	4500	6750	6750
11.00	4.7	4700	7050	6650
⋮	⋮	⋮	⋮	⋮
16.00	5.8	5800	8700	6075
17.00	6.0	6000	9000	6000
18.00	6.2	6200	9300	5925

to the right. Consequently, the market price will tend to fall. This process will stop only when there is no longer an incentive for new firms to enter the industry. This comes about when profits are reduced to zero, i.e., when total costs equal total revenues, or when average costs equal average revenues (= price). In our example this occurs when the price has dropped—because of the entry of the new firms—to $10.00.

Let us assume that the entry of 500 new firms into the industry is sufficient to make the market price drop to $10.00. Given this new price, each firm will try to determine its best output level. Each individual firm equates MC and MR to find its own optimal position. We find that MC equals MR at an output level of 4.5 tons. Each one of the 1,500 firms in the industry will produce 4.5 tons, resulting in an aggregate industry output of (1,500 times 4.5 tons) 6,750 tons.

Now each individual firm no longer makes any returns above and beyond what each input could have earned in its best alternative use, and there is no longer an incentive for firms to enter the industry. The industry had reached equilibrium when each firm operates at a level where $AC = AR$ (zero profit). Also, each firm is in equilibrium, because it produces in a situation where $MC = MR$.

Both the firm and the industry will be in long-run equilibrium when both of the above conditions are fulfilled:

$AC = AR$ (industry equilibrium; no new entry or exit)
$MC = MR$ (firm equilibrium; no output changes).

Both conditions are fulfilled when each firm operates at an output level of 4.5 tons, with the result that average costs equal marginal costs of $10.00, and market price equals average revenue equals marginal revenue also of $10.00.

Of course, if the price were initially *below* this $10.00 level, the process described above would be reversed: firms would make losses, and some would leave the industry in search of higher returns. The aggregate supply curve would shift to the left, and each individual firm would produce a bit more.

The long-run supply curve for the industry

Let us assume that we have an industry that purchases all its inputs in purely competitive markets. That is, the firms in that industry can buy as many inputs as they wish to purchase at a constant price. Then it will be possible for this industry to expand without the price for its inputs increasing. Because its costs of production do not increase, its output price can also remain constant.

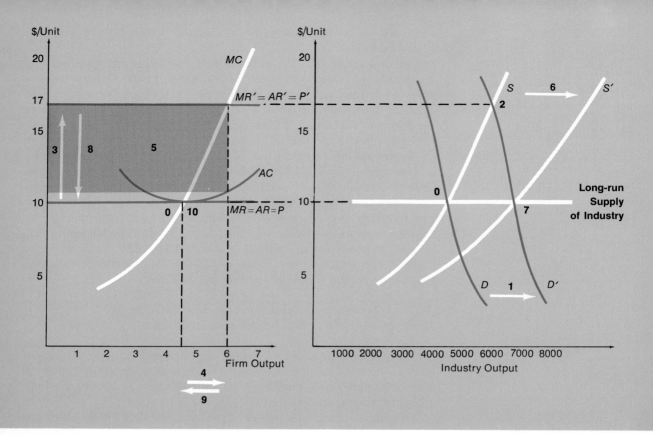

Figure 5-7

Adjustment to a demand increase *The initial equilibrium (Point 0 for both the firm and the industry) is disturbed by an increase in demand from D to D'. The text traces the ten steps of firm and industry adjustment to the new equilibrium.*

For instance, let us assume that the demand for the industry's product increases. The following chain of events which is depicted in Figure 5-7, is then likely to occur: (1) The aggregate demand curve for the industry's product shifts to the right. (2) The market price of the product increases to $17.00. (3) The increased market price means that each firm obtains higher marginal (and average) revenues. (4) Each firm will expand output to the point at which $MC = MR$ (6 units). (5) Each firm will make profits equal to the shaded area. (6) The profits will attract new firms to the industry, resulting in a shift of the industry short-run supply curve to the right. (7) Because of the increase in aggregate supply the market price will fall again to $10.00. (8) The lower market price will mean lower AR and MR ($= \$10.00$) for each firm. (9) Each firm adjusts to its new equilibrium by cutting back the quantity produced to 4.5 units. (10) Profits are reduced to zero, thus eliminating the incentive for firms to enter the industry. Equilibrium for the industry and all firms is attained.

At the new equilibrium, each firm again produces at the old level of output ($MC = MR$, no profits) but the industry as a whole has expanded by the addition of new firms. The market price has returned to its original level. Hence the industry as a whole can expand output without increasing the market price (except for a transitional period). The industry's long-run supply curve is a horizontal line: the industry is characterized by *constant costs*.

But let us remind ourselves that this case is based on the assumption that the industry as a whole can purchase its inputs at constant costs. For most industries, however, this assumption will not hold true. As the industry expands, the prices that have to be paid for the required inputs will go up. Hence, costs will increase as new firms enter the industry and each firm's cost curves shift upward. The result is that the long-run industry supply curve will slope upward. The whole industry will be characterized by increasing costs.

Summary

□ We distinguish between four basic market structures: *pure competition, monopolistic competition, oligopoly*, and *monopoly*. The last three market structures are frequently lumped together and called imperfect competition.

□ In pure competition we have a large number of firms that produce a homogeneous product. Furthermore, it is easy for firms to enter or leave the industry. As a consequence, purely competitive firms have no control over the price at which they can sell their product. They are *price takers*.

□ Each firm attempts to maximize its profits, which are the difference between total cost and total revenues. It can do this by (1) directly comparing total cost and revenue data, or (2) adding to its output, as long as the additional—or marginal—costs of one more unit of output are smaller than the additional revenues, and therefore increase the firm's profit.

□ By following this rule, the firm will maximize its profit at an output level where $MC = MR$. This is the firm's equilibrium position.

□ The *supply curve*, showing the quantity that the firm is willing to supply at a given price, is given by the *marginal cost curve* (above average variable cost) for the firm in pure competition.

□ The short-run *industry supply curve* is given by the addition of the individual firm's supply curves.

□ In a short-run situation, firms in pure competition may earn profits, i.e., a return above and beyond the return obtainable elsewhere. Profits serve as an incentive for new firms to enter the industry, thereby reducing and eventually eliminating the profits.

□ In the long run, a competitive industry may be able to expand output at *constant cost* (provided input prices do not increase). In that case, the *long-run supply curve* for a purely competitive industry is a horizontal straight line.

6

Imperfect competition

All markets that are not classified as *pure* competition are imperfectly competitive markets. In this chapter we will analyze two types of market structures that occupy much of the middle ground between the extremes of pure competition and pure monopoly. While there actually exists an infinite number of fine gradations between the two extremes, we will focus attention on monopolistic competition and oligopoly.

Monopolistic competition

Monopolistic competition is a market structure that is very similar to pure competition, but, as the label implies, some monopolistic elements are present. As in pure competition, we find in monopolistic competition many firms and free entry and exit into and out of the industry. The main difference between the two market structures is that while in pure competition all firms produce a standardized product, in monopolistic competition the products of the various firms are *differentiated*.

What do we mean by differentiated products? The products will vary slightly from firm to firm: they may carry brand names, have differences in design, manufacturing, and packaging. In addition, also, the service that is provided along with the goods bought may vary. Some firms will be willing to deliver their products to the purchaser; others will offer a free counseling service, or have especially well-trained or pretty salesgirls.

As a result of product differentiation, goods offered for sale by one firm are not perfect substitutes for goods offered by another firm in the same industry. Consequently, people will not be indifferent between buying their products from one or the other store. Hence, the demand curve facing each individual firm will not be a perfectly elastic, horizontal straight line, as in the case of pure competition, but will slope slightly downward to the right.

Demand

The downward-sloping demand curve is characteristic of all firms in imperfect competition. It shows that the firm can sell a larger quantity by lowering its price. By lowering the price the firm will (a) attract new buyers, who were not buying the product at the previous, higher price, and (b) lure customers away from other firms that offer similar products for sale. Because we find in monopolistic competition a very large number of firms selling very close substitutes, the elasticity of the demand curve of each firm is likely to be high.

Conversely, if a firm faces a downward-sloping demand curve, it is able to increase the price for the commodity it sells. For a firm in pure competition, the attempt to increase its price would prove futile: all its customers would switch to competitors, who would offer the same product for sale. The purely competitive firm is a price taker. The monopolistically competitive firm is not. Such a firm *can* increase its price without losing all its customers. It has some market power, because it faces a downward-sloping demand curve.

Marginal revenue

Let us return to the initial example of a monopolistically competitive firm, which slightly *lowers* its price to attract more business. Because the firm has to lower the price on *all* the units it sells—not just on

Table 6-1   Marginal revenue

Quantity	Price	Total revenue	Marginal revenue	Quantity	Price	Total revenue	Marginal revenue
0	$20	$ 0		10	10	100	
1	19	19	> $ 19	11	9	99	> −1
2	18	36	> 17	12	8	96	> −3
3	17	51	> 15	13	7	91	> −5
4	16	64	> 13	14	6	84	> −7
5	15	75	> 11	15	5	75	> −9
6	14	84	> 9	16	4	64	> −11
7	13	91	> 7	17	3	51	> −13
8	12	96	> 5	18	2	36	> −15
9	11	99	> 3	19	1	19	> −17
10	10	100	> 1	20	0	0	> −19

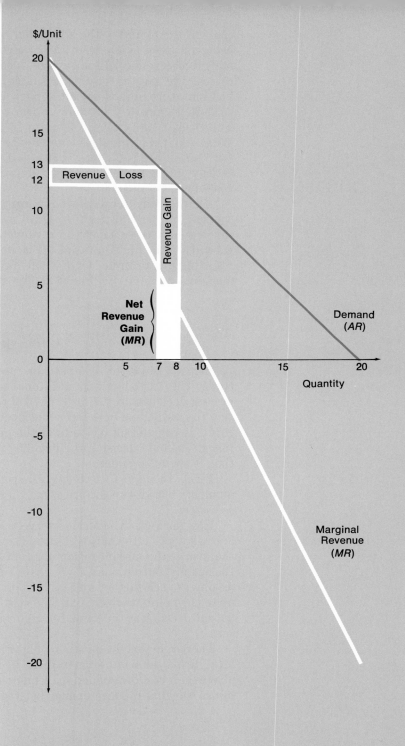

Figure 6-1

Demand and marginal revenue
If the demand curve slopes downward to the right, the marginal revenue curve must lie below it. The marginal revenue curve shows the additional revenue obtained by selling one more unit.

the additional units—the additional revenue that it obtains by lowering its price is *less* than the price obtained. As a matter of fact, marginal revenue will always be below the price that the firm receives. The reason for this is simple: the price cut required to sell just one more unit of output applies also to all other units of output sold. In Figure 6-1 we show a firm selling 7 units for $13.00 each. This firm is able to sell 8 units if it lowers the price to $12.00. What will its marginal revenue for the eighth unit be? Total revenues for 7 units are ($13.00 × 7) $91.00. For 8 units, total revenues are ($12.00 × 8) $96.00. Hence marginal revenues for the eighth unit are $5.00 ($96.00 − $91.00).

Another way of calculating marginal revenue would be as follows: the sale of the additional (eighth) unit brings in $12.00. But from this we have to subtract the revenue losses caused by the fact that we will sell the first 7 units at $12.00 instead of the old price of $13.00, resulting in a revenue loss of $7.00. Again, the change in revenue—or marginal revenue—will be ($12.00 − $7.00) $5.00.

Price searchers and mark-ups

All firms in imperfect competition face a downward sloping demand curve. This introduces an additional complication to the output and pricing decisions of the firm. We will recall that under pure competition the individual firm faces a perfectly elastic (horizontal) demand curve. It can sell all it wants at the going price. The firm is a price taker. The only decision the firm has to make concerns the quantity that it should produce.

Firms in imperfect competition have to decide not only on the quantity, but also on the price that they should charge. They are *price searchers*.

How does the firm decide its two problems of how much to produce and what price to charge? Let us remind ourselves that the goal of the firm is the maximization of profits. Thus the decision regarding the optimal output quantity is easy. The firm will produce more units as long as each further unit *adds* to its profits. That is, it will produce up to the point at which marginal cost equals marginal revenue. This output decision is the same for all firms, regardless of market structure.

There remains the question of how much to charge for the product. Most firms determine their price by charging a certain *mark-up* above their cost of production. A mark-up is nothing but a percentage figure showing the discrepancy between cost and price. An item that can be produced at a cost of $10.00 and sold at $12.00 is said to carry a 20 per cent mark-up. Or, the cost figure is multiplied by the *mark-up factor* 1.20 in order to obtain the sale price.

Of course, the question is *how* the firm determines the mark-up percentage that is optimal from its viewpoint. Most firms will apply some "rules of thumb" that they have determined by years of experience. Economic theory, however, can provide us with a simple formula, which we can apply directly to the mark-up problem.

First of all, let us remember that there is a definite mathematical relationship between the marginal revenue curve and the demand curve showing the price for each quantity demanded. This relationship says that marginal revenue is below price (or average revenue) if the demand curve slopes downward. The formula giving the exact relationship between marginal revenue and price is: $P = e/(e-1) \cdot MR$.* That is, marginal revenue can be multiplied by $e/(e-1)$ and we obtain the corresponding price or average revenue, where e is the elasticity of demand $(\Delta Q/Q/\Delta P/P)$ discussed on page 45.

Now we have to remember that marginal cost is equal to marginal revenue at the profit-maximizing output level. But if marginal cost is equal to marginal revenue, the above formula also applies to the marginal cost data:

$$P = \frac{e}{e-1} \cdot MR = \frac{e}{e-1} \cdot MC.$$

All we have to do to determine the optimal price to charge is to multiply marginal cost by the mark-up factor $e/(e-1)$.

$$P = \frac{e}{e-1} MC.$$

As an example consider Figure 6-2. Here we show a typical marginal revenue curve, *MR*, for a price searcher with a downward sloping demand curve. Consider now a firm with the marginal cost

---

*The mark-up formula can be derived with the use of some elementary calculus. Remember that the elasticity, e, is defined as the percentage change in quantity over the percentage change in price: $e = -dQ/Q \cdot P/dP$. Also, total revenue, *TR*, equals price times quantity: $TR = P \cdot Q$. Then we get:

$$MR = \frac{d(PQ)}{dQ} = P + Q\frac{dP}{dQ} = P\left(1 + \frac{dP}{P}\frac{Q}{dQ}\right) = P \cdot \left(1 + \frac{1}{e}\right) = P\left(\frac{e-1}{e}\right)$$

or, $P = \dfrac{e}{e-1} MR.$

Figure 6-2

The mark-up factor *Price searchers set their price by applying a mark-up factor to their marginal cost. Price = e/(e − 1) MC, where e is the elasticity of demand.*

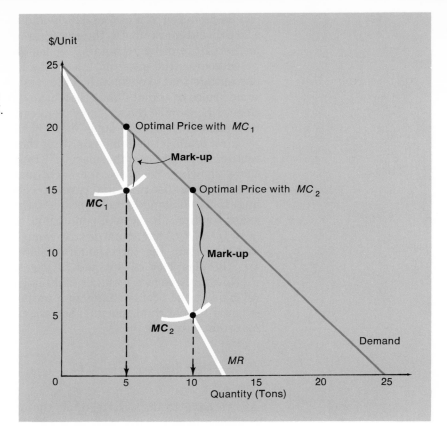

For MC_1: *Optimal output level = 5 tons:*
Elasticity (calculated over the 4-6 ton range)

$$e = \frac{\Delta Q/Q}{\Delta P/P} = \left| \frac{(4-6)/5}{(21-19)/20} \right| = 4 \qquad \text{Mark-up factor} = \frac{e}{e-1} = \frac{4}{3}$$

Price = MR × Mark-up factor = $15.00 × ⁴⁄₃ = $20.00

For MC_2: *Optimal output level = 10 tons:*
Elasticity (over 9-11 ton range)

$$e = \frac{\Delta Q/Q}{\Delta P/P} = \left| \frac{(9-11)/10}{(16-14)/15} \right| = 1.5 \qquad \text{Mark-up factor} = \frac{e}{e-1} = 3.0$$

Price = MR × Mark-up factor = $5.00 × 3.00 = $15.00

curve MC_1. The marginal cost curve MC_1 and the marginal revenue curve intersect at an output level of 5 tons. Because the $MC = MR$ rule is fulfilled, this must be the profit-maximizing output level. Next, we have to calculate the price to be charged. The elasticity of demand in the vicinity of the output level of 5 tons (calculated over the range from 4 to 6 tons) is equal to 4. For convenience we will drop the negative sign of the elasticity coefficient. The insertion of the elasticity coefficient $e = 4$ into the mark-up factor formula, $e/(e - 1)$, yields a markup factor of 1.33. Thus the optimal price will be 33 per cent higher than marginal cost. Given the marginal cost of $15.00, the optimal price will be $20.00.

If the firm had a different cost structure, for instance, such as the marginal cost curve MC_2, the mark-up would be different. MC_2 intersects MR at an output of 10 tons. The demand elasticity in the 9- to 11-ton range is $e = 1.5$. Hence the mark-up factor $e/(e - 1)$ is equal to 3.0. Multiplying marginal cost ($5.00) by the mark-up factor of 3.0, gives us the price to be charged: $15.00.

Note that a larger elasticity coefficient implies a smaller mark-up. In *pure* competition, where the demand curve facing the individual firm is perfectly elastic, $(e = \infty)$, the mark-up formula yields a mark-up factor of one or a mark-up percentage of zero. That is precisely what we found to be true for firms in pure competition: Price *equals* marginal revenue and marginal costs for the purely competitive firm in equilibrium. There is no mark-up at all.

For firms in imperfect competition, with some degree of market power, the elasticity of the demand curve facing the firm is smaller than infinity. As the elasticity of demand becomes smaller, the firm can charge a higher mark-up for its products. Hence it is to the advantage of a firm to try to influence the elasticity of the demand curve it faces. One way to do this is through advertising. When a firm advertises and establishes a brand name for a product, its buyers presumably become less inclined to switch to substitute products. The demand curve for the brand-named product will become less elastic, and the firm can charge a higher mark-up, hopefully more than recouping its advertising expenditures.

The short run

We are now in a position to consider the decision making of the individual firm in a monopolistically competitive industry. The firm's cost structure is given in Table 6-2 and graphed in Figure 6-3. The demand curve facing the firm (which is the same as the average revenue curve, *AR*) slopes downward to the right and the marginal revenue curve, *MR*, lies below it.

The firm maximizes its profits at an output level of 3.5 tons, where $MC = MR$. The elasticity of demand in the neighborhood of this

Figure 6-3

The monopolistically competitive firm *A monopolistic competitor will produce where MC = MR. If positive profits (shaded area) appear, other firms will enter into the industry.*

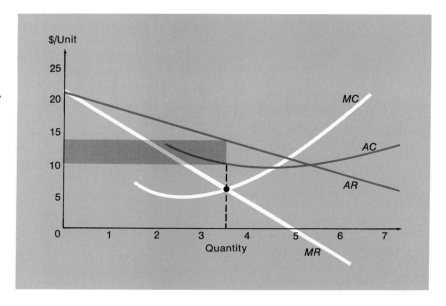

Table 6-2

Quantity	Average cost	Total cost		Marginal cost	Marginal revenue		Total revenue	Average revenue
0		0					0	0
1	$20.00	$20.00	>	$20.00	$19.00	<	$19.00	$19.00
2	14.00	28.00	>	8.00	15.00	<	34.00	17.00
3	11.00	33.00	>	5.00	11.00	<	45.00	15.00
4	10.00	40.00	>	7.00	7.00	<	52.00	13.00
5	10.00	50.00	>	10.00	3.00	<	55.00	11.00
6	10.67	64.00	>	14.00	−1.00	<	54.00	9.00
7	12.00	84.00	>	20.00	−5.00	<	49.00	7.00

At optimal output level of 3.5 units (measured over 3-4 ton range)

$$\text{Elasticity} = e = \frac{\frac{\Delta Q}{Q}}{\frac{\Delta P}{P}} = \frac{\frac{1}{3.5}}{\frac{2}{14}} = 2.00 \qquad \begin{array}{l}\text{Mark-up} \\ \text{factor}\end{array} = \frac{e}{e-1} = \frac{2}{2-1} = 2.00$$

output level (calculated over the range between 3 and 4 tons) is equal to 2.00. Hence the mark-up factor $e/(e-1)$ is 2.00. Marginal cost is $7.00, and the optimal price is twice that amount: $14.00.

But at an output level of 3.5 tons, average costs are only approximately $10.40. Hence the firm makes a profit of $3.60 on each ton it sells, or a total profit of $12.60 (indicated by the shaded area in Figure 6-3).

These profits constitute a return that is higher than the return obtainable elsewhere, and hence new firms will be attracted into the industry. Entry of new firms constitutes a long-run phenomenon and has to be analyzed separately.

The long run

In a monopolistically competitive industry, entry into the industry (and exit from it) is relatively easy—just as it is in pure competition. The appearance of profits serves as a signal for other firms to enter. As entry occurs, the new competitors will lure some customers away from the old-established firms. Hence the demand curve for each firm already in the industry will shift somewhat downward to the left: each firm is able to sell a smaller quantity than before at each and every price. (Compare the average revenue data in Tables 6-2 and 6-3.) As the firm's demand curve ($= AR$) shifts downward to the left, its marginal revenue curve will do the same. This will give us a new intersection of the marginal cost and marginal revenue curves. In Figure 6-4, MC equals MR at an output level of slightly less than 3 tons.

As the demand curve shifts downward, profits are reduced and eventually eliminated: average revenue is equal to average cost at the optimal output level. In Figure 6-4, both AC and AR are equal to approximately $11.00. The area showing excess profits has been eliminated completely. As firms can no longer earn in this industry a return that is higher than the return obtainable elsewhere, they will cease to move into the industry. Long-run equilibrium has been achieved.

Let us briefly repeat our findings. Each *firm* is at its equilibrium position when it produces at an output level where $MC = MR$. The whole *industry* is in equilibrium when no excess profits (or losses) lure new firms into (make them leave) the industry, hence, where $AC = AR$. Figure 6-4 shows a situation where both the firm and the industry are in equilibrium.

Figure 6-4

Long-run equilibrium in monopolistic competition *A monopolistically competitive industry will be in long-run equilibrium if there are no excess profits ($AC = AR$) at the same time that the firm is producing at its optimal output level ($MC = MR$).*

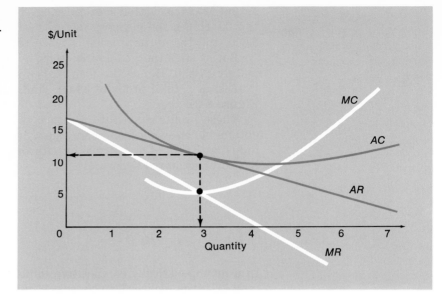

Table 6-3

Quantity	Average cost	Total cost	Marginal cost	Marginal revenue	Total revenue	Average revenue
0		0			0	0
			> $20.00	$15.00 <		
1	$20.00	$20.00			$15.00	$15.00
			> 8.00	11.00 <		
2	14.00	28.00			26.00	13.00
			> 5.00	7.00 <		
3	11.00	33.00			33.00	11.00
			> 7.00	3.00 <		
4	10.00	40.00			36.00	9.00
			> 10.00	−1.00 <		
5	10.00	50.00			35.00	7.00
			> 14.00	−5.00 <		
6	10.67	64.00			30.00	5.00
			> 20.00	−9.00 <		
7	12.00	84.00			21.00	3.00

Efficiency of monopolistic competition

A few comparisons may be made about the relative efficiency of purely competitive and monopolistically competitive industries in long-run equilibrium (see Figure 6-5).

1. The price charged by firms in monopolistic competition is slightly higher than the price charged by firms in pure competition.

Figure 6-5

Pure competition and monopolistic competition *Monopolistic competitors (as compared to pure competitors) charge higher prices, produce less output, have excess capacity, and charge more than the cost of producing the last unit of output.*

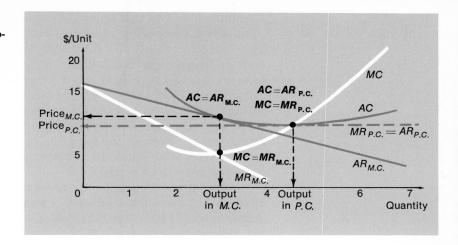

2. The volume produced by purely competitive firms is higher.
3. The purely competitive firm will produce at the minimum point of the average cost curve, while the monopolistically competitive firms produces at higher average cost and at lower capacity.
4. The price charged by the purely competitive firm is equal to the cost of producing the last unit of output $(P = MC)$, while the monopolistically competitive firm charges a price higher than marginal cost $(P > MC)$.
5. Both industrial structures have in common that all profits above and beyond a normal return for all inputs are eliminated by free entry into the industry.

Under which system is the consumer better off? That is difficult to tell. While he has to pay a slightly higher price in a monopolistically competitive framework, he will be able to obtain differentiated products. He has an opportunity to pick and choose between a variety of brands. The purely competitive industry sells its outputs at a slightly lower price, but it is a standardized uniform product. How much is it worth to be able to choose from a variety of products? That's a question that the individual must decide for himself.

Oligopoly

Another form of imperfect competition is oligopoly—competition among the few. The most important difference between a monopolistically competitive industry and an oligopolistic industry is simply the number of firms that sell in the same market area. In monopolistic competition there are many firms, in oligopoly there are only a few. The consequence of this difference in numbers is that firms in monopolistic competition will not be able to—and need not—react to every change in price charged or output produced by one of the competitors. Each one of the competitors is too small to make a substantial difference to the other firms. Not so in oligopoly. When there are only four, five, or six firms selling in a market, a price change made by one of the competitors will have a substantial influence on the other firms in the oligopolistic industry. The firms' decisions are *interdependent*.

Note that interdependence implies two things. First, the number of the other firms must be small enough so that their actions can be observed. If there were hundreds of competitors, it would be much too difficult to keep track of the various prices charged by them. Second, the actions of each firm have a substantial influence on the market conditions encountered by the other firms in the industry.

Examples of oligopolistic industries in the United States are many and varied: the automobile industry, steel, cigarettes, copper, and automobile tires. Note that while there is often a large number of brand names, there are frequently only a few producers of all these brands.

Economies of scale

Why do we find many firms in one industry and only a few in another? One important reason is the existence of economies of scale. Economies of scale refer to the phenomenon of decreasing average costs of production over a long range of output. Given a certain aggregate demand for a product, we will probably find many firms in the industry if average cost turns upward very early (see AC_1 in Figure 6-6). In that case the size of each individual firm will be limited by the increased costs of production at an early stage. If, on the other hand, technology is such that average costs fall over a large output range and turn upward only late (as shown by AC_2), then chances are that a few large firms will dominate the industry.

Also, if substantial economies of scale do exist, it will often be difficult for new firms to enter the industry. The established firms already enjoy low average costs of mass production, while the new firms are faced with high average costs. To be able to compete effectively against the established firms a newcomer must not only capture immediately a large share of the market, but he must also

Figure 6-6

Cost and industrial structure
If average costs of production turn upward very soon, many small firms are likely to be found in an industry. If average costs turn upward late, only a few firms may find room in the industry.

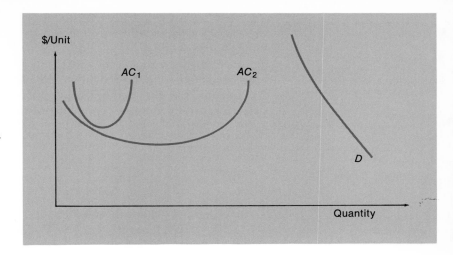

have the financial resources and the technological know-how required to establish a big firm. To raise the large amount of money required for such a risky venture may be difficult. In addition, the technical knowledge required may be protected by patents that are owned by the established firms. It is little wonder that we do not find new firms entering the automobile or steel business. Virtually the only new competition generally comes from firms that are located in other countries, where they already serve large markets and enjoy low costs of production. These firms are then able to compete with domestic manufacturers of the same product on a more or less equal footing.

Oligopolistic pricing

Firms in oligopolistic industries are just as interested in making profits as are firms in other industries. Hence they will follow the familiar pattern of decision making with respect to output produced and price charged. They will produce an output at which marginal costs equal marginal revenues. Then they will set the price by using the mark-up formula $P = e/(e - 1) \cdot MC$. This is shown in Figure 6-7 and Table 6-4 where $MC = MR$ at 3.5 tons and the optimal price is $14.00.

But once a price is established in the oligopolistic industry, this is where the similarity ends. The important new variable that now has to be taken into account is interdependence. If, for instance, a firm experiences a small increase in costs, it will normally charge a slightly higher price. But with oligopolistic interdependence, this is not necessarily so. A firm that would increase its price would probably find that the competitors would take away many of its old customers, and its sales would fall off drastically. Of course, this assumes that the other firms in the industry will not increase their price at the same time. But they are unlikely to do so, because they see a chance to substantially increase their share of the market. Hence the demand

Figure 6-7

Oligopolistic pricing *The oligopolist will set his price initially by applying a mark-up factor of e/(e − 1) to his costs of production.*

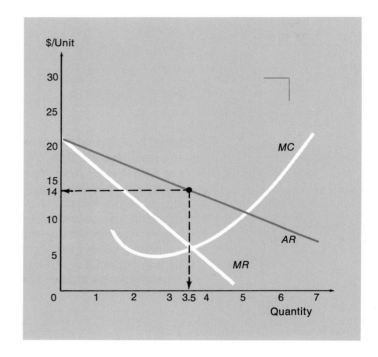

Table 6-4

Quantity	Total cost		Marginal cost	Marginal revenue		Total revenue	Average revenue
0	0					0.00	0.00
1	$20.00	>	$20.00	$19.00	<	$19.00	$19.00
2	28.00	>	8.00	15.00	<	34.00	17.00
3	33.00	>	5.00	11.00	<	45.00	15.00
4	40.00	>	7.00	7.00	<	52.00	13.00
5	50.00	>	10.00	3.00	<	55.00	11.00
6	64.00	>	14.00	−1.00	<	54.00	9.00
7	84.00	>	20.00	−5.00	<	49.00	7.00

curve above the established price is likely to be highly elastic, as seen from the vantage point of the individual oligopolist.

On the other hand, when one oligopolistic firm cuts its price, the other firms are likely to follow because they do not want to lose their customers to the price cutter. Because a price cut will probably be matched by the competitors, each firm will find that the quantity demanded increases only slightly. The demand curve below the established price is much less elastic than the demand curve above the established price. The demand curve as seen from the vantage point of one oligopolistic firm has a "kink" at the going price of $14.00.

This situation is shown in Figure 6-8 and Table 6-5 where the initial equilibrium output is 3.5 tons and where a price of $14.00 prevails. The demand curve that is relevant for price increases above $14.00 is highly elastic. For price cuts below the established price of $14.00, a much less elastic demand curve is relevant. The marginal revenue curves that correspond to the two sections of the demand curve are shown in the same diagram. It is evident that at the output level of 3.5 tons, where the demand curve has its kink, the marginal revenue curve has a discontinuity. As long as the marginal cost curve intersects the marginal revenue curve in this vertical segment, there is no incentive for the oligopolist to change his output level: maximum profit is maintained where $MC = MR$. In our example, as long as marginal cost at 3.5 tons is less than $10.50 and more than $3.50, there is no need to change output.

Note that the mark-up formula does not yield a unique result right at the kink in the demand curve. Precisely at the kink, the elasticity changes abruptly and its value is not defined uniquely. We can only calculate a value for the elasticity of demand just *above* or *below* the kink, and these elasticity values then can be used to calculate an upper and a lower limit between which the actual mark-up must lie.

Of course, if marginal costs were to increase or fall substantially, an intersection of MC and MR would be established at a different output level. But note again the implications. If just one oligopolist charges a higher price, and the others do not increase their price, chances are that the firm raising its prices will lose so many customers that eventually it will make losses and be forced to go out of business. On the other hand, if one firm cuts its price, and the others follow, a price war will result, in which the firms will match the price cuts of their competitors.

This establishes two characteristics found in many oligopolistic industries: (1) prices change only infrequently, and (2) if prices change, all firms in the industry change their price together. Interdependence between firms establishes the link between the individual decisions made.

Figure 6-8

The kinky oligopoly demand curve *An oligopolist who increases his price will often find that his competitors do not match the price increase: above the going price the demand curve looks to him very elastic. On the other hand, price cuts are likely to be matched, resulting in a less elastic demand curve. At the going price, the demand curve appears to have a kink in it.*

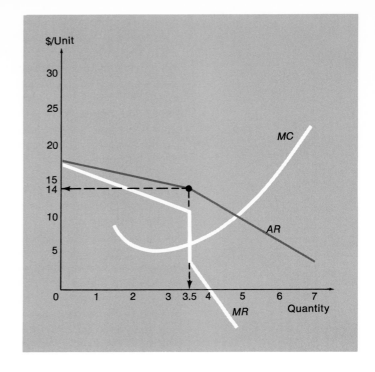

Table 6-5

Quantity	Total cost	Marginal cost	Marginal revenue	Total revenue	Average revenue	
0	0			0	0	
1	$20.00	> $20.00	$16.50	< $16.50	$16.50	
2	28.00	> 8.00	14.50	< 31.00	15.50	
3	33.00	> 5.00	12.50	< 43.50	14.50	
		> 7.00	10.50 to 3.50	< 50.00	12.50	kink
4	40.00	> 10.00	−2.50	< 47.50	9.50	
5	50.00	> 14.00	−8.50	< 39.00	6.50	
6	64.00	> 20.00	−14.50	< 24.50	3.50	
7	84.00					

Collusion

Because oligopolistic firms recognize their interdependence, there is a strong incentive to engage in collusion and to maximize joint profits. Such collusion may be formal or informal. Formal agreements regarding price, market area to be served, and output to be marketed may be established—but in most cases United States laws prohibit such collusion. A few exceptions do exist: for instance, most professional sports are exempt from the United States anti-trust laws, and the clubs may enforce rules that effectively eliminate competitive bidding between the clubs for the services of new athletes, limit the entry of new clubs, and the like.

Informal collusion may involve oral agreements made on the golf course, in a bar, or at a party. Of course, such agreements have no legal standing, but to make a formal agreement would be unlawful in the first place.

Price leadership is still another means by which price changes are coordinated in the industry. Generally by tradition, one firm—often the largest one—will change its prices and all the others will follow. Perhaps the price leader has an especially able economist on its staff who knows more about cost conditions or demand shifts, and whose judgment is respected by the firm's competitors. Or it may simply be the largest firm in the industry, and the smaller firms have no choice but to follow the leadership of the big fellow.

It is important to stress that the mere fact that in an oligopolistic industry prices change together provides no evidence that there is price fixing or collusion. It is simply the result of the strong interdependence between the oligopolistic firms. If one firm changes its price, the economic environment within which the other firms in the industry operate changes substantially, and they will—in all likelihood—react to the price change. But note that this reaction is due to purely economic motives.

Of course, as the number of firms in an industry increases, any formal or informal agreements to collude are more likely to be broken. One of the firms may think that it is to its advantage to break out of the group. Informal collusion agreements tend to break up in a relatively short time when the number of firms participating is very large. But as the number of firms in an industry increases, the degree of interdependence between them is decreased, in any case, and the industry may be closer to our model of monopolistic competition.

Product differentiation, research, and development

Because price competition is a very rare occurrence in oligopolistic industries, these firms often turn to other means of increasing their sales.

Product differentiation through distinctive styling, modern

design, and attractive packaging is often undertaken by firms in order to increase the demand for their product. Other possibilities include non-price competition in the form of trading stamps offered with a purchase, a more inclusive warranty, prettier salesgirls, better trained service personnel, and the like.

Also, an oligopolist may attempt to lower his own cost through research and development. By maintaining a fixed price and achieving a reduction in cost, the firm will be able to increase its profits. (Remember that the precise amount of mark-up was indeterminate in Figure 6-8.) Decreases in cost may be achieved by spending funds on research and development. Quite often it is not the spectacular scientific break-throughs that are important here, but the nickel or dime reduction in costs that is achieved through a determined effort. By keeping its own costs just below its rival's costs, a firm may be able to do rather well in the long run. The spectacular break-through innovation is much more likely to upset the oligopolistic equilibrium or lead to the manufacture of an entirely different product.

Summary

□ Various possible market structures form a continuous spectrum between the "extremes" of pure competition and monopoly. Two widely used reference points are *monopolistic competition* and *oligopoly*.

□ In monopolistic competition, we have many firms as well as easy entry into and exit from the industry. The products offered by the various firms are not identical—they are *differentiated*.

□ As a result of product differentiation, each firm faces a *demand curve* that slopes downward to the right: it can sell more if it lowers the price of its product.

□ If the demand curve (= average revenue curve) slopes downward, the corresponding *marginal revenue* curve must lie below it.

□ Because of the downward sloping demand curve, firms can determine the price that they charge for their product: they are *price searchers*.

□ Firms will produce the output quantity that will maximize their profits. They will follow the $MC = MR$ rule.

□ In determining the price to be charged, firms apply a *mark-up factor* to their marginal cost of production. The mark-up factor is: $e/(e-1)$, where e is the elasticity of demand facing the firm.

□ As in pure competition, the existence of profits will lure new firms into the industry. The industry will attain equilibrium when excess profits are eliminated, i.e., when $AC = AR$.

□ In *oligopolistic* industries we encounter only a few sellers of the product. Because there are only a few firms in the industry, the actions taken by one firm influence the economic environment of the other firms: the oligopolists are *interdependent*.

□ Typically, other oligopolists will match any price cuts made by competitors, while maintaining their own price when other firms raise theirs. As a result, the demand curve—as seen from the vantage point of an individual oligopolist—is more elastic above the present price than below the prevailing price: it has a "kink."

□ The *kinky demand curve* results in a corresponding marginal revenue curve with a discontinuity. As long as changes in marginal costs shift the *MC* curve only within the range of the discontinuity of the marginal revenue curve, the firm will not change its output or price.

□ Prices in oligopolistic industries typically change infrequently, but when they do change, all firms in the industry are likely to change their prices.

□ Because of the great interdependence between oligopolistic firms, it may be advantageous to engage in (generally illegal) collusion by fixing prices or agreeing on market shares.

□ In the absence of price competition, oligopolists will attempt to increase their profits by advertising and other promotional devices, or spending money on research and development in the hope of lowering their production costs.

7

Monopoly

A monopolist is the sole seller of a commodity that has no close substitutes. That only the sole seller of a good or a service may qualify as a monopolist is clear. The requirement that there be no close substitutes available is a bit more subtle. It brings us to the question of how to define a commodity. Is a Mustang in a commodity class by itself? But there are several close substitutes: Cameros, Firebirds, Chargers, and similar cars. Then, are passenger automobiles a commodity class? Again, substitutes exist in the form of buses and trucks. And even airplanes and railroads!

It is clear that there is no easy way to define a commodity class, such that there are no substitutes at all available. Hence monopoly power is a matter of degree. It is influenced by the closeness of the available substitutes, and no clear-cut borderline can be drawn between monopoly and other forms of imperfect competition.

Nevertheless, monopoly can be found in certain market areas. The post office has a monopoly on the carrying of mail, the local water company on water supplied to homes, the local telephone company on telecommunications, and perhaps a bus company on local transportation. What are the bases for such monopolies?

Barriers to entry

We have said that a monopolist sells in a market where there are no other sellers of the same or a similar product. In our discussion of pure and monopolistic competition, however, we saw that new firms tend to enter an industry as soon as returns higher than obtainable elsewhere can be earned in the industry. A monopolist may well enjoy such profits, and the question is, What keeps potential competitors from entering the industry and thereby breaking up the monopoly? The answer is found in a multitude of barriers to entry, which may protect the sheltered position of the monopolist. Without barriers to entry few, if any, monopolies would persist over time. We will discuss here only the main barriers to entry: economies of scale, ownership of essential raw materials, patents and research, and government licensing.

Economies of scale In some industries technology is such that average costs decrease over a substantial output range. Figure 7-1 shows a demand curve and three alternative average cost curves. If average costs turn upward at a relatively small output level, as in the curve labeled *CC*, there may be enough room in the industry for a large number of purely competitive or monopolistically competitive firms. If average costs turn upward later, as indicated by the curve *OO*, a few oligopolists may share the market. Finally, if the average cost curve looks like the *MM* contour, a monopoly may be established.

Given the average cost curve *MM*, as determined by technology and the prices that have to be paid for inputs, one firm can produce enough to satisfy the total market demand at a lower cost than two firms. Any new firm entering the industry and producing only a small number of units would be faced with higher costs than the established firm. Given these higher costs, it would be difficult for the newcomer to compete effectively and survive.

Industries that have a very high proportion of fixed costs are likely to have a declining average cost curve over a large range of output. The reason for this phenomenon is simple indeed. The fixed overhead costs can be "spread" over a larger and larger number of units as output increases. Hence each unit will have to bear a smaller and smaller share of the fixed costs of production. Public utilities are a group of industries for which fixed costs are typically very high in relation to variable costs. Once an electricity cable, a water main, or a gas pipe is installed in every street of the town, the additional

Figure 7-1

Costs and industrial structure
In industries where average costs turn upward early (CC), there may be room for many firms in an industry. If costs turn upward later (OO), only a few firms may comprise the industry. If costs increase very late (MM), a monopolist may dominate. The line DD shows the aggregate demand curve.

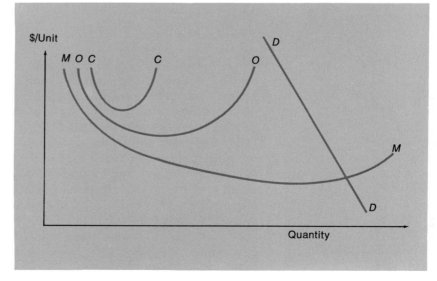

cost involved in providing service to another customer is small. So is the cost of increasing by a few units the amount of water or gas pumped into the pipe system. Clearly, it would be wasteful to duplicate the complete network of pipes and cables throughout the city just to offer the consumer a choice between service from two otherwise identical companies.

Ownership of essential raw materials If a firm manages to own all or most of some essential raw material needed in a production process, it may be impossible for a competitor to break into the market. All the monopolist has to do is abstain from selling the raw material to the potential competitor.

Patents and research The ownership of patents and special technological know-how established through research may have an effect very similar to the ownership of essential raw materials in preventing new firms from entering the industry. The object of the research, for instance, may be an essential formula required for the production of the commodity. And these research findings may be protected by a patent granted by the government. A patent is a right to the exclusive use of an innovation, which is granted to the originator by the government. For a specified time period—usually seventeen years—the government prohibits others from using the patented process. It grants these patent rights in order to foster new research and to protect the interests of the innovator who might have spent substantial sums in developing a new process. While patents offer an incentive to engage in research, they also provide a barrier to competition.

Government licensing We have already discussed an important case of government licensing: the granting of patents. Other cases of government licensing may involve exclusive franchises granted to certain gas, water, and electricity companies. Or to transportation enterprises, such as taxicabs in certain cities, buses, trains, and airlines. But government licensing of a wide variety of other goods or services also belongs under this heading: not everybody is allowed to produce atom bombs, be a doctor, run a TV station, or open a liquor store. In some cases the governmental license is used to establish certain minimum qualifications for the practice of a profession, but in others it serves to restrict entry of potential new competitors and thereby protect existing monopolies. Generally, when granting a license, the government reserves itself the right to regulate the licensee. The economic basis for such interference will be discussed later in this chapter.

Figure 7-2

The profit-maximizing monopolist *A monopolist maximizes profits by producing that output at which total revenues exceed total costs by the largest possible margin (upper diagram), or where marginal costs equal marginal revenues (lower diagram).*

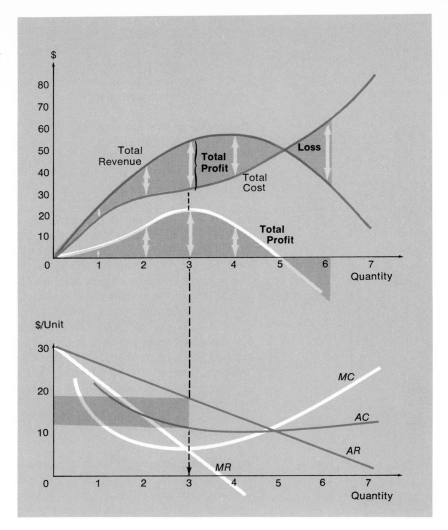

Profit maximization

By definition, the monopolist is the sole producer of a product, and consequently we no longer have to distinguish between the individual firm and the industry. In pure monopoly the firm *is* the industry. Thus the market demand curve—arrived at by aggregating the demand curves of all individual consumers—is the demand curve that the monopolist faces.

Table 7-1

Quantity	Average cost	Total cost	Marginal cost	Marginal revenue	Total revenue	Average revenue	Profit
0		0			0	0	0.00
			> $20.00	$26.00 <			
1	$20.00	$20.00			$26.00	$26.00	$ 6.00
			> 8.00	18.00 <			
2	14.00	28.00			44.00	22.00	16.00
			> 5.00	10.00 <			
3	11.00	33.00			54.00	18.00	21.00
			> 7.00	2.00 <			
4	10.00	40.00			56.00	14.00	16.00
			> 10.00	−6.00 <			
5	10.00	50.00			50.00	10.00	0.00
			> 14.00	−14.00 <			
6	10.67	64.00			36.00	6.00	−28.00
			> 20.00	−22.00 <			
7	12.00	84.00			14.00	2.00	−70.00

Elasticity at output = 3 tons (measured over 2–4 ton range)

$$e = \frac{\frac{\Delta Q}{Q}}{\frac{\Delta P}{P}} = \frac{\frac{2}{3}}{\frac{3}{18}} = 1.5 \qquad \text{Mark-up factor} = e/(e-1) = 1.5/0.5 = 3$$

The monopolist faces problems similar to other firms in imperfectly competitive markets with regard to output and price determination. First, he has to decide *how much* to produce, and second, he has to decide what *price* to charge. These same problems were already discussed in connection with firms in monopolistic competition, and in many respects the difference between monopolistic competition and the case of the pure monopolist is only a matter of degree, not kind. There is, however, one important difference: in pure monopoly we generally find the barriers of entry discussed above, while in monopolistic competition entry of new firms into the industry is possible. Hence the profits that were eventually eliminated by the entry of new firms in a monopolistically competitive industry will tend to persist in monopoly.

Of course, the monopolist is just as interested in maximizing profits as is any other firm. So he will operate at an output level at which marginal revenue equals marginal costs. This occurs in our example (Table 7-1 and Figure 7-2) at an output of 3 tons. Here total revenue exceeds total costs by the largest margin—$21.00. Note also that the total profit curve in Figure 7-2 has its maximum at 3 tons.

The second question pertains to the optimal price to charge. Again, we will use our mark-up formula to determine the optimal price. In the neighborhood of the output level of 3 units (calculated over the range between 2 and 4 tons), the demand curve has an elasticity of 1.5. The optimal price is found by applying the mark-up factor established in Chapter 6, page 90: $e/(e-1) = 3.00$. Marginal costs ($= MR$) amount to approximately $6.00, and multiplication by the mark-up factor of 3.00 yields an optimal price of $18.00. We could have determined this price also from our graph by simply reading off the price on the demand curve at which 3 tons can be sold, namely $18.00.

Elasticity and marginal revenue: a digression

We already know (Chapter 6) that there exists a direct relationship between the demand (or average revenue) curve and the marginal revenue curve. For the demand curve to slope downward, the marginal revenue curve must lie below it. In addition, the sign of the marginal revenue also says something about the elasticity of demand. Let us remind ourselves of the definition of the elasticity of demand (Chapter 3): demand is elastic ($e > 1$) if a lowering of the price *increases* total revenue. But for total revenue to increase, *marginal* revenue must be *positive*. Hence, as long as MR is positive, the demand curve in this output range must be elastic. (See Figure 7-3)

Also, unit elasticity means that a fall in price will not change total revenue. Unchanged total revenue means no change in marginal revenue, i.e., zero marginal revenue. Thus, wherever the marginal revenue curve cuts the horizontal axis, demand must be unit elastic at that output level.

Finally, a negative marginal revenue figure indicates that the demand curve in the same output range is inelastic.

As every firm incurs positive costs when it increases its output, the MC curve can cut the MR curve only at a positive value. But if MR is positive, the demand curve at that output level *must* be elastic ($e > 1$). Hence any firm will only operate at an output range at which its demand curve is elastic. This is also important for the use of our mark-up formula, as elasticities smaller than one would indicate a *negative* mark-up—obviously a nonsensical result.

Monopoly and profits

Let us repeat again that the barriers to entry will help to protect the profits of the monopolist. Only if a competitor manages to over-

Figure 7-3

Marginal, average, and total revenue *If a firm lowers its price in order to sell more and the demand curve (AR) is elastic, marginal revenue is positive and total revenue is increasing. If the demand curve is inelastic in that range, marginal revenue is negative and total revenue falls.*

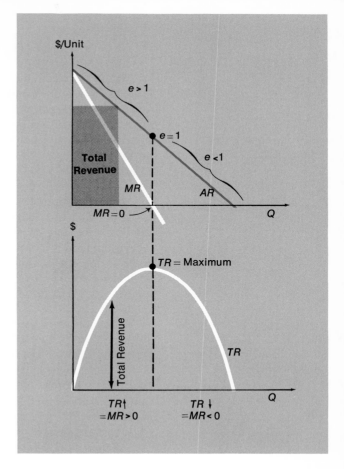

come the barriers to entry will the monopolist's profit position be endangered. Some economists argue that the mere danger of entry is enough to induce the monopolist to charge a lower price than he otherwise would. The lower price would mean lower profits, and therefore any outsider looking at the firm would not have such a great incentive to enter the industry.

One final word. There is no *necessity* that the monopolist must make any profits. Just consider what would happen if either the demand curve shifted downward, or the average cost curved upward. In both cases the monopolist's profits would be reduced and perhaps even completely eliminated or turned into a loss. Of course, if the monopolist made a loss in the long run, he would leave the industry. But if the only producer leaves the industry, the whole industry ceases to exist: the product disappears from the market.

Monopoly and competition compared

Let us briefly compare the performance of a purely competitive industry and a pure monopoly. Pure competition and pure monopoly mark the two end points of the broad spectrum of possible market structures. Pure competition provides a convenient reference point against which the performance of the other market structures can be assessed. What we will have to say about monopoly applies also to other imperfectly competitive markets—only to a lesser extent.

First of all, let us compare price charged and cost of production. The purely competitive firm will charge a price that is equal to the marginal cost of producing the last unit. This is due to the by now familiar fact that in pure competition the demand curve facing each individual firm is a horizontal straight line. Hence price and marginal revenue are the same to the pure competitor. He maximizes profits by setting $MC = MR$, and in addition we know that $P = MR$, which means, that his price will also be equal to the marginal cost of production: $P = MC$.

The monopolist faces the aggregate market demand curve for the product alone. The demand curve slopes downward, and hence the marginal revenue curve must lie *below* the demand curve. For the monopolist, it is always true that $P > MR$. The monopolist also maximizes profits by setting $MC = MR$, but because the price charged is above MR, price must also be above the marginal cost of production: $P > MC$. In Figure 7-4, $P_M > MC_M$. Hence we find that while in pure competition price accurately reflects the cost of production, in monopoly the price charged exceeds the cost of production. The extent of the differential is measured by the mark-up employed by the monopolist. The mark-up in turn depends on the elasticity of the demand curve and is given by the mark-up factor $= e/(e - 1)$.

Second, given the same cost and demand conditions, the monopolist will produce a smaller output than a purely competitive industry. This is due to the fact that a monopolist will produce where he finds $MC = MR$. But as we already pointed out, his MR curve lies below or to the left of the demand (AR) curve. The purely competitive industry produces where the industry supply curve (sum of all firm's MC curves) intersects the industry demand (AR) curve. The monopolist will produce less than that. In Figure 7-4, we find that the output produced by the competitive industry, Q_c, is greater than the output produced by the monopolist, Q_M.

Third, in the competitive industry, each firm produces at the minimum point of the average cost curve. Hence unit costs of production are as low as technology permits. On the other hand the

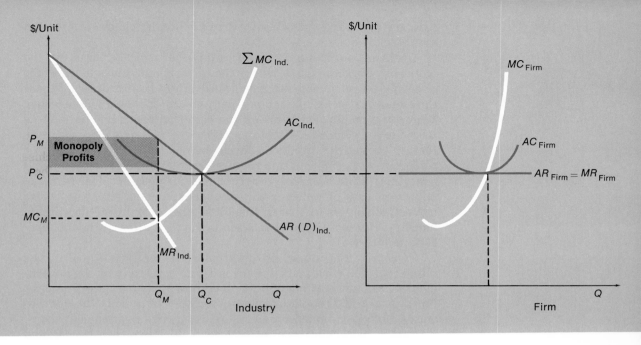

Figure 7-4

Monopoly and competition *In pure competition, we distinguish between the firm and the industry. The firm is a price taker, that faces a horizontal curve (right diagram). In monopoly, the firm and the industry are synonymous.*

monopolist will produce to the left of the minimum average cost point. As the monopolist does not produce at minimum average cost, we can conclude that lower production costs might be achieved if firms would in fact operate at minimum AC.

Finally, the monopolist may, but need not, make excess profits. In competition, these profits are competed away as a result of the entry of new firms into the industry. In monopoly, the barriers to entry discussed above serve to restrict the entry of new firms, and hence excess profits may prevail.

Monopoly regulation

We said that monopoly—in comparison to a purely competitive industry in similar circumstances—is likely to (1) charge a price above marginal cost, (2) produce less, (3) produce not at minimum average cost, and (4) enjoy profits higher than are obtainable elsewhere. Can anything be done about this?

One solution, it might appear, would be to try to break up the monopoly. In those cases where the government gives a franchise or license to the monopolist, this license might be withdrawn. Where the monopolist holds some important patents, these may be canceled. Where the monopolist owns all the essential resources, he may be forced to sell some of his holdings. Of course, this may not encourage further research, product development, and prospecting for resources—especially if this requires large monetary outlays—and hence may stifle economic progress. Also, it does not deal with the important case of a decreasing-cost industry, or a situation where market demand is just large enough to support only one firm in the industry. Hence a frequent solution is the regulation of the monopolistic industry.

Of course, the important question arises as to the goal of the regulation. If a regulatory agency is set up, generally by the government, it will try to attain certain objectives by its regulatory actions. For instance, the regulatory agency may try to remedy the discrepancies between monopoly and pure competition discussed above. Naturally, there is no guarantee that all objectives may be attained at the same time. In fact, it is likely that only one or two objectives can be attained.

The regulatory agency may set the price to be charged by the monopolist in such a way that it equals the marginal cost of production (point A in Figure 7-5). By that, output will expand to the level at which it would be in a purely competitive industry in the short run. Remember that only in a purely competitive industry MC is the supply curve. Now the monopolist will produce at an output level where supply and demand for the competitive industry would intersect. Price will be what it would have been in a purely competitive industry and, more importantly, it will also be equal to the marginal cost of production: $P = MC$.

A second principle that the regulators may follow is to make the monopolist produce at minimum average cost (point B in Figure 7-5). Of course, this applies only to average cost curves, which actually do have a minimum point in the relevant range. For decreasing-cost industries, this minimum average cost point may be at an output level much too high to be of practical importance.

The third principle may involve regulation to the extent that the monopolist can just make a "normal" return on all his investments. Because our cost data already include the monopolist's opportunity costs of using *all* his inputs in the production process, this involves setting the price in such a way that total costs equal total revenues.

Figure 7-5

Monopoly regulation *A free monopolist will produce his profit-maximizing output where MC = MR. Monopoly regulation may be designed to have the price reflect production costs (A), achieve minimum cost production (B), or eliminate excess monopoly profits (C).*

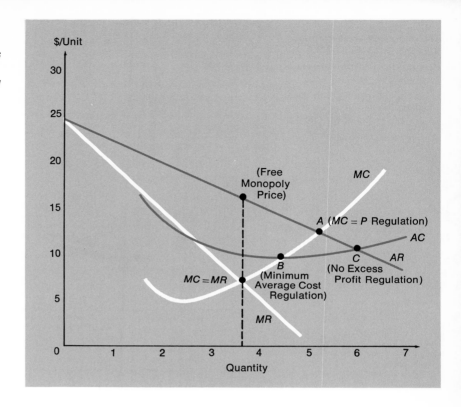

Or, average costs equal average revenues. Point *C* shows such a no-profit solution.

Of course, if we have three conflicting regulatory principles, we have to decide which one of the three principles we will actually follow. How do we decide between points *A*, *B*, and *C*?

If all other industries are purely competitive—so that in the rest of the economy price is equal to marginal cost and, in addition, all buyers of the products are also purchasing in purely competitive markets—so that the marginal utility derived from the last unit of purchase is equal to the price—*then* it follows that the regulatory rule that sets price as equal to marginal cost (point *A*) is optimal. Why? If, throughout the rest of the economy $P = MC$ and also $P = MU$, then it must also be true that $MC = MU$. That is, every product is produced in such a quantity that the additional utility gained by a consumer is exactly equal to the additional cost incurred by producing it. Now, the monopolistic industry is the *only* one where $P > MC$. But consumers still equate MU with P. It follows that for the output of the monopolistic industry $MU > MC$. But if $MU > MC$,

Figure 7-6

The decreasing-cost monopolist *A monopolist who enjoys decreasing average production costs may have to receive a governmental subsidy to cover his losses if he is to produce at the socially optimal production level.*

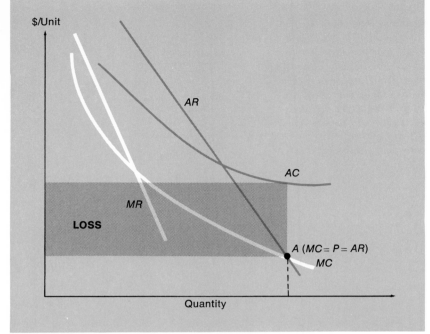

we could increase general welfare a certain amount by producing one more unit of that commodity. By restricting output so that $MU = P > MR = MC$, the monopoly leads to an underproduction of this good. Welfare for society as a whole is maximized when the marginal utility gained is equal to the price and the price in turn is equal to the marginal cost of production: $MU = P = MC$. Only then will it no longer be possible to increase somebody's welfare without making somebody else worse off.

But in decreasing-cost industries (Figure 7-6), because they are quite frequent in monopolistic situations, the optimal efficiency regulation of $P = MC$ may require the payment of a subsidy to the monopolist. If average cost is falling, this is because marginal cost is below average cost: $MC < AC$. If we now set price equal to marginal cost, and note that price is the same as average revenue, we get: $AR = P = MC < AC$, or simply $AR < AC$. Multiplying by the quantity, we can easily obtain the result that total revenue is smaller than total cost, i.e., the monopolist makes a loss. Thus, if we insist on efficient pricing even in decreasing-cost monopoly situations, we may have to subsidize the monopolist, so that he will produce the socially optimal quantity and still be able to avoid a loss which would force him out of business.

Summary

☐ A monopolist is the sole seller of a commodity for which there are no close substitutes available.

☐ The position of the monopolist is generally protected by barriers to entry. Such barriers consist in economies of scale that can be achieved only at large output volumes, the ownership of essential raw materials, special technological know-how, patents, and governmental licensing.

☐ The free monopolist will produce at an output level where he maximizes his profits ($MC = MR$).

☐ At the profit-maximizing output level, the marginal cost of production is lower than the price that the monopolist can obtain. If the rest of the economy is purely competitive, this will result in the misallocation of resources.

☐ The socially optimal governmental regulation policy is to force the monopolist to produce at an output level where price is equal to marginal cost of production. In decreasing-cost industries, this may lead to the necessity of having to grant governmental subsidies to the producer, as he will be making chronic losses because of the governmental regulation.

8

The public
sector

In the previous chapters we discussed the economic interactions taking place within the private sector of the economy. We looked at households in their role as consumers and at firms in their role as producers of goods and services. Only when discussing the special problems of economic efficiency created by the presence of monopolists in an economy characterized by competition in the other sectors, did we mention the role of government as a regulatory body.

In all this analysis we implicitly assumed that whatever is good for the individual is also good for the community as a whole. Each individual decision maker is motivated by his desire to make himself as well off as he can possibly be: the consumer is assumed to maximize his utility, and the entrepreneur is assumed to maximize the profits of the firm under his direction. It is private motives that are the guide for private decision.

The important question we have to ask now is, Will the individual actions of consumers and producers also lead to a maximization of welfare for society as a whole? Or to put it differently, Will private and social interests always coincide, or are there circumstances in which the two may diverge or even conflict?

In this chapter we will address ourselves to two aspects of this problem: first, we will deal with possible divergences between private and social welfare. That is, we will analyze the reasons for possible interference with the free market system as an allocative mechanism. Second, we will deal with a group of commodities called *public goods*— that is, those goods which are produced by the governmental sector of the economy for society as a whole. Governmental spending accounts for approximately 20 per cent of total spending on final goods and services in the American economy and thereby constitutes an important sector of the economic system, which cannot be overlooked.

We have talked at great length about the decision-making process in the private sector. We learned that costs and benefits (sometimes in the form of revenues, sometimes as utility) play an important part in any economic decision. Costs are the alternative opportunities that have to be forgone in order to purchase or produce a commodity. The benefits reaped may take the form of utility or satisfaction enjoyed by the consumer or revenue earned by a firm. The basic principle for welfare maximization that emerged was that we should produce or consume up to the point at which the additional costs were just balanced by the additional benefits, that is, marginal cost should equal marginal benefits: $MC = P = MB$.

But the focus of attention was directed clearly at *private costs* and *private benefits* that accrued to the economic unit making the decision in question. But in a modern integrated economy we frequently find that other economic units will also bear some of the burdens or enjoy some of the benefits of an economic decision. If this occurs, we speak of *spillovers* taking place. Spillover effects may harm or benefit other economic units. Hence we speak of spillover costs and spillover benefits.

Many economic actions are accompanied by spillover benefits as well as spillover costs. Take an airport, for example. Spillover costs imposed upon other economic units include the noise from the aircraft take-offs and landings, the street congestion resulting from additional automobile traffic, and the increased air pollution and its consequent hazards to health. All these economic costs are borne more or less involuntarily by the other economic units located in the vicinity of the airport. These are spillover costs. But at the same time, the airport's presence may confer certain benefits: industrial properties may increase in value because of their convenient location, hotels and restaurants may have more customers, and the airport may bring new employment opportunities. These are the spillover benefits.

Spillover benefits may reduce or even outweigh the spillover costs. All that is important for us is the *net* effect on the rest of society. Thus, if spillover benefits amount to $1,000, while spillover costs are only $400, we enjoy net spillover benefits of $600. Similarly, when spillover costs exceed spillover benefits, society will have to bear net spillover costs in addition to the private costs of production. Whenever we talk about the effects of spillovers in the following pages, we will have net spillover costs or benefits in mind.

As soon as spillover effects are present, private costs and benefits are no longer a true measure of the total costs and benefits associated with an economic decision. We need a more inclusive concept, one that will also take into account the possible spillover effects on other economic units. This broader concept measures the costs and benefits that are incurred not only by the private individual making the decision but by society as a whole. We will call them *social costs* and *social benefits*.

Spillover costs

In Figure 8-1 we show the supply and demand curves for a commodity subject to spillover costs. Let us assume that the industry under

Figure 8-1

Spillover costs *If a commodity creates spillover costs for other economic units, the free market will lead to overproduction and underpricing of that commodity.*

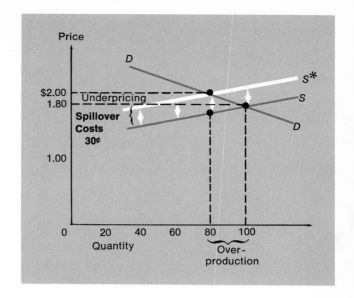

consideration is purely competitive, so that the free market supply and demand curves S and D accurately reflect the costs of producing the commodity and the utility or benefits derived from its consumption. The private supply and demand curves intersect at a market price of $1.80, and an output of 100 units.

If the economic activity under consideration imposes a net spillover cost of 30 cents per unit of output on the rest of society, the free market solution—which does not take account of these spillover costs—will lead us to too large an output and too low a price. If we were to add the spillover costs to the private costs underlying the supply curve S, we would obtain the new supply curve S^*, which includes the spillover costs. The supply curve S^* shows not only the private costs of production but also the social costs of producing the commodity. Taking social costs into account will lead to a higher price for the commodity, and a smaller output.

The precise amount by which the private market price will be below the price reflecting social costs depends on the elasticity of the demand curve for the product. If the demand for the product is inelastic, the market price and the price reflecting social costs of production will diverge more than if the demand curve is elastic.

Not only does the free market price fail to reflect accurately the social costs of production, but the output level, too, is nonoptimal. Because only the lower private costs are taken into consideration in the output decision, the output level will be greater than it would be if social costs were also considered. From the viewpoint of society as a whole, we have an *overproduction* of commodities, which imposes spillover costs on the rest of society—unless the community takes action to remedy this situation. What action may the community take to bring about a socially more optimal production level? We will briefly discuss four possible actions: outlawing the activity, "internalizing" the spillovers, taxation, and government takeover.

Outlawing the activity certainly results in the elimination of the spillover costs. But at the same time society forgoes the benefits of being able to enjoy the goods or services produced. To outlaw automobiles because they contribute to smog may force us to return to horses and buggies—which is not only a much slower mode of transportation but may also create new health hazards in the form of flies, horse droppings, and other "spillovers." Only in very extreme cases, where the economic benefits of an activity are minute in comparison to the social costs, may an outright prohibition be advisable. We may think, as an example, of a law prohibiting the burning of garbage in populated fire-hazard areas. Open fires would not only constitute a threat to houses, trees, and wildlife, but also endanger the lives of the population.

Internalizing the spillovers is accomplished by merging the units that create the spillovers and the units on which the spillovers are imposed. For instance, consider a small lake along whose shores a resort hotel and a chemical plant are located. The chemical plant may want to discharge dirty waste materials into the lake—which would make the resort hotel a less attractive place to tourists. The chemical plant would impose some costs on the resort hotel—a typical case of spillover costs. If the chemical plant and the resort hotel were owned by the same company, the chemical plant would have an incentive to stop polluting the lake, because it would decrease the profits of the resort. What used to constitute a spillover during separate ownership of plant and resort is internalized if both plant and resort belong to the same company. Now there is no longer any spillover cost imposed because the owner of both plant and resort bears the full cost of the chemical production.

But frequently it is impractical to merge the economic units creating and suffering from the spillovers. Were the chemical plant to pollute a river instead of a lake, the firm might have to buy all the property along the whole river in order to effectively internalize all spillovers. Automobiles create smog, and it would be virtually impossible to internalize this health hazard by appropriate mergers. Other solutions may have to be found.

Taxation is another possible solution. Here the government imposes on the creator of the spillover costs a charge that is equal to the costs that he himself imposes on the rest of society. Thus the total cost of production includes not only the private costs, but also the tax, which in turn is set to reflect the spillover costs. The costs of production including the tax then approximate the social costs of production. In several European countries, firms that discharge pollutants into rivers are taxed in such a way. The firm has the option of eliminating the pollution by installing water treatment equipment or paying the tax. If it chooses to adopt the latter course, the government will then take the tax proceeds, construct its own water treatment plant, and clean up the water. In effect, the firm is paying the government to perform this service. In either case, the firm will have to bear the full social costs of production.

Finally, *governmental takeover* of industries that are subject to large spillovers is a possibility. The government would simply provide the optimal amount of the commodity and charge a price that reflects the total social costs of production.

Spillover benefits

Spillover benefits are the opposite of spillover costs. Here an economic activity imposes positive benefits on the rest of society. Health, education, and public transportation are examples of industries for which the claim of positive spillovers is frequently made. A person who is immunized against polio, diphtheria, or smallpox not only benefits personally; his neighbors also benefit, because the immunized person cannot become a carrier of the disease and transmit it to the rest of the population. If everybody else was immunized, I wouldn't even have to take the shots myself, because there would be nobody I could catch the disease from!

An educated person may vote more intelligently and stay off the welfare rolls, and his friends may benefit from his good advice and stimulating dinner conversation. Public transportation systems not only benefit the people who ride in the buses or subways; but by easing road congestion and smog, they also benefit the persons who elect to drive their own automobiles.

Again, the free market does not take account of the spillover benefits, because the regular supply and demand curves (*S* and *D* in Figure 8-2) take account only of the private costs and benefits. If spillover benefits are present, the free market will lead to *underproduction* and too high a price for the commodity creating the spillover benefits. Again, there exist several possible means of correcting the free market solution.

Subsidies or *tax incentives* may be used as an additional inducement for firms to expand output. The government might give out-

Figure 8-2

Spillover benefits *A commodity that confers spillover benefits on others is underproduced and overpriced if the free market is the sole allocation device.*

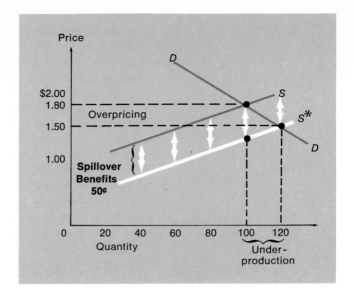

right grants to firms in industries that produce positive spillovers. Or it might offer special tax deductions as an incentive. Thus the government gives direct grants to private educational institutions through the National Science Foundation and other agencies. In addition, it offers exemption from taxation to all nonprofit educational institutions. The same is true for nonprofit hospitals and medical research facilities.

It has been suggested that a reduction of the automobile vehicle tax and the gasoline tax for vehicles that are pollution-free may be offered as an incentive to install pollution-free engines and to use low pollution gasolines—whose private production costs may be higher, but whose spillover costs would be lower.

Internalizing the spillovers by mergers of the two units is again a possible solution in some cases. An apple orchard owner may also go into the honey production business, because bees provide a useful service in pollinating the apple blossoms and thereby create positive spillover benefits. Even if the honey business were not very profitable in itself, it might pay the orchard-owner/beekeeper to buy some more beehives because the additional bees would pollinate the apple blossoms more effectively and increase the profits from the orchard. Similarly, airlines have bought or constructed large hotels in the cities served by them, and offer special low airline tour fares to people buying a "package" that includes hotel accommodations in addition to the air transportation.

Governmental takeover may constitute another alternative. This solution is used frequently in industries where the spillover benefits are very large compared to the private benefits accruing to the operator of the plant or service. In the extreme case, we can identify commodities that are virtually all spillover. Unlike an overcoat, where only the owner benefits by its purchase, with little or no spillover benefits accruing to other persons, so-called public goods are all spillover. They benefit anybody and everybody who cares to utilize the service. We will now turn to an analysis of the case of these public goods.

Public goods

Public goods are those commodities from whose enjoyment nobody can be effectively excluded. Everybody is free to enjoy the benefits of these commodities, and one person's utilization does not reduce the possibilities of anybody else's enjoying the same good. Using our previous terminology, we might say that public goods are cases in which we have a complete spillover of all benefits.

Examples of public goods are not as rare as one might expect. A flood control dam is a public good. Once the dam is built, *all* persons living in the area will benefit—irrespective of their own contribution to the construction cost of the dam. The same holds true for highway signs or aids to navigation. Once a lighthouse is built, no ship of any nationality can be effectively excluded from the utilization of the lighthouse for navigational purposes. National defense is another example. Even a person who voted against military expenditures or did not pay any taxes will benefit from the protection afforded.

If it were up to private individuals to provide for these public goods, it is unlikely that they would be provided in sufficient quantity—if at all. It would be in the narrow self-interest of any individual to do nothing and to hope that his neighbor might construct the flood control dam, erect signs at dangerous intersections, and volunteer for the army. But if it is in everybody's interest to wait until somebody else takes the action, nobody will take it and we will fail to provide for the production of public goods that will benefit everyone. Hence, a collective or governmental action is the only feasible solution.

There are two important questions that have to be considered in this context. First, how large should the governmental sector be, and second, what and how much of each public good or service should the government provide?

How large should the governmental sector of the economy be?

To find an answer to this question we must remind ourselves that any activity undertaken by the government is costly, in that it will use resources that could otherwise be utilized in the private sector. The effective means of transferring resources from the private to the public sector is taxation. When the government taxes its citizens, the citizens will have less money to spend for their own activities and the government can increase its purchases. Fewer resources are used by the private sector and more are made available to the public sector. Hence the opportunity costs of governmental activity are the private goods and services that have to be forgone.

We stated previously that the maximization of welfare requires that marginal costs equal marginal benefits. This rule may here be restated: the optimal balance between the public and the private sector is achieved when the marginal benefits of the last dollar of *public* expenditures is equal to the marginal benefits of the last dollar of *private* expenditures. Then no further reallocation of resources that will increase total social welfare is possible between the two sectors of the economy.

The second question pertains to the optimal amount of each public good to be produced. Welfare maximization requires that marginal costs and benefits are equated throughout the economy. Hence the government should provide the different public goods in such a quantity that the marginal social costs are equal to the marginal social benefits. This point is reached in Figure 8-3 at the intersection of the marginal social cost (*MSC*) and marginal social benefit (*MSB*) curve.

An alternative way of determining the optimum quantity to be provided is again given by the total cost-total benefit approach. Here the government will select the output level at which total social benefits (*TSB*) exceed total social costs (*TSC*) by the largest possible margin, thereby maximizing the net social benefits associated with that public good.

Of course, it is no easy task to determine the social costs and social benefits associated with a public good. In the private sector of the economy, the free market in which commodities are purchased and sold provides a convenient measuring rod: the market price determines the value of a commodity. But for a public good there exists no market place. There is no practicable way of charging drivers for looking at highway signs, seamen for watching a lighthouse, and citizens for the security provided to them through national defense. Because the market does not provide the necessary signals, economic analysis has to be substituted for the impersonal judgment of the market place.

Before public expenditures are undertaken, economists can eval-

Figure 8-3

Public goods *Public goods should be provided in a quantity that will result in the greatest excess of total social benefits over total social costs, or where marginal social costs equal marginal social benefits.*

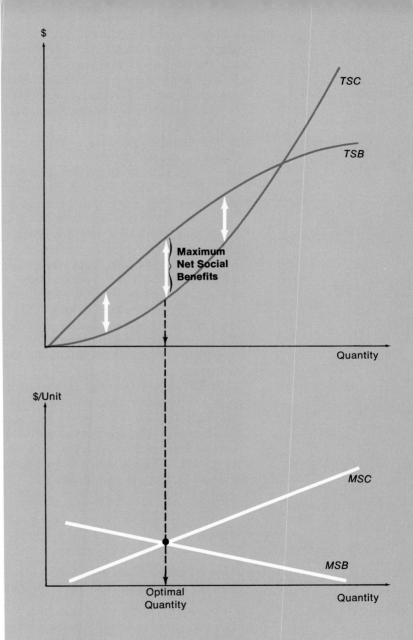

uate the expected social costs and benefits associated with the project. Economic cost-benefit analysis provides a framework for the systematic exploration of the many ramifications of any public expenditure. In addition, the competent analyst can provide the policy maker with a whole array of alternative courses of action. For each alternative, the associated social costs and benefits can be estimated and the best alternative can then be chosen.

For instance, protection against floods may be provided by building one gigantic dam, or a series of smaller dams, or a dike along the total length of the river, or a flood diversion canal, or perhaps even other means. Cost-benefit analysis will provide the person or committee responsible for the decision making with a complete list of all the social costs and benefits associated with each alternative. While one large dam may be cheaper than a series of small dams, the big dam may create a much larger lake, which will flood a bigger area of land on which crops could have been raised. The dike along the river may have lower construction costs than either the large dam or the series of small dams—but the dams may have the advantage that they could be used to generate electric power as a by-product. The flood diversion canal may provide spillover benefits in the form of irrigation by channeling water to hitherto arid lands. Lakes created by the dam projects can do double duty as water reservoirs and recreation areas.

It certainly is no easy task to accurately estimate all the social costs and benefits associated with the various alternative projects, especially in view of the fact that many of the costs and benefits may accrue only years from now. But quantifying and analyzing the costs and benefits will lead to a more rational decision than would be possible in the absence of cost-benefit analysis and on the basis of hunches and guesses alone.

Summary

□ Private individuals will take account only of the costs and benefits accruing to them in their decision-making process.

□ Frequently, *spillover effects* exist which will impose costs or benefits upon other economic units. In that case, the private costs of production do not accurately reflect the cost of production to society as a whole.

□ *Spillover benefits* emerge when the economic activity of one unit positively benefits other economic units. *Spillover costs* harm other economic units.

☐ Because private decision making takes account only of private costs and benefits alone, spillover costs will lead to *underpricing* and *overproduction*, while spillover benefits lead to *overpricing* and *underproduction*.

☐ Governmental *regulation* may compensate for these spillover effects and restore the equality between private costs (or benefits) and social costs (and benefits).

☐ Regulation may include legal prescriptions, taxation or subsidy payments, the merging of economic units affected by the spillovers, or governmental takeover.

☐ *Public goods* are "all spillover," in that nobody can be effectively excluded from their benefits. Typically, the government will provide these goods and services.

☐ The optimal size of the governmental sector is governed by the rule that the last dollar spent by the government should yield equal benefits to the last dollar spent by the private sector.

☐ Each governmental activity should be pushed to the point at which marginal social costs are equal to marginal social benefits; thereby assuring the maximization of welfare for society.

☐ Because there exists no free market for public goods the market mechanism must be replaced by economic analysis of the costs and benefits associated with any economic project.

☐ *Cost-benefit analysis* provides a framework within which the possible alternative courses of action can be evaluated, and the best alternative chosen.

9

International trade

Specialization is the basis for exchange. We saw how individual firms specialize in the production of certain commodities and then sell these commodities to other economic units. What holds true for individual economic units also holds true for countries as a whole. But let us remember that international trade is carried on by *individuals*, i.e., households and firms, which do so for their own advantage. Individual firms export their commodities to other countries, or import foreign goods for resale to their customers. Hence, in order to explain international trade, we have to look at the motivations of individual economic units. International trade between countries offers the opportunity of reaping gains similar to those that accrue to individual firms and households because they specialize and engage in mutually advantageous exchange.

Excess supply and demand

We found that we can derive an industry supply or demand curve, showing the aggregate supply or demand for a commodity, by summing horizontally all the individual supply or demand curves. Figure 9-1 shows some hypothetical aggregate supply and demand curves for wheat in the United States. We see that at a market price of $1.00 per bushel, the market will be cleared: the quantity of wheat supplied will equal the quantity of wheat demanded, namely, 800 million bushels.

Now consider the quantities supplied and demanded at other prices. At a price of $1.50 per bushel, farmers are willing to produce a total of 1,200 million bushels, while consumers will buy only 700 million bushels. Hence, in this hypothetical example, there is an *excess supply* of 500 million bushels on the American market. If the wheat market is restricted to American buyers and sellers, this wheat surplus will have a depressing influence on the market price. But consider what will happen if we permit foreign trade. The excess supply of 500 million bushels may now be offered for sale in the world market at $1.50 per bushel. While we do not know yet whether foreigners would be willing to buy 500 bushels of wheat at $1.50 per bushel, we do know that Americans would be willing to sell or export

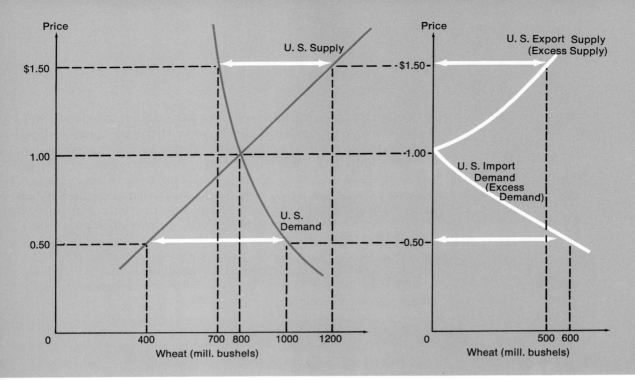

Figure 9-1

The U.S. supply and demand curves

The United States export supply and import demand curves show the quantities that the United States is willing to export or import at various prices.

Figure 9-2

The U.S. export supply and import demand curves

that quantity at that price to foreigners. We may derive a new curve showing the excess supplies that Americans would be willing to export at various prices. These excess supplies are shown in Figure 9-2, and they are given by the horizontal difference between the domestic supply and demand curves of Figure 9-1. Numerically, the excess supplies may be obtained by subtracting the aggregate domestic demand from the aggregate domestic supply at each and every price and labeling the differential "excess supply," or quantities available for export. The excess supply curve of Figure 9-2 is also called, simply, the *export supply curve*.

At prices lower than $1.00 we find the opposite phenomenon. American consumers are willing to buy a larger quantity of wheat than American producers are willing to produce at such low prices. For instance, were the price of wheat to fall to 50 cents, total domestic demand would amount to 1,000 million bushels, while domestic supply would fall to 400 million bushels. This would leave an unfulfilled *excess demand* of 600 million bushels at that price. The excess demand for wheat is given by the horizontal difference between the domestic demand and supply curves, and is identical to the *import demand* at the various prices. It is graphed also in Figure 9-2.

Figure 9-2 now shows the export supply (excess supply) as well as the import demand (excess demand) curves for wheat viewed from the vantage point of the United States. Let us note that at a price of $1.00 per bushel, where domestic supply just equals domestic demand, the export supply and import demand curves touch the vertical axis: no amounts are available for export or are demanded by importers. At the $1.00 price, the United States is not willing to engage in foreign wheat trade.

Let us assume that the United States trades only with Germany. (We may let Germany stand here for all other countries with which the United States maintains trade relations, because the analysis will be considerably simplified if we restrict ourselves to just one foreign country.) We now have to construct some hypothetical supply and demand curves for wheat in Germany. To render our prices comparable to each other, we will have to convert the German prices, which are stated in marks, into dollars. Let us assume that the exchange rate between the two currencies is fixed, and that we are always able to exchange $1.00 for 4 German marks and vice versa. In Chapter 15 we will deal explicitly with the analysis of foreign exchange rates, and we will study the effects of changes in the exchange rate. But for the time being we will adopt the convention that $1.00 always equals 4 marks.

Given the 1:4 exchange rate, we are able to show the supply and demand for wheat by Germans in terms of United States dollar prices. Figure 9-3 shows the hypothetical German domestic supply and demand curves for wheat. Again we derive the export supply and import demand curves by plotting the horizontal differences between the domestic supply and demand curves in Figure 9-4.

Figure 9-5 reproduces both the American and German excess supply and demand curves for wheat. Let us first delineate the possible price range within which trade between the two nations is possible. At prices *above $2.00* per bushel, both Germany and the United States will want to export wheat. Hence *no* trade between the two countries will be possible, because when both want to act as exporters of wheat, there will be no willing buyer or importer. If both countries attempt to sell wheat at a price above $2.00, no buyers will be found, and consequently the price of wheat will have to drop to at least $2.00. The situation is exactly reversed at prices *below $1.00*. Now we find that both Germany and the United States

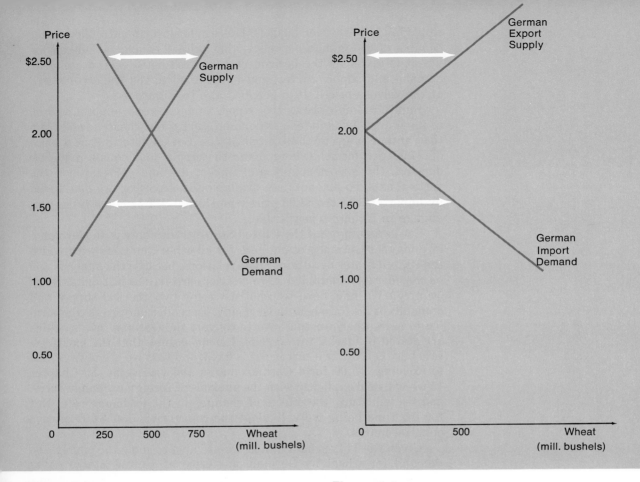

Figure 9-3

The German supply and demand curves

Figure 9-4

The German export supply and import demand curves

The German export supply and import demand curves show the quantities of wheat that Germany is willing to export or import at various prices.

will want to import wheat. As both countries have an excess demand for the product, its price is going to be bid up at least to $1.00.

We have now established the upper and lower limits for the international market price of wheat. The upper limit is provided by the price that will prevail in Germany if that country does not engage in international trade at all, but lives under conditions of autarky. The lower limit to the possible price range is provided by the American autarky price of $1.00. Mutually profitable trade is possible somewhere in the price range between $1.00 and $2.00.

The exact international market price and the quantity that will be traded between the two nations is determined by the intersection of the United States export supply curve and the German import demand curve. In our hypothetical example, the two curves intersect at a price of $1.50 and a trade volume of 500 million bushels of wheat. Hence the United States will export that quantity of wheat and Germany will import it.

As a result of free international trade between the two countries the price of wheat will be equalized in the two nations. (That is, of course, under the assumption that transport costs are zero and that there are no other obstacles to free trade, such as tariffs, quotas, and the like.)

Can we say anything additional about the effects of international trade on the production and consumption patterns in the two countries? In the United States, pretrade equilibrium prevails at a price of $1.00 per bushel, with 800 million bushels being produced and consumed. After trade opens up and the price of wheat climbs to its new international equilibrium of $1.50, United States wheat output will expand to 1,200 million bushels, while consumption will decline from 800 to 700 million bushels. American wheat production expands, while American consumption of wheat declines. But at the same time the export earnings allow the United States to import other goods from Germany and to increase the consumption of these goods.

The reverse is true in Germany. Here we find a pretrading equilibrium price of $2.00 and an output of 500 million wheat bushels.

Figure 9-5

The international market *The international market price and the quantity traded are determined by the intersection of the United States export supply and the German import demand curves.*

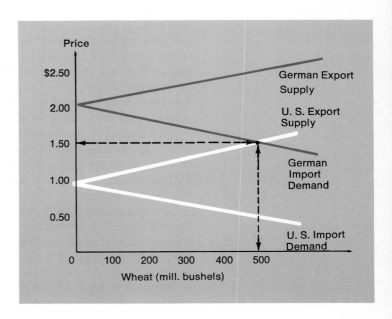

After trade is started and the wheat price drops to $1.50, German wheat producers cut production to 250 million bushels. Consumers, on the other hand, take advantage of the lower prices and increase their purchases to 750 million bushels.

It is clear that German consumers are now able to purchase their wheat at a lower price—but German farmers also receive a lower price. Conversely, American farmers receive a higher price than formerly for their product, while American consumers also have to pay a higher price. If we look at the wheat market in isolation, international trade certainly seems to be a very mixed blessing. In order to make any more conclusive statements about its desirability we must analyze what happens to the resources that are released in Germany by the cutback in wheat production, as well as finding out where the resources are coming from that are being used to expand the American wheat output. To look at the wheat market in isolation cannot provide the answer. As usual, we must look at the opportunity costs involved in the changes in production and consumption. To do this, we must look at the other commodities that are affected by international trade.

Comparative advantage

The cost of a commodity was defined earlier as the sacrifices that we have to make in order to obtain that commodity. In our simple partial equilibrium model used above, the cost of a bushel of wheat is the amount of money that we have to pay in order to obtain the wheat. But in a more fundamental sense, the cost of wheat consists of the other commodities that we have to forgo so that the released resources may be used to acquire the wheat. Now we shall turn to a two-commodity analysis of the effects of international trade.

In Chapter 1 we encountered the production possibility curve, which shows the maximum quantities of two goods that we can produce with our given resources and technology. Figure 9-6 shows a hypothetical production possibility curve for wheat and beer for the United States.

Let us assume that in the initial pretrade or autarky position the United States is producing 800 million bushels of wheat and 600 million gallons of beer. The exchange ratio of wheat against beer is given by the slope of the production possibility curve at the autarky point A.

Now let us consider what happens after trade is initiated. In the previous section we saw how both the American and German supply

Figure 9-6

International exchange *The production possibility curve shows the maximum commodity combinations that a country can
produce under autarky. The trade possibility curve shows the various commodity
combinations that can be reached by international exchange.*

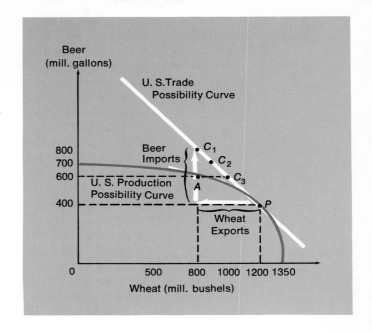

and demand curves together determine the price that will prevail
in world markets. Let us assume that the new international exchange
ratio between beer and wheat is one gallon of beer for one bushel
of wheat. This exchange ratio is shown by the slope of the United
States trade possibilities curve. It will be advantageous for the United
States to produce more wheat, up to the point at which it has to
sacrifice exactly one unit of beer for one unit of wheat. This optimum
production point is reached at P, where the United States produces
1,200 million bushels of wheat and 400 million gallons of beer.

But this new wheat/beer combination may not be the optimal
combination of the two commodities that Americans wish to consume
at the new prices. By trading away some wheat in exchange for beer
(at the 1:1 ratio), Americans are able to modify the commodity bundle
represented by point P. For instance, we may trade 200 million
bushels of wheat against 200 million gallons of beer from Germany.
By this we reach the commodity combination C_1. At C_1, we have just
as much wheat to consume as we had under autarky, namely, 800
million bushels. But our beer consumption has increased from 600
to 800 million gallons. The 200 million gallon consumption increase
represents the gain from trade that accrues to the United States.

Alternatively, we may engage in different amounts of trade and
reach commodity combinations C_2 or C_3. Commodity combination C_2
offers us 700 million gallons of beer and 900 million bushels of

wheat—a gain of 100 million units of each commodity over the autarky position. Commodity combination C_3, on the other hand, enables us to consume 200 million bushels more wheat than under autarky, while maintaining our beer consumption. Whichever commodity combination we actually select, C_1, C_2, C_3, or somewhere in between, we will wind up with a beer-wheat combination superior to the one that we could have attained under autarky. These gains result from the United States having first increased its production of the commodity that it can produce relatively more cheaply than Germany, namely, wheat, and then having traded some of that wheat against beer.

In Germany the process of specialization is reversed. Germans will produce more of the good that they produce relatively cheaply— beer—and then they will trade some of that beer for wheat from the United States. The German gains from trade are similar to the ones enjoyed by the United States, in that each country is enabled to increase its commodity consumption over the amount that it would be able to produce for itself alone.

We have established now that the country as a whole will derive certain benefits from engaging in free trade with other countries. But we also know from our previous supply and demand analysis of the wheat market that prices of individual commodities do change after free trade is introduced. As individual prices change, there will be some economic groups who will gain and other groups who will lose. In particular, the former producers of the commodity that will now be imported will have to undergo adjustments, and until a new equilibrium in that industry is reached, economic hardships may have to be borne.

But it is important to point out again that the country as a whole will be better off as a result of free trade. Hence it might pay those economic groups that will reap the benefits from free trade to pass some of these benefits on to those economic units that will incur losses. But while it is easy to state this general principle, it is much more difficult to identify precisely the dollar amount of the gains made by the beneficiaries and the losses incurred by the losers, so that proper compensations may be made. The problem is additionally complicated by the fact that while the gains may be enjoyed by a large number of consumers in the form of slightly lower prices on import commodities, there will probably be a few producers who will suffer sizable losses. It may be that the few individuals who are sustaining large losses will be much more vocal about the situation than the large number of small gainers, and therefore carry more political weight.

The basis for comparative advantage

We said that different prices prevailing under autarky are the cause for international trade. Only if pretrade prices differ will there be a profit incentive for traders to ship goods across international borders. There are three factors that can be identified as the main reasons for the emergence of price differentials between countries: differences in resource endowments, differences in production functions, and differences in tastes.

Differences in resource endowments We recall that resources like land, labor, and capital are the inputs that are used in the production process. We also know that—often because of an historical accident or simply by nature—different countries have different relative endowments of resources. For instance, Australia has a large land area in relation to its population, when compared to other countries. The reverse holds true for Japan, where we find a large number of persons crowded onto a relatively small group of islands. The United States and the industrial countries of Western Europe have relatively large amounts of capital at their disposal, while in the underdeveloped regions of Latin America, Africa, and Asia, capital is relatively scarce. We might expect that as a consequence of these differing resource endowments the prices of these resources would also differ between countries. For instance, we would expect that in Australia or Canada land would be relatively cheap, and that the same would hold true for labor in Japan or Hong Kong and for capital in the United States and Western Europe.

The second important observation we can make is that different products use the productive inputs in various proportions. The raising of sheep or the growing of wheat require large land areas; hand tailoring requires many man-hours of labor; and much capital equipment is needed in automobile production, milling steel, and oil refining.

Our theory says that a country will specialize in the production of those commodities that use a relatively large amount of the inexpensive (or abundant) resources. Australia will specialize in the production and subsequent export of wheat, which uses large land areas. Hong Kong will manufacture hand-made suits, which require many hours of the cheap labor abundant there, and the United States and Western Europe will specialize in and export capital-intensive products such as automobiles. Each country will produce and export those products that will take the greatest advantage of the country's resource endowments. Because commodities will tend to be produced where the resources mostly used in their production are the cheapest, this will lead to a world-wide lowering of production costs and thereby benefit all concerned.

Differences in production functions Another reason for the emergence of international relative price differentials, which serve as the basis for profitable international trade, is found in different production functions in different countries. A production function shows *how* various resources are combined in the production of the commodity. Some countries may have special engineering knowledge, or, for environmental reasons, be particularly well suited to certain production processes. For instance, tropical countries are well adapted to citrus fruit production. The same quantities of land, labor, and capital will yield a far larger output of oranges in Morocco than in Denmark or Norway. Other countries perhaps have populations with special engineering skills or technical know-how on which they might base their production superiority. Whatever the reasons, a nation that is able to do a better and more efficient job than its rivals will be able to undersell its competitors, and thereby gain a comparative advantage in those commodities it produces best.

One special type of comparative advantage based on production functions is found in industries characterized by *increasing returns*. In industries where economies of large-scale production prevail, additional units of output can be produced at ever lower unit cost. It follows that any firm (or country) that is already established will be able to undersell a potential competitor who is starting out from scratch. In an international setting, this means that the country that initiates production of the commodity subject to increasing returns will be able to undersell other countries, and thereby become the world's major supplier (or at least one of a few major suppliers) of the commodity.

Differences in tastes Fortunately, not all the world's people have identical tastes. If many residents of a country have a preference for certain commodities, the price of these commodities will be bid up and the country may become an importer of those goods. For instance, some people argue that in spite of the fact that the United States may have a comparative cost advantage in automobile production based on supply considerations alone, she is actually an importer of automobiles, because Americans have a strong preference for automobiles. Thus, the United States winds up as an importer of Volkswagens, Ferraris and Datsuns—in spite of the fact that looking at the production side (input endowments and production functions) alone, we would expect the United States to be an exporter of automobiles. If such a reversal of the trade pattern—which is expected on the basis of supply considerations alone—comes about, economists speak of a *demand reversal* of the trade pattern.

Clearly, the *actual* trade pattern between countries is influenced by all the factors we have just mentioned: resource endowments, production functions, and tastes. They all play their role in determining comparative advantage. Whichever commodity has a lower price relative to the other commodity will become the country's export good, while the relatively high-priced commodity will be imported. For equilibrium to prevail, the total value of all exports must also equal the total value of all imports. What happens if this condition is not fulfilled will occupy our attention in Chapter 15, when we talk about the balance of international payments.

Barriers to international trade: tariffs

We have dealt with the reasons for the emergence of international trade and we have analyzed the trade pattern that will prevail if countries permit free and unhampered exchange of commodities. Now we have to turn our attention to possible impediments to trade. There are a variety of obstacles that may be placed in the way of free trade. Countries may impose quotas, licensing requirements, tariffs, import surcharges, and a whole array of other obstacles. The two most important trade restrictions are quotas (quantitative limits placed on the amount of a commodity that may be imported) and tariffs (charges that are imposed and collected by the government). We will deal here only with tariffs.

Tariffs are frequently imposed by the government when a foreign-produced good crosses the nation's borders. Typically, the tariff will increase the price of the good to the domestic residents, who not only have to pay the manufacturer the price he is asking but also the duty collected by the government. While it is clear that a tariff will in most cases raise the product's price to consumers, it is somewhat less clear—but just as important—that a tariff will generally lower the amount that the foreign manufacturer receives for his product.

To see why tariffs in general lower the price received by the foreign exporter of the commodity, consider Figures 9-7 and 9-8. Here we reproduce the American and German supply and demand curves for wheat that were introduced in Figures 9-1 and 9-3. The pretrade or autarky price of wheat in the United States is $1.00 and in Germany it is $2.00. We find that if free trade is allowed to prevail between the two countries, a world-market wheat price of $1.50 will be established, and the United States will export wheat to Germany.

Now consider what happens if Germany imposes a tariff. Let us assume that the German wheat tariff will amount to 50 cents per bushel. The price to German consumers will rise above the free trade price of $1.50, as can be seen in Figure 9-8. But now Germans do not want to import the same amount of wheat as before. At the new, higher, price, German consumers will want to import less wheat, which in turn means fewer exports for American producers. Hence the market price for wheat in the United States will fall. In Figure 9-7 the United States price falls to $1.25, but the precise amount obviously depends on the elasticity of the supply and demand schedules for wheat. In our example the 50 cent tariff is evenly split between an increase in wheat prices to German consumers (from $1.50 to $1.75) and decreased export proceeds (from $1.50 to $1.25) for American producers. The tariff revenue itself goes to the German government.

Terms of trade effects

We learned that a tariff lowers the amount that the importing country pays to the exporting country. Thus a tariff will permit a country to import the commodity at a lower price. It is still true that consumers pay a higher price, but the differential goes to the government. While the tariff revenues are collected by the government, there is good reason to believe that these revenue collections will improve the welfare of the citizens. For instance, the government may use the revenue it collects for public works projects, to lower the income, sales, or profit taxes that it levies, or even to rebate the tariff proceeds to the citizens in the form of lump-sum cash payments. What is important from the standpoint of the nation as a whole is that the price actually paid to the foreign supplier is reduced. This price effect, or terms of trade effect, is beneficial for the country. Economists refer to the lowering of the price paid for the import goods (assuming a constant price for our own export commodities) as an improvement in the terms at which our trade is conducted. As the terms of trade improve, the quantity of imports that we receive

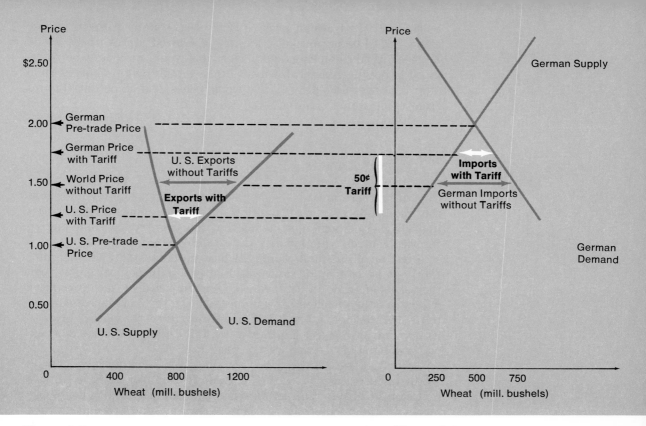

Figure 9-7

The United States market

The imposition of a tariff will reduce the trade volume and make the prices prevailing in the two countries unequal.

Figure 9-8

The German market

in exchange for a given amount of exports will increase. It costs us less to obtain the same quantity of commodities as before: the terms at which we conduct our trade improve.

Prohibitive tariffs

We can overdo a good thing. While a tariff may lead to an improvement of the terms of trade, it will also lead to a *reduction of the trade volume.* The higher the tariff, the smaller the quantity that we shall be importing. Finally, a point may be reached at which all trade will cease, because the tariff is prohibitively high. This will always happen if the tariff is at least as high as the pretrade price differential. In our example, the pretrade United States wheat price is $1.00 per bushel and the German price is $2.00. If Germany were to impose a tariff of $1.00 per bushel, the price of United States wheat would be $2.00 to German consumers. Germans would no longer be interested in buying American wheat, because their own producers could offer it at the same price. Trade would cease, and all potential gains from trade would be eliminated too.

The optimal tariff

Obviously, there must be some golden mean. If a country finds that the imposition of a tariff will lower the price it has to pay for its imports (net of tariffs), it means that this country has some degree of price control, which it may use to its own advantage.

First of all, a small country, which purchases only an insignificantly small portion of total world output, is in no position to turn the terms of trade in its favor. A tariff imposed by such a country will have only one effect. It will increase the price of the commodity to its own residents, but it will *not* lower the world market price to its own advantage. Such a country will find that the terms of trade will not improve if it imposes a tariff.

Second, other countries may retaliate. If Germany increases its wheat tariff to turn the terms of trade in its favor, other countries may not sit idly by and let this happen. Instead they may impose tariffs on the goods they buy from Germany, and attempt to turn the terms of trade back in their own favor. Who will win in such a tariff war? Theory does not provide a unique answer. It will all depend on the various elasticities of supply and demand of the goods involved. Any outcome is possible: Germany might emerge as a winner from the tariff war; the other countries might win; all might lose. This latter result is especially likely if the tariff war is protracted. As all countries involved impose higher and higher tariffs, these tariffs will eventually become prohibitive and all gains from trade will be eliminated because trade itself will cease.

These are two major restrictions on a country's ability to impose tariffs. But let us assume that the country is an important importer of foreign commodities and that it does not have to fear retaliation. Under these—admittedly very limited—circumstances, a country may exploit some of the market power it possesses by imposing an optimal tariff, which will turn the terms of trade in its favor while still allowing a considerable amount of trade to flow.

Infant industry tariffs

Another argument for tariff protection is particularly applicable to industries that experience decreasing costs over a considerable output range. As we may recall, a decreasing-cost industry is characterized by relatively high starting costs, but once a larger output volume is reached the cost of production drops off. Let us assume that the automobile industry is a decreasing-cost industry. If this assumption holds true, it is very difficult indeed for any new firms to enter the automobile market. New firms have to face the high starting costs, while their established competitors are already enjoying the low costs of large-scale production.

Applied to an international setting, this means that a country that has a *potential* comparative advantage in automobile production, but does not now produce automobiles, will have a very hard time indeed competing against the established foreign producers. The recommendation is, therefore, that the country should levy an initial tariff, so that the "infant" automobile industry can develop without having immediately to compete against foreign producers. Then, once the industry is well established in the home market, the protective tariff may be removed and the country's products be allowed to compete against the foreign manufacturers on an equal footing.

Let us note that this infant industry argument is valid only for those industries in which the country will eventually enjoy a comparative advantage, and where the current foreign selling price is below the starting costs incurred by an industry that is starting from scratch. Only a careful long-run economic analysis can tell whether a given country enjoys a potential comparative advantage in a product.

Also, once the infant industry has come of age, the protective tariffs must be removed, if the full gains from international specialization are to be reaped. Frequently it happens that an industry is started under tariff protection and becomes accustomed to the tariff shelter it enjoys. Clearly, it is in the industry's own interests to lobby for a continuance of the tariffs, so that the industry can exploit its monopolistic position at home. But at the same time all the domestic consumers are forced to pay higher prices. The country as a whole is better off if the tariff is eventually removed and consumers are free to buy from the least-cost supplier—be it a domestic or a foreign firm.

Tariffs for self-sufficiency

The argument is often made that countries might want to maintain a certain degree of self-sufficiency for political or military purposes. If a country is dependent on foreign suppliers for essential foodstuffs or military goods, it is easy for that country to slip into a position of dependency on the foreign suppliers. In an emergency situation, the country may face starvation or an inability to arm itself to counter the foreign threat. There is some truth to this argument.

But by levying a tariff relative prices will be distorted. For instance, a tariff on wheat imports will increase the domestic wheat price and bring about increased domestic wheat production. At the same time, the high price of wheat will lead domestic consumers to cut down on their wheat purchases and buy other, less expensive goods instead.

The way out of the dilemma lies in lump-sum subsidies to domestic producers of the commodities deemed essential. For instance, if domestic wheat producers face a loss should they sell their product at the low price prevailing in international wheat markets, the government may elect to give them a lump-sum payment to cover their losses and thereby allow them to earn a normal return on their investment. The wheat producers can then sell their product at the low international price, and consumers are able to purchase the commodity cheaply. This encourages them to consume more wheat than if the price were kept artificially high—thereby contributing to the development of a large wheat industry. In addition, there are no distortions in consumption patterns, resulting from artificially high prices.

At the same time, the lump-sum subsidies paid to the wheat producers by the government make explicit the economic cost of the domestic wheat production support program. If the lump-sum payments to farmers have to be budgeted, the government has a clear idea of the total cost of the program, and thereby of the cost of self-sufficiency. If, instead, tariffs are used to bring about self-sufficiency, the costs are no longer explicit, but hidden in the form of higher consumer prices and market distortions. By making explicit all the costs associated with self-sufficiency, everyone concerned will be able to judge more intelligently whether protection and self-sufficiency are really worth the costs involved. Or, to put it differently, this action enables us to compare the economic costs with the political and military benefits associated with self-sufficiency.

Trade and economic stability

Finally, we have to deal with the argument that international trade introduces additional instability into the economic system. If a country were to isolate itself from the rest of the world, no economic disturbances emanating from abroad would affect its own economy. If, on the other hand, a country engages in international trade, fluctuations in the rate of economic activity, changing demand patterns, technological innovations, and other changes that take place abroad will also affect the domestic economy. Thus a new source of instability is introduced. To have to make constant economic adjustments is costly. Resources that are invested may become useless, human skills that were acquired only with years of experience lose their value, established income and wealth patterns will be changed. In this way, international trade may impose some transitory costs on an economy. In Chapter 15 we will deal in greater detail with the alternative ways in which the economy as a whole adjusts to external disturbances. It will suffice here to say that a country that contemplates any changes in its tariff structure—be they in the upward or downward direction—may be well advised to make the change gradually, rather than in one abrupt step. For instance, if a country grants an infant industry some protection, it may be difficult to remove the entire tariff in one jump at the end of a five-year "growing-up" period. Economic disturbances will be minimized if the tariff adjustment is spread over a number of years, so that producers can slowly adjust to the new foreign competition. By making the adjustment gradual, resources can be shifted slowly, men can be retrained, and other inputs will not be faced with extreme fluctuations in their demand and supply.

International trade opens up new avenues of prosperity for everyone. But it also imposes certain adjustment costs upon the country. By making the necessary adjustments in a gradual fashion, these adjustment costs can be minimized and the maximum gains from international trade can thereby be realized.

Summary

□ The *gains* from trade are the result of international specialization.

□ The difference between the quantities supplied and demanded at each and every possible price determines the country's *export supply schedule.* (If the quantity demanded exceeds the quantity supplied, it gives the *import demand schedule.*)

□ The international market price will lie between the prices prevailing under autarky conditions.

□ The precise *international market price* and the quantity traded are determined by the intersection of the export supply and import demand curves.

□ A country will export the commodities in which it enjoys a comparative advantage. Comparative advantage may be based on differences in resource endowments, production functions, or taste patterns between countries.

□ *Tariffs* are charges that are imposed on commodities that cross international borders.

□ Tariffs tend to raise the price to consumers in the importing country and lower the price received by the producers in the exporting country—the differential going to the government that imposes the tax.

□ If the importing country imposes a tariff, it may succeed in lowering the price paid to the foreign producers, and thereby turn the terms of trade in its favor.

□ An *optimal tariff* is designed to maximize the advantage derived from the lower prices paid for the import goods, while minimizing the quantity reduction in the volume imported.

□ A *prohibitive tariff* is high enough to eliminate any price differential that may have existed before trade opened up. Imposition of such a tariff will eliminate *all* trade.

□ An infant industry tariff is designed to protect a new industry that will eventually enjoy a comparative advantage. Infant industry tariffs should be eliminated gradually over a few years, so that the industry can then compete effectively against the foreign competition.

□ Tariffs designed to promote self-sufficiency for political or military purposes distort price patterns and lead to economic inefficiency. Direct lump-sum subsidies paid to the producers in industries that are deemed essential are superior to tariffs because they do not distort relative prices; in addition, they make the cost of self-sufficiency explicit.

10

The national income and product accounts

In the first half of this book we analyzed the behavior of individual households, firms, and governmental units. We adopted a microeconomic viewpoint by focusing attention on the actions of the individual component units that make up the economic system. Now it is time to look at the aggregate manifestation of economic behavior. The center of attention will be macroeconomics, which is concerned with the sum total of the individual economic actions.

Looking at individual households, we analyzed how these economic units decide on the amount of each good they purchase and how they allocate their total expenditures between various goods and services. Now we will deal with the determinants of aggregate consumption expenditures of households and will try to find out what determines this total amount of spending. The composition of total consumption expenditures will be of little concern to us.

In the theory of the firm, we looked at the factors responsible for the firm's decision as to what should be sold and how it should be produced. Now we will focus attention on the total volume of production in the economy. Earlier, we considered the firm's decision to expand or to contract output, and we analyzed the circumstances in which new firms will be set up in an industry. All this involved investment in new machinery and equipment. We will determine now the aggregate manifestations of investment activity in the economy as a whole.

The government in a modern economy serves two important roles: it provides the public goods and services, as we discussed in the microeconomic section, and it acts as a stabilizer for the economic system as a whole. Microeconomic analysis tells us about the proper balance between the private and public sectors, as well as the optimal amount of the various public goods to be provided by the government. Macroeconomic analysis focuses attention on the government as a stabilizer of the economic system.

Finally, in the analysis of the foreign trade sector, we adopted a microeconomic approach to what goods and how much of them will be exported or imported. The total amounts of exports and imports are recorded in the national balance of payments, and here again certain macroeconomic problems emerge that affect the economic system as a whole.

Measures of economic activity

Before we can talk in any meaningful way about the level of economic activity taking place within an economy, we have to develop some yardsticks that will allow us to measure the total volume of commodities produced and the income earned in the production process.

The greater the volume of commodities produced by the economic system, the greater the economic well-being of the residents of the country. If more commodities are available for consumption, more wants can be satisfied, more hunger stilled, more housing provided, and so on. But let us note that any economic yardstick measuring the volume of production or income in the economy merely provides an idea about the *economic* well-being of the residents. It tells us something about their material standard of living.

However, satisfaction and happiness in life do not come solely from economic well-being. Social, cultural, religious, and a wide variety of other influences together determine the quality of life, our basic sense of fullfillment. But this is a book on economics, and therefore we will concentrate on measures of economic well-being.

Of course, if we want to use one common yardstick for all economic activity, we have to have a joint denominator, which will allow us to add up the various economic activities taking place. This common measuring rod is provided by the monetary value of the goods and services that are produced in the economy.

The sum total of the monetary values of all goods and services produced is called the *national product* of the economy. The national product measures the amount of money which is spent on goods and services during a certain time period—usually a year. Obviously, the money spent represents income to somebody else. Hence we are able to devise an alternative measure: *national income,* or the total amount earned by economic units during a time period.

Spending and earning are just two sides of the same coin. The amount you spend on a haircut constitutes an expenditure from your viewpoint, but from the barber's viewpoint it represents an earning. Hence national product and national income must be equal to each other at all times. If we succeed in measuring one, we know the other.

There are some important definitional conventions of national income or national product, which we customarily adhere to. Some of these definitions are arbitrary conventions, but they have been found highly useful when working with these aggregate numbers.

Single unit actions   There are many economic actions that affect only a single unit within the economic system. One person might spend a day at the beach, paint a self-portrait, or write a diary. These actions do not involve any other economic units, and there are no market transactions taking place. It is a matter that concerns only the person involved in doing these various things. What is the economic value of these activities? It is virtually impossible to determine this value with any degree of accuracy. Your self-portrait may be very dear to you, but its value to anybody else might be zero. There is no easy way out of this dilemma. Economists avoid these valuation problems generally by not considering as part of the national product or income any actions that do not involve transactions between different individual economic units.

Nonmarket transactions   Another group of economic actions, while involving different persons, does not take place in the market place. Again there is no easy way to determine the value of these non-market transactions. The standard example is the family. Husband and wife provide many and varied services for each other and their children, yet no transactions are taking place in the market place. Generally, the husband does not buy each dinner, window washing, or hug from his wife, and it would certainly be difficult to estimate the aggregate value of the services provided. Hence they are excluded from the traditional measures of national product. Similarly, if your uncle helps you to repair your roof, if you have friends over for Thanksgiving dinner, or if you teach a neighborhood kid how to read, no market transactions are involved, and therefore these goods and services are not counted in the official statistics.

Nonproductive transactions   Transactions that involve a mere exchange of existing assets are also excluded because they do not represent any *new* production. Thus, if you sell a used item to somebody else, this does not contribute to the total amount of commodities produced. It represents a mere exchange of existing assets.

In addition to secondhand sales, transfers and exchanges of financial assets do not contribute to new production. A transfer is a payment—or gift—made to another person without receipt of any good or service in return. Social security and unemployment payments are transfers from the government to private individuals. Birthday presents or the allowance received by a student from his parents are transfers within the private sector of the economy. Similarly, exchanges of financial assets, such as stocks, do not create any new income for society as a whole, nor are new assets produced. Only an exchange of existing assets takes place, and that is not counted in current national income or product.

Quality changes   Changes in the quality of a product affect the utility or satisfaction that we derive from the commodity. But unless price changes reflect the improvements in quality, they will not be measured in the national income or product statistics.

Value-added and final products approaches

There are two alternative ways of determining the aggregate amount of economic activity taking place in an economy. These two approaches are the value-added and the final products methods. We stated earlier that nonproductive transactions are excluded from our measure because they do not add anything to national income or product. These transactions represent a mere passing on of existing goods. Similarly, we have to guard against the possibility of counting the same commodity twice or even three times as it passes through various stages in the production process. Two possible ways of avoiding double counting are presented by the final products and the value-added approaches.

The *final products approach* considers only goods and services purchased for *final* use. Thus, anything that is bought as an input into a production process or for the purpose of being resold is excluded. Often it is difficult to determine what is a final product. Consider the purchase of a loaf of bread. If you purchase a loaf of bread to consume it, this clearly is a final purchase. But if a restaurant owner purchases the bread, he may use it to make sandwiches. In that case the sandwiches constitute the final product, and the bread is nothing but an input into the production of the sandwich. Only the sandwiches count as final products.

The *value-added approach* sums the *additions* to the value of the product as it passes through the various stages of the production process. We have to ask at each stage of the production process: "How much more are the firm's outputs worth than the inputs purchased from other economic units?" The difference represents the value

Table 10-1

Stage of production	Value of output		Value added
1. Farm (output: wheat)	$ 500	>	$ 500
2. Mill (output: flour)	700	>	200
		>	300
3. Bakery (final product: bread)	$1,000	=	$1,000

added by that particular firm. For instance, a farm might sell a ton of wheat to a flour mill for $500; the miller might sell the flour for $700 to a baker; and the baker might sell the bread for $1,000 to consumers. The value added by the farmer to the final product is $500; the miller adds another ($700 − $500) $200; and the baker ($1,000 − $700) $300. The sum of the values added in each stage ($500 + $200 + $300) equals $1,000, or the total value of the final product. Numerically, the value-added and the final products approaches will always yield the same result, as shown in Table 10-1.

Real and monetary magnitudes

One last potential complication in our national income and product data has to be dealt with. It concerns the effects of a change in the average price level of the economy. It was noted earlier that we use the prices of individual commodities to determine their value, and thereby their contribution to national product. Money, in effect, serves as a measuring rod by which we can evaluate the contribution of diverse commodities to the nation's output.

As long as the general price level remains unchanged, no problems arise. But if, for instance, we experience a general increase in prices, an increase in the measured national product no longer denotes a corresponding increase in the quantity of goods and services produced. *Inflation*, as a general increase in prices is called, merely means higher prices for goods and services, but it does not mean that an increased quantity of goods and services actually becomes available.

Now we have to differentiate between "real" and "monetary" measures of national income and product. Real magnitudes measure the nation's output at *constant* or fixed prices. Monetary magnitudes measure the nation's output at *current* prices. Thus the difference between real and monetary national product or income is accounted for by general price-level changes. If the general price level remains constant, real and monetary magnitudes—or changes therein—are identical. But if the general price level changes, then the difference between the change in real national income or product and the change in monetary national income or product is equivalent to the change in the price level.

For instance, let us assume that the nation's product is equal to $1,000 billion in 1970. If it increases to $1,100 billion in 1971, this represents a 10 per cent growth in the national product figure. But if the general price level increases during the one-year period by, let us say, 4 per cent, then $40 billion of the $100 billion increase is only caused by inflation. While the *monetary* national product,

Figure 10-1 (opposite)

The circular flow *The total amounts earned by the four main sectors of the economy are national income, and the total amounts spent are national product.*

measured in current prices, increases by 10 per cent, the *real* (inflation-corrected) increase in national product is only $60 billion or 6 per cent. If the general price level *rises*, monetary measures grow faster than real measures. The reverse is true during periods where the general price level *falls*.

Gross national product

Gross national product, or GNP, is the broadest measure of economic activity within a nation. GNP measures the total dollar value of all goods and services produced during a given year. Or, alternatively, GNP measures the total amount of earnings for productive activity. Whether measured by the total production or the total income method, GNP must yield the same numerical value because each dollar spent on a product represents income to someone.

The relationship between spending on products and income earned by the main sectors of the economy is illustrated in Figure 10-1. All transactions between the various units comprising the economic system of a nation are recorded in the gross national product account—subject to the qualifications discussed in the previous section.

GNP calculated according to the total spending on final products approach consists of (1) household consumption expenditures for goods and services, (2) all firms' investment expenditures on machinery, equipment, inventories, and construction, (3) the total spending by federal, state, and local governments on goods and services, and (4) net exports to other countries. Net exports are the difference between exports and imports. Exports are clearly part of domestic production and they generate income payments to the producers of these exports. Hence exports should be counted as part of GNP. Spending on imports, however, leads neither to domestic production nor to earnings by domestic producers: any spending on imports should therefore be excluded from GNP. Here we will follow the customary procedure and simply present the *net* effect of the foreign trade sector, i.e., the difference between exports and imports. It should be pointed out that this number may be positive (if exports exceed imports) as well as negative (if imports exceed exports). These four sectors are shown in Figure 10-1; see also Table 10-2, page 168.

GNP calculations according to the total income approach would be easy if we merely had to add up the total incomes earned by all the inputs used in the production process. Unfortunately, there are several factors that complicate the simple accounting framework

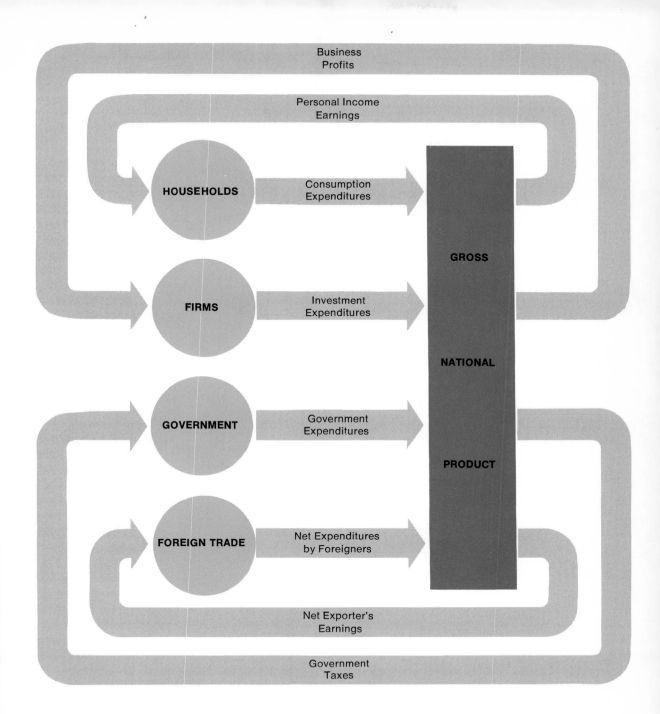

Business
Profits

Personal Income
Earnings

HOUSEHOLDS

Consumption
Expenditures

GROSS

FIRMS

Investment
Expenditures

NATIONAL

GOVERNMENT

Government
Expenditures

PRODUCT

FOREIGN TRADE

Net Expenditures
by Foreigners

Net Exporter's
Earnings

Government
Taxes

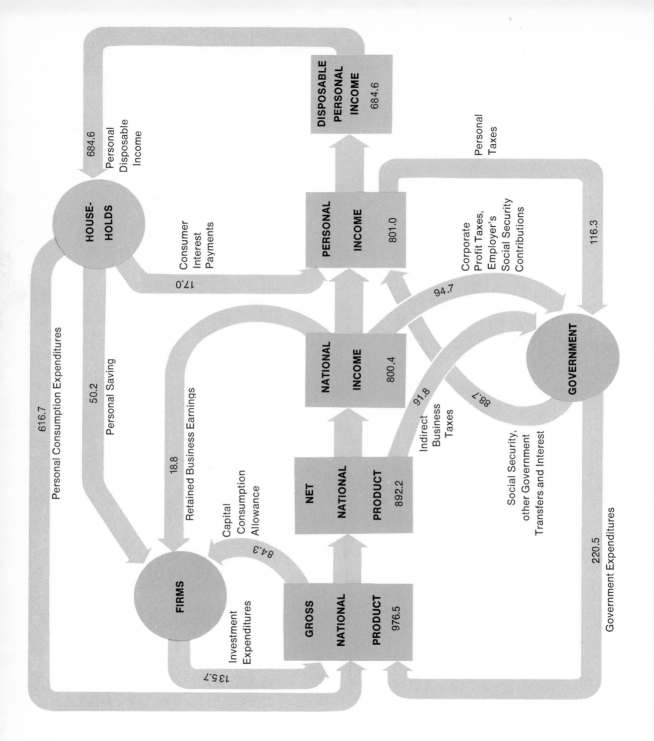

DISPOSABLE PERSONAL INCOME 684.6

Personal Disposable Income 684.6

Personal Taxes 116.3

HOUSE-HOLDS

Consumer Interest Payments 17.0

Corporate Profit Taxes, Employer's Social Security Contributions 94.7

PERSONAL INCOME 801.0

GOVERNMENT

Personal Consumption Expenditures 616.7

Personal Saving 50.2

NATIONAL INCOME 800.4

Retained Business Earnings 18.8

Indirect Business Taxes 91.8

Social Security, other Government Transfers and Interest 88.7

Capital Consumption Allowance 84.3

NET NATIONAL PRODUCT 892.2

FIRMS

Investment Expenditures 135.7

GROSS NATIONAL PRODUCT 976.5

Government Expenditures 220.5

166

Figure 10-2 (opposite)

Measures of economic activity
In the circular-flow diagram we may devise several measures of economic activity in an economy. Compare the figures in the flow chart to the data in Tables 10-2 and 10-3.

Data are 1970 figures in billions of dollars. Totals may not add exactly because the foreign sector is not shown and because some units may have run surpluses or deficits during the year.

Source: *Survey of Current Business* and *Federal Reserve Bulletin*

presented in Figure 10-1. The main factors of complication are transfer payments made between economic units, which are not payments for productive services, taxes levied by the government on firms and households, and the fact that capital equipment, such as machines, tools, and the like, will wear out in the production process or depreciate. Consequently, various alternative measures result, depending on whether we want to include or exclude one particular tax, depreciation allowance, or transfer payment. There are five main measures, which are illustrated in Figure 10-2.

1. *Gross national product* is a highly aggregate measure of economic activity in a country, which actually overstates the amount produced without entrenching on the existing capital stock. We know that capital equipment is used in the production of goods and services. But machines and tools wear out in the production process, and if we neglect to replace worn-out machinery, the total amount of capital equipment becomes smaller and smaller. We may distinguish two components of investment: that amount which represents merely replacement of worn-out machinery (called the *capital consumption allowance* or *depreciation*), and the new additions to the existing capital stock or net investment. Because worn-out machinery has to be replaced, we subtract the capital consumption allowance from GNP to obtain *net* national product.

Gross national product	$976.5 billion
− Capital consumption allowance	− 84.3
Net national product	$892.2

2. *Net national product* is a more useful measure than GNP, if we are interested in the total amount of products that the economy is capable of producing in any given year on a sustained basis—that is, without entrenching on the existing stock of capital equipment.

But the total net national product is not equivalent to the total earnings of the factors of production or inputs. First, the government levies so-called indirect business taxes. These taxes are imposed on the production of commodities, rather than on the profits made by firms. What remains after the government has taken its share is the national income that accrues to the factors of production.

Net national product	$892.2 billion
− Indirect business taxes	− 91.8
National income	$800.4

Table 10-2 Gross national product (1970)

Total spending approach (billions)		Total income approach (billions)	
Personal consumption	$616.7	Compensation of	$599.8
Gross domestic	135.7	employees	
investment		Proprietor's income	67.6
Government purchases	220.5	Corporate profits	77.2
Net exports	3.6	Rental income	22.7
		Net interest	33.5
		Capital consumption	84.3
		allowance	
		Indirect business tax	91.4
Total spending	$976.5	Total income earned by	$976.5
on products		sale of products	

3. *National income* is earned by the various owners of the inputs used in the production process. The amounts accruing to the different input categories are shown in Table 10-2.

But before the national income reaches its final recipients—the individuals who are the owners of the various factors of production—a few more adjustments have to be made. First, we will have to subtract out all the earnings retained by corporations—and therefore not passed on to individuals—as well as the corporate profit taxes and employer's social security contributions paid to the government. Then we have to add in interest and transfer payments (social security, unemployment, and disability payments) made by the government to individuals, as well as interest payments received from other persons. The end result is the personal income received by individuals.

National income	$800.4 billion
− Corporate profits tax	37.6
− Retained business earnings	18.8
− Social security contributions	57.1
+ Government interest + transfers	88.7
+ Interest from households	17.0
Personal income	$801.0

4. *Personal income* is the amount received by individuals. But before they can start to spend this amount, the government collects personal income, sales, and property taxes. What is left over is the disposable income of individuals.

Personal income	$801.0 billion
− Personal taxes	−116.3
Disposable personal income	$684.6

5. *Disposable personal income* earned is then spent by individuals as they see fit. Most of it goes for the purchase of consumption goods and services, some of it for interest payments, and the rest represents personal saving.

Disposable personal income	$684.6 billion
Personal consumption	616.7
Interest payments	17.0
Personal saving	50.2

Which one of the five measures is the most important one? There is no easy answer to this question. It all depends on the purpose for which the data are required. If we are interested in the total dollar amount spent by economic units in the country, we use the GNP figure. If we want to know about take-home pay, disposable personal income is relevant. Also, some of the figures are easier to collect than others and therefore give more current information.

Summary

□ To measure the total economic activity taking place within an economic system, such as a nation, we have to develop a *measure of aggregate economic activity.*

□ Two alternative approaches are open to us: we may measure the total value of the *products produced* by the economy or calculate the total *incomes received* by factors of production. The two measures yield identical amounts.

□ When calculating national income or national product, we *exclude* (1) economic actions that do not involve any other economic units, (2) economic transactions that do not take place in the market place, and (3) nonproductive exchanges of existing assets.

□ *Quality* changes of products are not reflected as changes in national income or product, unless accompanied by price changes.

□ When determining the total value of all products produced in an economy, we must avoid *double counting*. This is done by either considering only *final products*, or adopting a *value-added* approach.

□ *Real* GNP shows the nation's output at *constant* prices; *monetary* GNP evaluates it at *current* prices. The difference between monetary and real GNP is an indicator of the change in the general price level that has occurred over the time period under consideration.

Table 10-3   Measures of economic activity

Gross national product (GNP)	$976.5 billion
— Capital consumption allowance	84.3
Net national product (NNP)	$892.2
— Indirect business taxes	91.8
National income (NI)	$800.4
— Corporate profits tax	36.6
— Employer's social security contribution	57.1
— Retained business earnings	18.8
+ Government transfers and interest	88.7
+ Interest paid by individuals	17.0
Personal income (PI)	$801.0
— Personal taxes	116.3
Disposable personal income (DPI)	$684.6
Consumption	616.7
Interest payments	17.0
Savings	50.2

□ We have five measures of aggregate economic activity which are summarized in Table 10-3: (1) Gross national product (GNP), measuring the total amount of goods and services produced within a year. (2) Net national product (NNP), which allows for the replacement of worn-out machinery by subtracting a capital consumption allowance from GNP. (3) National Income (NI), which shows the total income earned by the factors of production. Indirect business taxes collected by the government are subtracted from NNP to arrive at this figure. (4) Personal income (PI) is the amount actually received by individuals. Payments made by businesses to government as well as retained earnings are excluded in this measure, but transfer payments received by individuals are included. (5) Disposable personal income (DPI) is the amount left over from personal income after personal taxes have been paid to the government. The disposable personal income is then spent on consumer goods, interest payments, and the rest represents personal savings.

11

Aggregate private expenditures: consumption and investment

In the last chapter we adopted the accountant's view of the national income and product accounts. Now we will have to take a closer look at the individual components comprising the nation's output. We showed the two alternative ways to derive the gross national product (GNP) as either the sum of total *expenditures* on final products taking place in the economy or the sum of all *income* earned by the factors of production. Largely for its greater simplicity, we will focus on the *total expenditure approach* to national income determination.

The four main categories into which total expenditures on the nation's product may be classified are personal consumption, business investment, governmental purchases, and net exports. In the first half of the book we analyzed the composition of each one of these expenditures: we asked how much a household might spend on each one of a wide variety of consumer products; how firms decide on when to expand, and to enter new industries; what is the role of government in providing public goods and services; and what are the determinants of the volume of exports and imports.

In this chapter we will look at the determinants of the aggregate amount of expenditures in the first two of these categories: private consumption and investment. As the data presented in Chapter 10 show, these two components account for approximately 80 per cent of GNP and constitute the total spending of domestic private economic units on the nation's output. The two remaining components, governmental expenditures and net exports, will be discussed in greater detail in Chapters 13 and 15. The role of aggregate governmental expenditures is fundamentally different from that of expenditures by private individuals and should therefore be treated separately. The analysis of the foreign trade component may be conveniently postponed until the end of the book, and attention focused first on the domestic sector.

The consumption decision

In Chapter 4 we analyzed the role of prices in the consumer's decision as to how much he should spend on each one of a variety of commodities. Now our problem is to decide on the *total* amount of consumption expenditures. Figure 11-1 shows the budgetary expenditure patterns for individual households. As household income increases, expenditures on the major groupings of commodities also increase. It is noteworthy that the relative amount spent on various items in the budget varies: very poor families spend a high proportion of their total income on food and beverages, with a relatively small share going to education, medical care, and recreation. The bare survival needs have first claim to the family income. Families in higher income brackets spend a smaller proportion of their income on food, while expenditures on education, medical care, and recreation increase more than in proportion. Their basic needs are satisfied, and consequently they can spend their money on items that the poorer families just cannot afford.

But perhaps one of the greatest luxuries of all is to be able to *abstain* from consumption. Only families that attain a certain minimum income level are able to save. Saving represents the amount not consumed. It opens up the possibility of deferred consumption—the purchase of goods and services at a later date. But only when their current minimum needs are satisfied are people willing to engage in saving.

Figure 11-1

Income and spending *As the level of income increases, households spend more on the various items in their consumption budget—but part of the income increase is saved.*

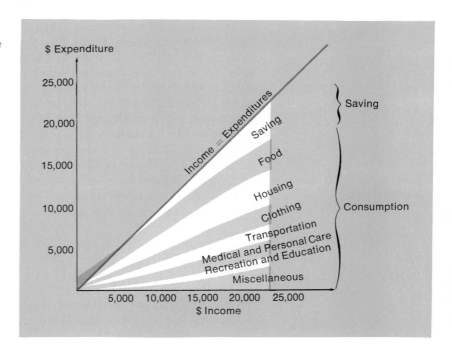

The consumption function

The amount of income that each family has available after taxes is the main determinant of its total consumption expenditures. In Table 11-1 we show a simplified relationship between family income and consumption expenditures. The simplified *consumption function*, as the relationship between income and consumption is generally called, is graphed in Figure 11-2 and is similar in shape to the one plotted in Figure 11-1.

In our hypothetical example, we find that at an income level of $2,000 all income earned is also spent on consumption. This amount of income allows the family to "break even" by spending all its income on current consumption. There is no new saving, but the family does not have to go into debt nor take money out of its savings account.

At income levels lower than $2,000, (to the left of the break-even point) the family is spending more dollars on consumption than it earns in current income. How is this possible? There are two solutions that offer themselves: one, the family is *dissaving*, i.e., it is drawing down the balances in its bank account or it is forced to sell the family car or the TV for cash in order to be able to pay the bills for its current consumption expenditures. The other alternative is that the family is *borrowing* funds, i.e., the family goes into debt. If current income is only $1,000 and current expenditures on consumption goods amount to $1,250, the family must be dissaving or borrowing $250.

At income levels greater than $2,000, the family does not spend all of its income on consumption items. Some of the current income is saved. For instance, if family income is $5,000, $4,250 may be spent on consumption and the remaining $750 can be saved.

Note that saving is a residual: it is the amount of income which is left over after all consumption expenditures have been accounted for. In terms of Figure 11-2, saving is the difference between the 45-degree line showing the amount of income earned by the family and the amount spent on consumption as shown by the white consumption function. The vertical distance between consumption and income shows the amount saved.

Of course, saving may be directly shown in a graph. The amount not spent on consumption, or, in other words, saved, is graphed in Figure 11-3. Note that the break-even point at an income level of $2,000 is now indicated by zero saving (all income is spent on consumption). To the left of the break-even point, saving is *negative*. Negative saving is nothing but the dissaving or borrowing referred

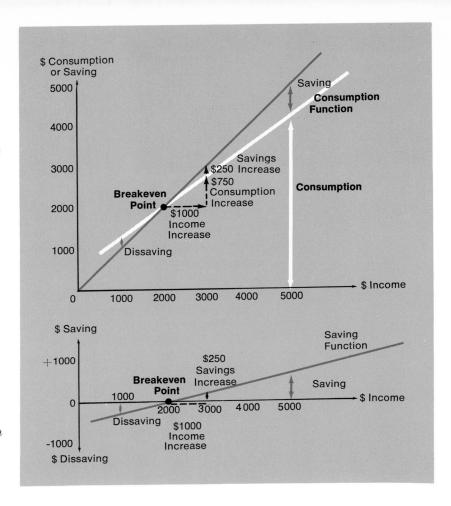

Figure 11-2

The consumption function
The consumption function shows the relationship between income and total consumption. The marginal propensity to consume gives the change in consumption that results from an income increase: $MPC = \Delta C/\Delta Y$.

Figure 11-3

The saving function *The saving function shows the amount saved at various income levels. It is equal to the vertical distance between the consumption function and the 45° line in Figure 11-2.*

Table 11-1   Income, consumption, and saving

Income (Y)	Consumption (C)	Marginal propensity to consume $\Delta C/\Delta Y$	Saving (S)	Marginal propensity to save $\Delta S/\Delta Y$
$1,000	$1,250		$ −250	
2,000	2,000	> .75	0	> .25
3,000	2,750	> .75	+250	> .25
4,000	3,500	> .75	+500	> .25
5,000	4,250	> .75	+750	> .25
6,000	5,000	> .75	+ 1,000	> .25

to earlier. Finally, to the right of the break-even point, saving is positive. The saving function shows the amount saved at each and every level of income.

Marginal propensities to consume and to save

Economists are very interested in finding out what happens to consumption and saving if income increases just a little bit. The relevant question is, How will my consumption expenditures and the amount saved change if income increases by a certain amount? Consider Figure 11-2 and Table 11-1. Let us assume that income initially is at the $2,000 level. If the family experiences an increase in income of $1,000, we find that consumption expenditures increase from $2,000 to $2,750—an increase of $750. The change in consumption expenditures, ΔC, over the change in income, ΔY, is called the *marginal propensity to consume (MPC)*.

$$MPC = \frac{\text{Change in consumption}}{\text{Change in income}} = \frac{\Delta C}{\Delta Y} = \frac{\$2,750 - \$2,000}{\$3,000 - \$2,000}$$

$$= \frac{\$750}{\$1,000} = 0.75.$$

Clearly, the *MPC* is nothing but the ratio of *additional* consumption expenditures in which the family will engage to the *additional* income earned.

In Table 11-1, we show various income levels for a family in steps of $1,000. The dollar amount spent on consumption increases in steps of $750. Hence the marginal propensity to consume is 0.75 for the whole schedule.

Graphically, the *MPC* is given by the slope of the consumption function. In Figure 11-2, we show an increase in income from $2,000 to $3,000, indicated by a horizontal arrow. The increase in consumption that will accompany this income increase is shown by a vertical arrow and is equal to $750. The slope of the consumption function is a graphical measure of the marginal propensity to consume. In our example, it is equal to $750/$1,000, or 0.75.

From these examples it is also clear that the *marginal propensity to save (MPS)* must be equal to 0.25. The MPS measures the increase in saving that accompanies an increase in income. As income increases, part of it will go for increased consumption, and the residual will be saved. Hence, if income increases by $1,000, and $750 is spent on further consumption, the residual of $250 must be saved.

$$MPS = \frac{\text{Change in saving}}{\text{Change in income}} = \frac{\Delta S}{\Delta Y} = \frac{\$250 - 0}{\$3,000 - \$2,000}$$

$$= \frac{\$250}{\$1,000} = 0.25.$$

The *MPS* shows the fraction of each additional income dollar that is saved, and the *MPC* the fraction that is consumed. The two measures together must add up to *one* by definition: an additional dollar of income must either be saved or consumed.

$$MPC + MPS = 0.75 + 0.25 = 1.00.$$

Or, put still differently, the *MPS* is equal to $1 - MPC$, or, in our example, $1 - .75 = .25$.

There is no necessity for the *MPC* to remain constant throughout the consumption function, and some economists have argued that the *MPC* declines as income increases. But much of the statistical evidence points to a relatively constant *MPC*. Also, the assumption of a constant *MPC* simplifies our analysis considerably, and we shall adopt it henceforward. If the *MPC* is constant, the residual showing the *MPS* must be constant too.

Aggregate consumption and saving

So far, we have talked about the consumption function and saving function for one household or one family. Our next task is to derive the aggregate consumption function and the aggregate saving function for *all* households in the economy.

As the income of the individual households increases, the income of the nation as a whole increases. As individual families move further to the right on their consumption functions, the nation as a whole moves along its aggregate consumption function to the right.

But the shape of the aggregate consumption function for the nation as a whole depends also on the *income distribution* that prevails. To make this point clear, consider the difference in aggregate (national) consumption that exists if we have a nation composed of 3 million households, each earning $2,000, and a nation composed

Figure 11-4

The aggregate consumption function *The historical aggregate consumption function for the United States resembles closely the hypothetical consumption function of Figure 11-2.*

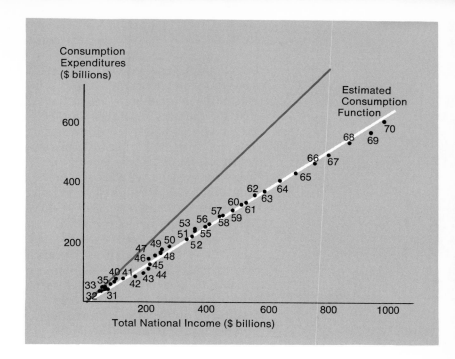

Table 11-2 *Income distribution and aggregate consumption*

Number of households	Household income level	Household consumption expenditures	National income	National consumption expenditures
3 million	$2,000	$2,000	$6 billion	$6 billion
1 million	$6,000	$5,000	$6 billion	$5 billion

of 1 million households each earning $6,000. In both cases, the national income amounts to $6 billion. But given identical consumption functions for all the households in our example (data from Table 11-1), total consumption for the first nation amounts to (3 million households at $2,000 each) $6 billion, while aggregate consumption expenditures for the second nation come to (1 million households at $5,000 each) $5 billion (see Table 11-2). Hence the income distribution does make a difference in the aggregate consumption expenditures of the nation as a whole.

Figure 11-4 shows the historical relationship between gross national income (equal to GNP) and consumption expenditures during the last forty years (1930-70). A line is drawn through the points to show the approximate relationship between income and consumption during the period under consideration. This historical consumption function corresponds closely to the theoretical consumption function discussed earlier. Also, the individual observations plotted lie reasonably close to the straight line drawn in, showing that for the nation as a whole the marginal propensity to consume stayed approximately constant during the time period covered. The only noteworthy exception is provided by the years of World War II, when administrative controls were in effect that limited consumer spending. Hence wartime consumption was below the long-run trend indicated by the straight line drawn through the points.

One of the most remarkable characteristics of the consumption function is that it has remained extremely stable throughout the whole period for which we have data. The only major exception is provided by the World War II years just alluded to. But during all other times consumption exhibited a very close and stable relationship to income. From this observation we might conclude that private consumption expenditures *in the aggregate* do not represent a source of substantial disturbances to the economy as a whole.

This last statement should be qualified somewhat. Frequently shifts in consumer demand from one product to another do occur, and these shifts in consumer demand may have repercussions on the level of economic activity. These shifts may occur in response to changes in relative prices of commodities or may be caused by changes in tastes or living habits. These changes in consumer demand may then in turn affect the investment decisions taken by business men. As producers realize that consumers want different products, they will invest in new machinery and equipment that can produce these commodities. As a result, private investment may change in response to consumer demand changes. To this topic we will turn next.

Investment and capital

The second major component of GNP that has to be considered is investment. Investment spending is undertaken for the purpose of *adding* to the total amount of resources that are available for production. It is spending not for present consumption, but for the construction of man-made equipment, machinery, buildings, and the like, which can be used in the production of other goods and services. The total stock of these man-made resources in existence is referred to as *capital*.

Let us look a bit more carefully at the relationship between investment and capital. Production, as we learned earlier, can take place only if we have certain inputs available that can be used in the production process. A broad classification scheme of inputs used in production would group all inputs into the categories of land, labor, and capital. The categories land and labor are self-explanatory. Capital consists of all man-made resources that are used in the production process. By this it is clear that the first man did not find any capital equipment at his disposal. First, he had to engage in investment. In order to engage in investment, he had to abstain from present consumption. That is, he had to save. The amount saved he could then invest in order to build up his capital stock and thereby increase his future production possibilities.

Investment represents nothing more than the *additions* to the capital stock that are undertaken during a certain time period. For instance, the total stock of capital equipment that a certain firm possesses on January 1 may amount to $100,000. If, during the year, the firm invests an additional $20,000 in capital equipment, its capital stock on December 31 amounts to $120,000.

It would be sufficient to differentiate merely between capital and investment if it were not for the unpleasant fact that capital equipment has the tendency to wear out or to *depreciate*. As we use the machinery, tools, and equipment in the production process, these resources will eventually wear out. If we do not replace the worn-out equipment, the stock of capital equipment will continuously diminish and eventually disappear. Hence part of our current investment has to be used to replace the worn-out equipment and to keep the capital stock intact.

It is useful to distinguish between the investment that is undertaken merely to keep the capital stock intact and the investment that represents a new addition to the capital stock. The total amount of investment undertaken in any year (including both the replacement investment and additions to the capital stock) is called *gross investment*. If we subtract from this magnitude the amount that represents replacement of depreciated capital, we arrive at *net investment*. Figure 11-5 illustrates the pertinent relationships. Let us assume that on January 1 our firm has a capital stock of $100,000 in machinery and equipment. If this capital stock depreciates at an annual rate of 12 per cent, the total amount of depreciation for the year will come to $12,000. If the firm has a gross investment of $20,000 budgeted for the year, $12,000 of this gross investment will go for the replacement of depreciated capital. Hence only $8,000 represents a new addition to the capital stock, or net investment. The capital stock in existence at the end of the year will be the initial amount of

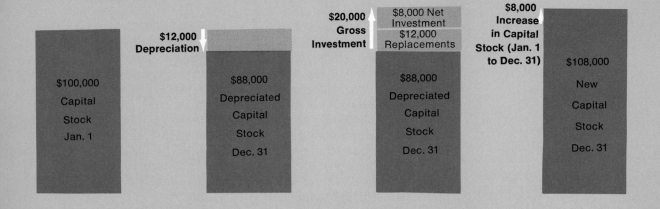

Figure 11-5

Investment and capital *The capital stock in existence depreciates, and new investment is needed simply to replace the worn-out capital equipment. Gross investment shows the total amount of investment in a given year, while net investment is equal to gross investment minus depreciation.*

$100,000 plus the new net investment of $8,000, that is, a total of $108,000.

Alternatively, we can determine the new capital stock as the end result of the following calculation.

Capital stock on January 1	$ 100,000
− 12 per cent depreciation	12,000
	$ 88,000
+ new *gross* investment	20,000
Capital stock on December 31	$1,008,000

We may note that net investment may be a negative figure. This result comes about if gross investment is smaller than depreciation. If gross investment is not enough even to replace all the depreciated capital equipment, the capital stock itself is shrinking. Net investment is defined as the net *addition* to the capital stock, and hence it will be a negative figure in this example.

Determinants of investment

Investment is undertaken by business firms to add to their productive capacity. Thus we have to determine the motivating forces that will lead businessmen to invest in new capital equipment. This topic was already touched upon briefly in Chapters 5 and 6, when we talked about the role of profits in making the existing firms expand their productive capacity and—in the long run—induce new firms to enter the industry. We learned that the main motivating force in the businessman's investment decision is the expectation of future profits.

There are an extremely large number of possible investment activities that we might engage in. We might build a new steel plant, a ski lift, a new automobile factory, or a bridge across a river. What factor determines which one of the literally millions of different investment projects that might be undertaken will actually be carried out? One highly important factor in this decision is the *rate of return* that the project will yield to the investor.

What is the rate of return of an investment project, and how is it determined? The rate of return is the annual earnings (or yield, or pay-off) that accrue to the owner of the investment. For instance, a car rental agency may have a $3,000 investment in one of its automobiles. If this car yields a return of $300 dollars per year after all the operating expenses have been accounted for, the annual rate of return is 10 per cent ($300 on a $3,000 investment). Would that be a wise investment to undertake? That depends on the alternative investment opportunities that are open to you. If you know of a different investment that will yield 20 per cent to you with the same degree of certainty, you will probably choose the investment yielding the higher rate of return.

If we rank all investment alternatives according to their expected rate of return, we obtain a curve that slopes downward to the right. (See Figure 11-6.) There are a few projects that are very lucrative and yield a high rate of return. Then there are others, which yield a lower, but still respectable rate of return. Finally, there are some projects where the expected rate of return is extremely small. Economists refer to the schedule showing the rate of return obtainable on various investment projects as a *marginal efficiency of investment schedule.*

After we have ranked all feasible investment projects in the nation according to their expected rate of return, how do we know the total amount of investment activity that will be undertaken? One important determinant (among others to be treated later) is the *rate of interest.* The rate of interest is the percentage that one must pay for the use of borrowed funds. A bank or finance corporation may be willing to lend money to businessmen—for a certain rate of interest. Clearly, businessmen will want to borrow these funds only if the rate of return that they expect to achieve on their investment is greater than the rate of interest that they have to pay to the bank. If the expected rate of return on an investment is 15 per cent annually, and you have to pay only 5 per cent to the bank for the use of the borrowed money, you will realize a net profit of 10 per cent

Figure 11-6

Investment and the rate of return *The graph shows the quantity of investment projects that yield a certain rate of return. At a high rate of interest, only projects with a high rate of return will be undertaken.*

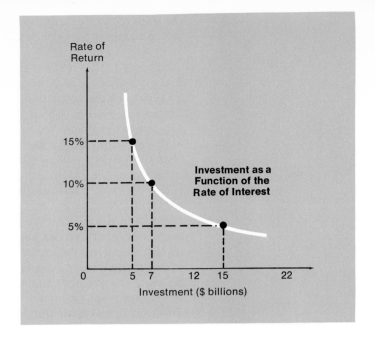

on this investment. This would be a good investment. On the other hand, if you have to pay 5 per cent to the bank and the investment yields only 3 per cent per year, you will lose out, so if you were smart and had the proper foresight you would avoid spending money on this venture.

In terms of Figure 11-6, we find that there are $5 billion of investment opportunities that yield at least a rate of return of 15 per cent. Thus, if the rate of interest that has to be paid for the use of borrowed money is 15 per cent, we might expect that up to $5 billion of investment might be undertaken in the economy. If the rate of interest falls to 10 per cent, profitable investment opportunities totaling $7 billion exist. A further fall of the interest rate to 5 per cent opens up $15 billion of investment opportunities for which the rate of return exceeds the interest that has to be paid on the funds invested.

From what has been said so far, it is evident that there are two factors that play a role in the investment decision: (1) the expected rate of return that can be achieved on the investment, and (2) the rate of interest that has to be paid for the use of funds. The rate of return that may be achieved depends partly on new innovations that are taking place, partly on the discovery of new business opportunities, and also on changes in the demand for individual products.

It is clear that most of these factors are relatively *unstable*. Innovations do not take place at a regular pace. Sometimes the inventor will be lucky and hit upon a new formula that may eventually serve as a basis for a whole new industry—but there are other times when even a determined effort does not bring forth anything new. New discoveries that increase the efficiency of production or improve the quality of the product add new investment opportunities to those already in existence. Hence the investment schedule will shift to the right. Also, businessmen will invest in new machinery and equipment if they expect that the demand for their product is going to increase. This expected increase in demand may or may not materialize; nevertheless, investment activity is guided by these expectations. Thus one of the most important facets of investment behavior is the *instability* of its determinants; innovations occur at a pace that is difficult to predict, and expectations of demand changes are certainly not characterized by great stability.

The other ingredient, the rate of interest, may also change from time to time in response to the factors influencing the aggregate supply and demand for funds. One powerful factor in this realm is the influence exercised by the Federal Reserve, the monetary authority of the United States. The precise way in which the Federal Reserve influences the rate of interest, along with the quantity of money and other variables of importance for the pace of economic activity will be analyzed more fully in Chapter 14, when we deal with monetary policy. Suffice it to say here that changes in the rate of interest and the availability of funds may change rapidly and that the rate of investment activity is strongly influenced by these changes.

A certain cushioning effect against changes in the rate of interest is provided by the fact that many firms rely on *internal funds*, rather than borrowed money, for the financing of their investment projects. Firms reinvest some or all of their retained earnings. Retained earnings are that portion of the difference between the firm's total revenues from sales and the costs of production and governmental levies which is not distributed to the stockholders in the form of dividends. These nondistributed profits or retained earnings may be used by the firm to finance its new investment spending.

It is clear that the use of these internal funds involves opportunity costs—that alternatives have to be forgone—but it is also evident from the actual behavior of business firms that the opportunity cost of utilizing internal funds for investment activities is not reassessed with each and every change in the market rate of interest.

Risk plays another important role in investment decisions. There is quite a bit of difference between an investment project that yields a rate of return of 10 per cent with certainty, and one in which there is only a fifty-fifty chance of actually realizing the 10 per cent or nothing at all. In the latter case, the "expected" or risk-adjusted rate of return is probably more in the neighborhood of 5 per cent. In any case, the attitudes of businessmen toward risk are very mixed indeed. Some businessmen are willing to assume enormous risks in the expectation of a high pay-off if their gamble materializes. Others prefer a more modest, but certain return on their investment. Attitudes toward risk are also influenced by the general economic outlook. In a boom period, one will find many more people willing to assume risks than in a depression. All this adds another unstable influence to the determinants of investment activity.

One variable that has only a modest influence on the rate of investment spending is the current level of *national income*. We may have an economy with a relatively low level of GNP but a high rate of investment spending or an economy with a high level of GNP and low investment spending. When we *graph* GNP and investment spending, there is no clear relationship between the two variables. The best we can do is to draw a horizontal straight line which shows that the current level of investment activity is consistent with any level of GNP. This is done in Figure 11-7.

The level of investment activity is determined mainly by the other

Figure 11-7

Investment and GNP *Current investment activity is independent of the current level of GNP. The investment function shown shifts up and down in response to changes in the rate of innovations, the rate of interest, changes in demand, attitudes toward risk, and other factors.*

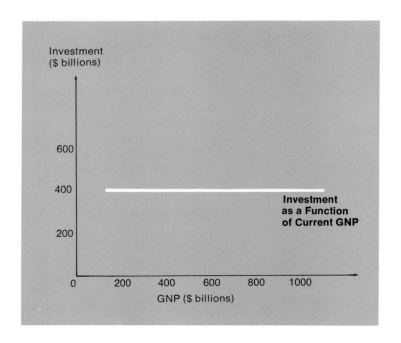

factors mentioned: innovations taking place, the prevailing rate of interest, the attitude toward risk, the general economic outlook, changes in consumer demand, and many other, mostly unstable forces. All this means that the investment schedule as drawn in Figure 11-7 is far from being stable; indeed, it shifts violently up and down. The consequences of this irregular rate of investment activity for the stability of the economic system as a whole will be assessed in greater detail in the following chapter.

Summary

□ In this chapter we analyzed the determinants of private *consumption* and *investment* behavior.

□ Income earned by households is either spent or saved. The relationship between income and consumption is expressed in the *consumption function*. The residual between income and consumption is *saving*, and it may be shown separately as the saving function.

□ A household that spends all its current income on consumption is said to *break even*. At that income level, the consumption function crosses a 45-degree line through the origin (consumption equals income), and the saving function crosses the horizontal axis (saving minus zero).

□ The *marginal propensity to consume* shows the additional consumption that will result if income is increased by one dollar. The marginal propensity to save shows the additional saving out of the same dollar.

□ Because additional income will either be saved or consumed, the marginal propensity to save and the marginal propensity to consume must add up to one.

□ The aggregate consumption function shows the total amount consumed by all households in the nation at various income levels. Note that the aggregate consumption function is influenced by the *average household's income* as well as the *income distribution* between households.

□ The main determinant of aggregate consumption and saving is the level of national income.

□ *Investment* is the addition to the *capital stock*—the total amount of man-made resources—made during a specified time period. We distinguish gross and net investment. *Gross* investment is the total amount of investment taking place. *Net* investment is the addition to the capital stock after allowance is made for depreciation of worn-out capital equipment.

◻ The level of investment activity is determined by the rate of new innovations, the rate of interest, the riskiness of investments, and other highly variable factors.

◻ While the *consumption* function, relating consumption and income, is highly stable over time, we find that the relationship between income and investment is very unstable.

National income determination

The purpose of the present chapter is twofold: first, we will specify in some detail the standards or goals by which we will judge the performance of the nation's economy, and second, we will develop a simple model of national income determination.

This chapter builds largely upon the material presented in the previous chapter; at the same time, it lays the foundations for the chapters that follow, which are concerned with fiscal and monetary policy as control instruments that enable us to achieve the goals of economic policy.

Three economic goals

Most economists agree that the triple goals of *full employment, price stability*, and a *high growth rate* are the most important objectives of the national economy. We will first analyze the goals of full employment and price stability; only at the end of the chapter will we be concerned with the goal of a high growth rate.

While it may be obvious to most people why these three goals are desirable, let us say a few words about the economic costs that have to be borne if these goals are not achieved. That is, we will concentrate on the economic costs of unemployment and inflation.

The costs of unemployment

If economic resources are unused, this means that goods and services are forgone because the economy is operating at less than capacity. If the economy operates at less than capacity, the *actual* GNP that is being produced falls short of the *potential* GNP that the economy is capable of achieving. Actual GNP measures simply the current level of national production. Figure 12-1 shows the actual GNP that was achieved by the American economy in the last fifteen years. In the same graph we also show the potential GNP that the economy could have achieved if it had operated reasonably close to full employment. Clearly, the definition of "reasonably close" is important. Many

Figure 12-1

Actual and potential GNP *If the actual level of GNP falls short of the potential GNP the economy is capable of producing, a GNP gap exists.*

Source: Council of Economic Advisors

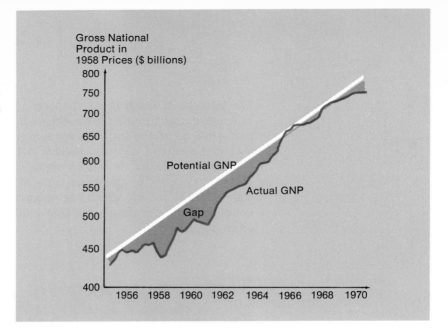

economists argue that the best we can hope for is an unemployment rate of 3.5 or 4 per cent. There will always be some people who are between jobs; people who have quit their present jobs and are looking for new and more exciting or rewarding ventures; people who want to move to a different region; and people who have been fired and are therefore forced to take different jobs—but whose new jobs may start only next month. All these persons represent, in the economist's jargon, *frictional unemployment.* They are not the long-run unemployed people we may find in a depressed region or in the urban ghettos, nor are they persons displaced by automation. Instead, they are just between jobs—a normal phenomenon in a growing and changing economy. Hence the definition of potential GNP takes into account a frictional unemployment rate of approximately 3.8 per cent. In Figure 12-2 we show the unemployment rate and the bottom area shows the frictional unemployment that is considered normal. Note how the unemployment peaks above the frictional unemployment rate of Figure 12-2 correlate with the GNP gap of Figure 12-1.

The economic costs of unemployment do not only include the output and wages forgone by having men unemployed, but also the products that could have been produced by idle machines, on untilled land, or in empty buildings. In an economy that is capable of operating at a level of $1,000 billion—or $1 trillion—a 1 per cent underutili-

Figure 12-2

Unemployment *The unemployment rate closely parallels the GNP gap. In a dynamic economy there will always be some "frictional" unemployment (bottom area in the figure).*

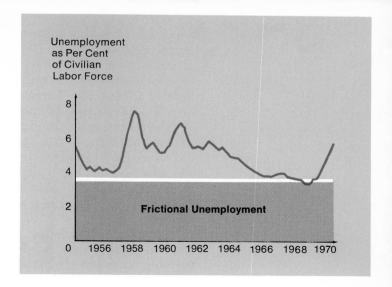

zation of capacity amounts to $10 billion annually, or an amount equivalent to the total GNP of Austria or Norway. The products forgone by a 2½ per cent underutilization equal the total amount spent on new residential construction in the United States.

The total cost to society of unemployment may exceed these purely economic costs. Typically, unemployment rates among teenagers and minority groups are a multiple of the unemployment rates of married white workers. The potential for social unrest, riots, and criminal activity may be far more costly to society than the mere output forgone, as measured by the GNP gap.

The costs of inflation

If the total expenditures on goods and services exceed the capacity of the economy to produce these commodities, inflation will be the result. First, a *bottleneck inflation* is likely to occur as the economy approaches capacity. Some sectors will hit the full-employment barrier sooner than others, and price increases will first be observed in those areas. Eventually, as the whole economy strains under the pressures of excess demand, a general inflation will be the result.

What are the costs of inflation? Here we will discuss only the most important effects of inflation: *income and wealth redistribution* and economic *efficiency*. When inflation, defined as a general increase in the price level, occurs, we find that it will affect the value of all assets denominated in fixed dollar terms. Anybody holding cash, demand deposits, savings deposits, bonds, and the like owns an asset that has a certain value, given by its purchasing power. As the general price level increases, the purchasing power of assets whose value is stated in fixed dollar terms decreases. Hence the holder of these assets will be worse off because of inflation.

The reverse holds true for anybody who owes a debt that is fixed in monetary terms: a loan from your bank, a mortgage on your home, and so on. As inflation proceeds, the real value of the debt goes down. The debt is repaid in dollars whose purchasing power is less than at the time when the debt was incurred. Hence debtors stand to gain from inflation. There is a wealth redistribution from creditors to debtors.

A similar redistribution takes place for people whose income is fixed in dollar terms. A widow living on a pension, or somebody deriving his income from interest earned on his savings will be hurt by inflation because his income is fixed, while the prices he has to pay for the goods and services he purchases go up. On the other hand, anybody who has an obligation to pay each month a certain dollar amount as alimony payments or child support will feel less and less of a burden as inflation progresses.

These redistributive effects are especially pronounced when an inflation occurs unexpectedly. Then people on fixed incomes or people who hold assets whose value is stated in fixed dollar terms will truly be "caught." If inflation is expected, that is, if everybody anticipates correctly that an inflation is going to occur, people will negotiate their contracts in a way that will take account of the expected decrease in purchasing power. Lenders will ask for a higher interest rate, labor unions for a greater wage increase, business firms writing long-term contracts will insist on a higher rate of return, and so on. The higher *nominal* rate of return ensures that the people who expect to be hurt by the inflation will still receive an appropriate *real* rate of return. The real rate of return, of course, is simply the nominal (or stated) rate of return corrected for any price changes that may take place.

Economic efficiency is also likely to be impaired—especially in a fast-paced inflation—because money will lose some of its usefulness as a medium of exchange, store of value, and unit of account. If prices rise, it means that the value of money will fall. People will substitute other commodities for money, and money can no longer perform its useful functions to the fullest extent possible. People may resort to bartering real goods against each other, and consequently economic exchange will become more cumbersome and costly. People will also tend to hold their assets in the form of commodities whose value is likely to increase, such as precious stones, gold, or land. Much of this investment will be in basically unproductive assets, thereby retarding the potential growth of the economy. In a very mild inflation, these effects may be small enough to be neglected, but as the rate of inflation increases, the economic costs will start to mount rapidly. In hyperinflations, such as were experienced in Germany after World War I and in Hungary after World War II, money loses virtually all its usefulness, and the economic dislocations caused by this process are most severe.

Having analyzed the economic costs of unemployment and inflation, we can now turn to our model of national income determination. This model will help us to determine the actions that have to be undertaken to remedy any existing underemployment and/or inflationary situation.

Potential GNP

In Chapter 1 we learned about the production possibility curve, which shows the maximum commodity combinations that we can produce with our existing resources and the current technology. There is a physical limit to the amount of output that the economy is capable of producing. This is the *potential GNP* alluded to earlier.

In Figure 12-3, we show the relationship between total spending and real GNP (real output). As long as there is unused capacity in the economy, more spending will result in a corresponding increase in the nation's product. For instance, if monetary expenditures increase from $500 billion to $800 billion, output will also increase from $500 billion to $800 billion.

But there is the absolute barrier to real output that is set by the economy's productive capacity. In Figure 12-3, this potential GNP is indicated by the vertical line. It is assumed that the productive capacity of the economy is reached at an output level of $800 billion.

If monetary expenditures expand beyond this $800 billion level—to let us say $1,000 billion—then the real output of the nation can no longer increase to the same level. But because people will spend their $1,000 billion, prices will increase and an inflation will ensue.

In our example, if expenditures on commodities are below the $800 billion mark, unemployment will result, and we will experience a GNP gap between actual and potential GNP. If money expenditures are above $800 billion, an inflationary situation exists.

Figure 12-3

Potential and actual GNP *The full employment barrier sets a limit to the size of the real GNP. The actual GNP is determined by the level of aggregate expenditures.*

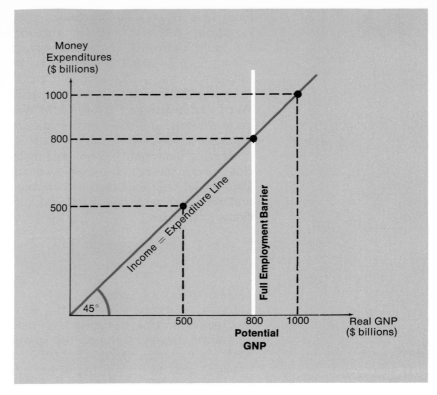

Next, we have to determine the actual level of expenditures that consumers and firms wish to engage in.

National income and expenditures

Both private consumption and private investment are components of the nation's aggregate expenditures. If we forget for the time being about the governmental sector and foreign trade, we may say that aggregate expenditures are equal to total consumption and investment expenditures.

In Figure 12-4, we measure national income along the horizontal axis and total expenditures along the vertical axis. We show the aggregate consumption function for the economy as a whole. It relates the aggregate amount of consumer spending to the nation's income level. In the same figure, we show the investment function.

Figure 12-4

The total expenditure function *The total expenditure function of the private sector is the sum of private consumption and investment expenditures. The total expenditure function shows how expenditures vary with income.*

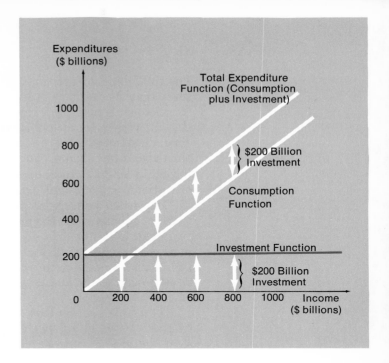

Table 12-1   *Total expenditure and its components*

Total income (billions)	Total consumption (billions)	+	Total investment (billions)	=	Total expenditures (consumption plus investment) (billions)
$ 0	$ 0		$200		$200
200	150		200		350
400	300		200		500
600	450		200		650
800	600		200		800
1,000	750		200		950

We shall assume that the forces determining the level of investment are such that businessmen are willing to spend $200 billion for investment, irrespective of the current income level. Hence, the investment function is a horizontal straight line. The addition of the amounts spent on consumption and investment at each and every level of national income yields the desired total expenditure function, which is depicted in Figure 12-4 and Table 12-1.

Equilibrium

The total expenditure function shows the total amount of expenditures that the nation's economic units are going to engage in as a function of their income. In other words, the total expenditure function answers the question: "If total income is x dollars, what will total expenditures be?" There are hundreds of different possible income and expenditure "pairs," but only one pair of numbers for which total income is *equal to* total expenditures. This is the *equilibrium level* of national income and expenditures which occurs at $800 billion.

Only when aggregate income equals aggregate expenditures is there no tendency for the level of GNP to change. Conversely, if the two magnitudes are not equal to each other, forces will be set into motion that will work for a restoration of their equality. Just as supply and demand determine the price and the quantity traded, so do national income and aggregate expenditures determine the level of GNP.

Let us take a closer look at the determination of equilibrium GNP by the interaction of income and expenditures. In Figure 12-5 we show the level of aggregate spending by households and firms along

Figure 12-5

Equilibrium income *Equilibrium income exists when expenditures are equal to income. If this condition is not fulfilled, forces will be set into motion that return the economy to equilibrium.*

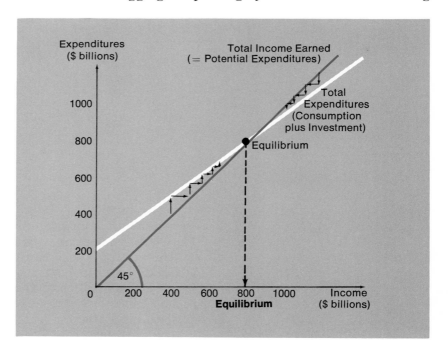

the vertical axis, and the level of total national income along the horizontal axis. First, we draw a 45-degree line, which shows the current income that is available for spending. If the total income of all economic units in the nation is equal to $500 billion, then these units have a spending potential of $500 billion. If the total income goes up to $600 billion, then spending can go up to $600 billion, too. Hence the line showing the income earned during the current time period that is potentially available for spending is a 45-degree line, that is, its slope is always equal to 1.0.

Next, we draw the actual total expenditure function previously derived. Its most important property for us at this juncture is that it is less steep than the 45-degree line. The slope of the total expenditure curve is *smaller* than 1.0.

Given the two curves, we find that they intersect at the $800 billion level. This is the GNP level at which total income equals total expenditures. Only when income is equal to expenditures can the economy be in equilibrium. To show why this statement is true, let us consider what happens if this condition is not fulfilled. The relevant data are presented in Table 12-2. Consider an income level of $600 billion. At that income level, economic units will spend an aggregate amount of $650 billion. The additional $50 billion are coming out of previously accumulated savings. But if spending on goods and services is equal to $650 billion, then income in the next period will go up to $650 billion, too. The old income level of $600 billion does not remain unchanged. It is not an equilibrium level. And as long as current spending exceeds current income, the level of income will tend to increase.

Equilibrium is reached when income equals expenditures. This is true in our example at an income level of $800 billion. Expenditures

Table 12-2 Equilibrium income

Total income (billions)	Total expenditures (billions)	Pressure on national product and income
$ 400	$500	upward
500	575	(greater spending
600	650	means higher
700	725	income)
800	800	equilibrium
900	875	downward (lower spending
1,000	950	means lower income)

are now also equal to $800 billion, and the income-equal-to-expenditure condition is fulfilled. Hence there is no further tendency for GNP to change.

Finally, let us consider what happens when income exceeds expenditures. For instance, at an income level of $900 billion, households, firms, and governments will engage in only $875 billion of expenditures. Hence, income in the next period will be only $875 billion. There will be a downward pressure on aggregate income and product. This downward pressure will cease to exist when the equality of total income and total expenditures is again restored at the $800 billion equilibrium level.

Full employment once again

We stated that there exists a barrier beyond which physical output cannot expand: full employment of all resources. If all resources are fully employed in their best possible use, and if technological know-how remains unchanged, no further expansion of output is possible. If aggregate demand—as evidenced by expenditures on goods and services—continues to increase, only prices but not output can increase, and inflation will result. The full-employment level of national income serves as a highly important reference point for the economic policy maker.

Figure 12-6 shows the same features as Figure 12-5: we have a total income curve (45-degree line) and a total expenditure curve. In addition, we show the full-employment barrier of potential GNP by a vertical line.

The full-employment level is determined by (1) the amount of resources that are available, and (2) the state of the technological knowledge that is used to convert resources into goods and services. An increase in the amount of resources available, such as land, labor, or capital, will result in a rightward shift of the full-employment level. Similarly, improved production methods, that is, more efficient ways of converting inputs into outputs, will result in a rightward shift of the full-employment barrier. Both processes, the increases in resources and the improvements in technology, will open up the possibility for economic growth to occur, in that these processes shift the full-employment barrier to the right.

Let us note carefully the difference between full employment and equilibrium. *Full employment* (or potential) GNP is given as a capacity limitation on the economy. The productive capacity depends, as we noted previously, on the amount of resources and the technology

Figure 12-6

Equilibrium and full employ-ment *If equilibrium (actual) GNP falls short of full employment (potential) GNP, a GNP gap exists.*

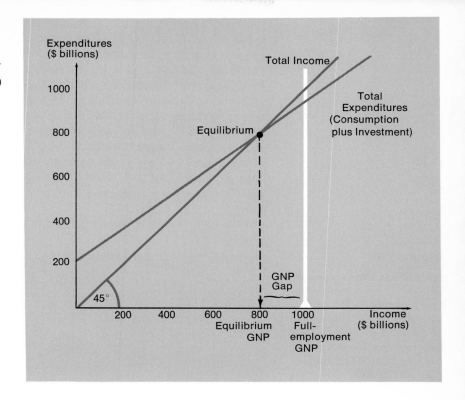

available to us. The *equilibrium* (or actual) GNP that is being achieved depends on the level of aggregate expenditures on goods and services. There is no necessity for the two to coincide at all times.

If the equilibrium level of national income is *below* the full-employment point and prices and wages are relatively inflexible in the downward direction, unemployment is the natural result. If the equilibrium level is above the full-employment point, real output cannot expand, and instead prices will increase. The result is inflation. A rightward shift of the full-employment barrier opens up the possi-bility for economic growth, which is realized when the equilibrium level of GNP increases commensurately.

Output and prices

In Chapter 5 we learned that a competitive industry that experiences an increase in demand for its output can expand its production in the long run at essentially constant prices—provided that the price it has to pay for its inputs does not rise. As long as there are unused resources in the economy—that is, unemployed workers, unused machinery, and unused land—firms that desire to expand output can do so at constant costs. They can hire additional workers at the going wage rate, purchase more machines, and rent more land at prevailing prices. Because output can be increased at constant cost of production, there is no necessity for prices to increase. This means that a curve showing price changes as a function of the output level is a horizontal straight line, as long as we have general excess capacity, that is, as long as we do not get close to the full-employment barrier. This situation is shown in Figure 12-7 by the horizontal portion of the curve.

We must remember to be careful in our definition of full employ-

Figure 12-7

Inflation and excess capacity
If there is considerable excess capacity in the economy, expansion is possible at constant prices. As the capacity barrier is approached, bottleneck inflation results. When capacity is reached, further expansion results in pure inflation.

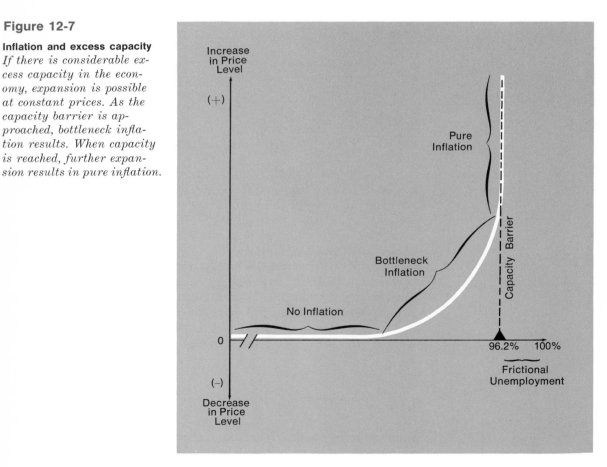

ment by taking into account the inevitable frictional unemployment. As aggregate output approaches the full-employment barrier, some sectors of the economy are likely to reach their capacity barrier sooner than others. While the automobile industry may be working at capacity output, and no trained automobile workers may be looking for jobs, other industries, such as construction, may still have considerable excess capacity and unemployed workers. There is no requirement that all sectors of an expanding economy reach the full-employment barrier at the same time. In fact, this would be a most unlikely event.

But as some sectors reach full employment, prices in these sectors are likely to rise, because buyers will bid up the prices of the products for which they compete. This means that in these sectors prices will tend to rise, although no such tendency manifests itself in the sectors where excess capacity is still available. The result is an increase in the *average* price level, which is composed of the rising prices in the industries with excess demand and constant prices in the industries with excess capacity. This is what economists often call a bottleneck inflation. In Figure 12-7 this is represented by the upward-sloping part of the curve, just before full employment is reached.

If further expansion occurs, the economy will finally reach a stage of general excess demand—all sectors will experience full employment and inflationary pressures. Aggregate output can no longer expand, and only prices will rise. This is the case in a *pure inflation*. As the general price level drifts upward, real output is no longer expanding. The apparent increases in GNP are a purely monetary phenomenon. Changes in physical output—measured by real GNP—no longer accompany the changes in monetary GNP. This situation is depicted by the vertical stretch of the curve of Figure 12-5.

As long as no changes in the aggregate price level are occurring, the monetary GNP will be identical to real GNP, measuring the actual physical output. But as inflation occurs—first in the form of bottleneck inflation and finally as pure inflation—increases in the measured monetary GNP overstate the changes that are occurring in real GNP (which corrects for the price changes).

A final note on the relationship between price level changes and unemployment is in order. As an economy expands, it is likely that the *output changes* occur *first*. Only when there is a certain time lag will firms change their prices, laborers ask for higher wages, and higher rents be negotiated. Hence, as the economy approaches the full-employment barrier, changes in real output will occur first, followed at a later date by price increases. In an economic downswing, the same order is likely: first, output will contract and employment levels will fall. Only then will price and wage increases become smaller and smaller, until they finally disappear. Figure 12-8 shows the trade-off between inflation and labor resources utilization as it manifested itself during the last fifteen years in the United States. Note that the actual path of price changes and employment rates during the period 1956-61 lies above the heavy white line showing the approximate average relationship between inflation and unemployment. During this period the GNP gap (see Figure 12-1) widened. While this period could not be classified as a genuine depression, it marked a slowdown in the growth rate of the American economy. Unemployment increased and the rate of inflation decreased. The same graph shows two generally expansionary periods: 1954-56 and 1961-68. During these periods the GNP gap in Figure 12-1 was closed. Unemployment was reduced, but the rate of inflation increased. In periods during which the GNP gap is closed, output tends to expand first, followed by the price increases. (The colored line with *upward*-pointing arrows lies below the white line showing

Figure 12-8

Inflation and unemployment
Historically, there has existed a trade-off between inflation and the rate of unemployment. As full employment is approached, the price level tends to rise.

Source: Council of Economic Advisors

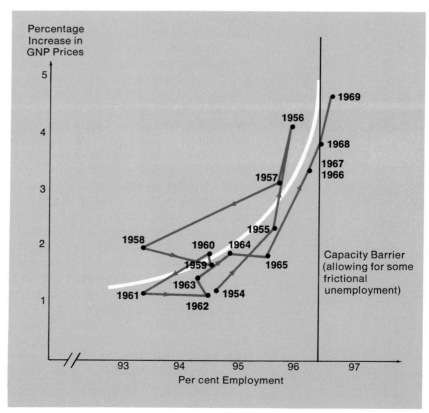

the average response.) In times of a widening GNP gap, the order of events is reversed. Increases in unemployment are likely to be felt right away, while a substantial slowdown in the rate of inflation may take more time. (The colored line with *downward*-pointing arrows lies above the white line.)

There is no easy solution to the policy dilemma posed by the unemployment-inflation trade-off. Clearly, it would be best if we could avoid the undesirable consequences of both inflation and unemployment. It is here that different persons are likely to disagree strongly on the more desirable state of the world. If you are living on a pension, or if most of your assets are fixed in dollar terms, you would probably favor no inflation—even if this should mean substantial unemployment. If you are a wage earner who is likely to lose his job during a period of economic slowdown, you would probably be willing to have a bit of inflation, if this means that you will be able to retain your job.

Cost-push inflation

Another significant complication is introduced by the phenomenon of *cost-push inflation*. Cost-push inflation refers to the ability of economic units with monopoly power to increase the price of their product or the wage rate charged above the level that would prevail in purely competitive conditions. In Chapter 7, we learned that a monopolistic seller is able to charge a higher price for his product by restricting his output. The same applies to economic unions, which have some monopoly power and which can obtain higher wages by limiting access into the union and thereby into the labor market. If firms or unions exercise such monopoly power to increase their prices or wages, cost-push inflation is the result.

Note that this kind of inflation is independent of the level of general economic activity. Thus, even in times where we have substantial excess capacity in the economy as a whole, monopolistic firms and unions are able to increase their prices and wages. This complicates our simple analysis presented in this chapter, because it introduces an additional upward bias into the price-level determination. We argued in Chapter 7 that governmental regulation may be one possible way of limiting the exercise of the monopolist's price-setting power. It has been suggested by some economists that the government has an obligation to regulate the pricing behavior of monopolistic firms and check the wage demands made by strong unions. But such governmental interferences with the free market pricing of resources and commodities will generally also be accompanied by decreases in the efficiency of resource allocation. Economists are not in general agreement on the social desirability of governmental regulation of monopolistic pricing by firms and unions.

Economic growth

Not much has been said so far about economic growth. Economic growth occurs when the economy as a whole expands in real terms. Two conditions have to be met for this process to occur. The first is that the full-employment barrier must be shifted to the right, permitting a larger GNP to be produced. There are two ways in which this rightward shift of the full-employment barrier may come about. (1) We may experience an increase in the quantity of the resources used in the production process. The labor force may increase because

Figure 12-9

Growth and equilibrium *For economic growth to occur, the full employment barrier must shift to the right. Potential GNP is increased. But it takes an increase (upward shift) in the total expenditure function to bring the equilibrium (actual) GNP up to the potential.*

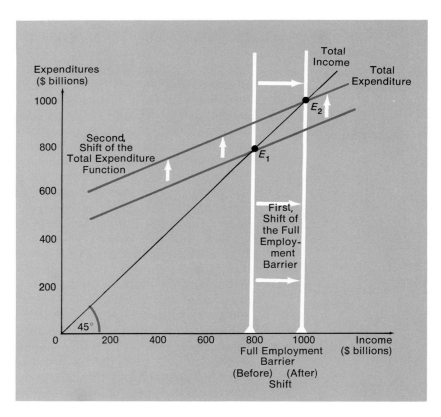

more people reach the age at which they start their productive activity. The area of useful land may increase. Swamps may be drained, deserts irrigated, and poor soil fertilized. The amount of capital equipment, such as machinery, tools, and buildings, may increase as a result of new investment in these man-made resources. (2) The production function may change. The production function shows the technological relationship between resources (inputs) and commodities (outputs). If a technological advance occurs, we are enabled to produce a larger quantity of output with the same quantity of resources as before. Thus, either *quantitative* increases in land, labor, and capital, or *qualitative* increases in the methods of production will lead to a rightward shift of the full-employment barrier, thereby permitting a larger quantity of output to be produced, and opening up the possibility for economic growth.

But a rightward shift of the full-employment barrier means only that the potential for economic growth is created. For actual output to expand, the second condition we referred to earlier must be fulfilled: total expenditures (aggregate demand) must increase too. Only after an increase in aggregate demand will the *equilibrium* level of GNP increase. The rightward shift of the full-employment barrier represents the precondition for an expansion of real output. Its realization depends on an increase in aggregate expenditures, which will put the new resources or the new technology to work. See Figure 12-9.

Full employment, price stability, and growth

The economic policy maker, then, would like to avoid the economic costs of unemployment and inflation, and at the same time reap the benefits of economic growth. That is, in ideal circumstances economic growth will proceed at the maximum feasible rate, while both price stability and full employment are maintained. That this is no easy task to accomplish should be obvious. It is somewhat like shooting from a moving car at a target that itself is moving. The moving target is provided by the full-employment level, which is shifting to the right as resources increase and technology is improved. Aggregate expenditures are the means by which the target of full employment and price stability can be attained. One additional complication is provided by the trade-off between unemployment and inflation that we discussed previously. It may not even be possible to attain all three goals at the same time.

Actual economic policy may have to involve a compromise between two or even three of the goals. Clearly, if the ideal state is unattainable, we will try to choose the solution that improves the welfare of the citizens to the greatest possible extent, or, put differently, that will impose the least cost on the nation. But let us remember that the costs of unemployment fall mainly on the unemployed, and the costs of inflation on the aged and retired whose income or wealth is fixed in monetary terms. Economic growth provides one bright light, because a growing GNP provides an increasing "economic pie," which means that there doesn't have to be *any* losers at all. If more commodities become available, the gainers may gain, while the less fortunate people at least are able to maintain their present position. Hence, some inflation or some unemployment may be economically bearable if this means that the rate of economic growth is substantially increased.

It is easy to agree on the ideal of complete full employment and absolute price stability with maximum growth—but such an ideal may be difficult to attain in the imperfect world in which we live. In the following chapter we will take a first look at the problems faced by a national government that tries to attain the triple goals of full employment, price stability, and a high growth rate.

Summary

□ Full employment, a stable price level, and a high growth rate are the most frequently mentioned economic *goals*.

□ Unemployed resources impose a *cost* on the economy because the actual GNP falls short of the potential GNP. Some *frictional* unemployment, however, is considered unavoidable in a dynamic economy.

□ *Inflation* is accompanied by a *redistribution* of income and wealth and thereby imposes hardships on some people. Money loses its usefulness in hyperinflations.

□ The national economy is in *equilibrium* when the amount that economic units wish to spend is equal to the amount that they receive as income.

□ The *full-employment* level of the national economy is given by the productive capacity. Both the amount of available resources and the state of the technology determine the full-employment GNP.

□ If the equilibrium level of employment is below the full-employment level, unused capacity exists in the economy. The gap between equilibrium and full employment is the *GNP gap,* which shows the amount by which real income could increase.

□ If the equilibrium level is above the full-employment level, *inflation* will result.

□ *Bottleneck inflation* occurs when some sectors are already reaching the full-employment barrier, forcing prices up there, while other sectors still have excess capacity.

□ *Cost-push inflation* may occur if firms or unions can exercise monopoly power and force prices or wages up, even if unused capacity exists.

□ Economic *growth,* caused by increases in resources or improvements in technology, increases the *potential* for economic expansion by shifting the full-employment barrier to the right. But aggregate demand has to increase, too, to bring the equilibrium (actual) level of GNP up to the full-employment (potential) GNP.

13

Fiscal policy

In the last few chapters, we have talked about the effects of *private* economic activity on the national economy—now the time has come to turn our attention to the ever-increasing importance of the *public* sector of the economy. Governmental economic activity accounts for almost 25 per cent of GNP, and the relative size of the governmental sector is growing. In particular, we will focus attention on the role of government spending and taxation in influencing the level of economic activity in the country as a whole. In the following chapter, we will analyze monetary policy as another way in which the government can influence the economy.

Governments, as the elected representatives of the people, have an obligation to promote the economic well-being of the citizens. Governments help to determine the economic environment within which we all have to operate. Laws prohibit the sale of certain drugs, while requiring a doctor's prescription before others can be dispensed. Laws restrict the sale of other commodities to various population groups—such as forbidding the sale of liquor to minors, for instance. Governments regulate some firms and determine the prices that they can charge for their products—especially in the public utilities industries. Governments provide public goods and services to the citizens—fire protection, police, highways, and street lighting are examples.

It is clear that governmental actions do influence economic activity, and given that the government is supposed to act on behalf of society as a whole, we may argue that the government has an obligation to act in a way that will maximize the welfare of the whole nation.

This governmental obligation was explicitly recognized in the Employment Act of 1946. More specifically, the federal government was charged in the Act with the obligation to work for a high level of employment, a stable price level, and a high growth rate of the economy. At the same time, the Council of Economic Advisors was created to analyze economic problems, and to assist in the implementation of economic policy.

On a national level, then, economic policy is largely concerned with the attainment of the triple goals of full employment, price stability, and a high growth rate. In this chapter we will focus on *fiscal policy*, that is, the deliberate use of governmental expenditures and taxes to influence economic activity.

In the previous chapters, we looked at the private sector, and especially aggregate consumption and investment as being the main components of private spending. We learned that while consumption expenditures have a relatively stable and consistent relationship to income, investment activity occurs in spurts and leaps and is mainly influenced by factors other than current income. There is no necessity for income and spending to expand smoothly. Instead, we might experience strong fluctuations of total private expenditures. Moreover, there is no requirement that the *actual* or equilibrium level of GNP coincides with the *potential* or full-employment level of GNP, and it is probable that the private sector alone will generate periods of unemployment or inflation.

The role of the government may then be described as exercising a stabilizing influence on the economic fluctuations generated in the private sector. By acting as a stabilizer the government may help the economy as a whole to achieve the triple goals of full employment, stable prices, and a high growth rate.

Inflationary and deflationary gaps

Economists find it useful to consider the amount of total expenditures relative to total income *at the full-employment level*. In Figure 13-1 we show three alternative aggregate expenditure curves. If aggregate expenditures are as shown by the line E_1E_1, equilibrium national income will be $400 billion, for the alternative line E_2E_2 it will be $800 billion, and for the total expenditure line E_3E_3, equilibrium income is $1,100 billion.

Full employment of all resources is reached when the economy operates at an income level of $800 billion. Clearly, then, if the aggregate expenditure curve E_3E_3 prevails, the equilibrium income level will be greater than the full-employment income level. This is a situation that will lead to inflationary pressures, which will result in a general price-level increase. In a situation such as this, the government has to ask the question, By how much does aggregate demand for goods and services, as indicated by the total expenditures curve, have to decrease in order to remove the discrepancy between equilibrium and full employment? That is, by how much do we have to shift the total expenditure curve E_3E_3 downward to bring the equilibrium and full-employment income levels together and thereby eliminate a cause for the inflation? The amount of the downward shift required is given by the difference between total expenditures at full employment ($950 billion in terms of Figure 13-1 and Table

13-1) and full-employment income ($800 billion). A reduction of aggregate expenditures by $150 billion would remove the inflationary pressures, in that the new total expenditure curve would be E_2E_2, and equilibrium GNP would now coincide with full-employment GNP of $800 billion. Economists call the excess of planned expenditures (at full employment) over full-employment income an *inflationary gap*. The inflationary gap, which in our example is equal to $150

Figure 13-1

Inflationary and deflationary gaps *The inflationary (or deflationary) gap measures by how much the aggregate expenditure function has to be shifted downward (upward) to bring about full employment without inflation.*

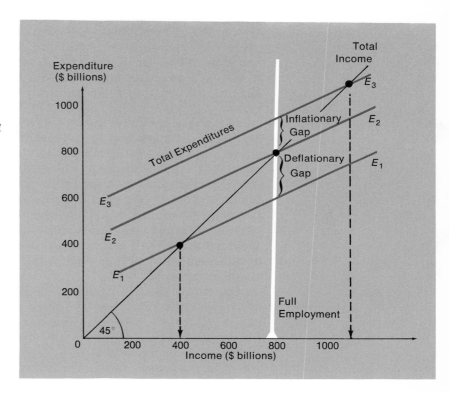

Table 13-1 Inflationary and deflationary gaps

Total expenditure curve	Equilibrium income level (billions)	Full-employment income level (billions)	Total expenditures at the full-employment income level (billions)	Inflationary or deflationary gap (billions)	
E_3 E_3	$1,100	$800	$950	$150	Inflationary gap
E_2 E_2	800	800	800	0	
E_1 E_1	400	800	600	200	Deflationary gap

billion, measures the inflationary pressures that manifest themselves in the economy. A reduction of expenditures by that amount would eliminate the inflationary gap and thereby the upward pressures on prices.

Similarly, if the aggregate expenditure curve E_1E_1 prevails initially, equilibrium income will be smaller than full-employment income: there will be unemployment or a deflationary situation. Again we have to ask the question regarding the shift required to make full employment and equilibrium coincide. In terms of our example, the full-employment level is at $800 billion, and the total expenditure curve E_1E_1 indicates that at full employment total expenditures would be $600 billion. Hence a *deflationary gap* of $200 billion exists. If the aggregate expenditure curve E_1E_1 is shifted upward by that amount, the deflationary (or unemployment) situation will be eliminated.

Let us note carefully that the size of the inflationary or deflationary gap is *not* measured by the numerical difference between full-employment and equilibrium income levels. It is measured by the amount of the downward or upward shift of the total expenditure curve that is required to bring full-employment and equilibrium GNP together. That is, the gaps are measured in terms of the *vertical* distance between the prevailing expenditure curve (E_3E_3 or E_1E_1 in our examples) and the desirable curve (E_2E_2). Or, put still differently, the gaps are given by the numerical difference between the full-employment income and the total expenditures at the full-employment level.

But clearly there is a relationship between the size of the inflationary or deflationary gap measured at the full-employment level and the difference between actual and potential GNP discussed in the previous chapter. If the inflationary or deflationary gap is eliminated, the economy will actually operate at its full-employment potential. The inflationary and deflationary gaps merely show by how much the aggregate expenditure function has to be *shifted* to bring the equilibrium and the full-employment levels of GNP together.

The multiplier

The link between the various gaps is provided by the *multiplier,* a phenomenon based on the fact that additional expenditures—for instance, by the government—will create new income and that part of this new income will be spent, thereby again creating additional income, which can be spent, and so on.

Let us consider in greater detail what happens to the level of equilibrium GNP when there is a shift of the expenditure function. What happens, for instance, if the government increases its spending by $50 billion? Clearly, the $50 billion represents income to the producers of the goods ordered, and GNP will increase immediately by that amount. But that is not where the story ends. The producers will spend some of their additional income just earned. Let us assume that the marginal propensity to consume is equal to .75. That is, out of every additional dollar of income, people will spend 75 cents on consumption, while saving 25 cents. Then out of the additional $50 billion of income earned by the producers, 75 per cent or $37.5 billion will go into additional consumption expenditures, and 25 per cent, or $12.5 billion, will go into saving. But the $37.5 billion spent on consumption goods represents income to still somebody else. And yet again, consumption by these people will increase. We will have a chain reaction, and the end result is an increase in GNP that is a *multiple* of the initial increase in investment.

In our example, the total increase of GNP caused by the $50 billion additional governmental expenditures will amount to $200 billion. How do we arrive at this figure? A simple formula, called the multiplier, can be used to compute the total change in GNP. The total change in GNP depends on two magnitudes: the initial change in expenditures and the percentage of each additional dollar earned that will be devoted to consumption. Clearly, the greater the amount of new income generated for other people, the greater also will be their spending. The multiplier formula reads:

$$\text{Change in GNP} = \frac{1}{1 - MPC} \times \text{Change in expenditures.}$$

The *MPC* is our familiar marginal propensity to consume, shown by the slope of the consumption function. In our case the *MPC* (the amount spent on additional consumption after an income increase of one dollar) is equal to .75. The initial change in expenditures was $50 billion. Using these figures, the formula yields

$$\text{Change in GNP} = \frac{1}{1 - .75} \times \$50 \text{ billion} = 4 \times \$50 \text{ billion}$$
$$= \$200 \text{ billion.}$$

Alternatively, we could have used the familiar relationship that the sum of the *MPC* and *MPS* equals one (a one-dollar increase in income will lead to a one-dollar increase in consumption *plus* saving, by definition) and rewrite the multiplier formula simply as

$$\text{Change in income} = \frac{1}{MPS} \times \text{Change in expenditures}$$

$$= \frac{1}{.25} \times \$50 \text{ billion} = \$200 \text{ billion}.$$

Thus, total national product will expand four times as much as the initial increase in expenditures. The multiplier in this case is equal to four. If the marginal propensity to consume would have been larger, say, .80, the multiplier would have been larger too. *More* of each additional dollar earned would have gone into consumption spending, and would therefore have boosted income in each spending round by a larger amount. Given the higher *MPC* of .80, the multiplier would have been equal to 5. [Multiplier = $1/(1 - MPC)$ = $1/(1 - .80) = 1/.20 = 5$.] In that case, the total GNP expansion due to the initial increase in expenditures of \$50 billion would have amounted to \$250 billion.

But let us not fail to add that the multiplier works also in the downward direction. If government spending had decreased by \$50 billion, our GNP would have *dropped* by \$250 billion, given the *MPC* of .80. All changes in spending caused by extraneous forces will be magnified in their impact on GNP by the workings of the multiplier.

The multiplier provides the link between the deflationary gap and the discrepancy between actual and potential GNP. The deflationary gap shows by how much expenditures have to increase to close (with the help of the multiplier) the gap between actual and potential GNP.

Of course, the opposite holds true for the inflationary gap. If there is an inflationary gap, equilibrium GNP also exceeds full-employment GNP. Because production can no longer expand, inflationary pressures will make themselves felt. The inflationary gap shows the decrease in aggregate expenditures necessary to bring about (again with the help of the multiplier) equality between actual and potential GNP.

Government expenditures

The inflationary and deflationary gaps are important measures for the governmental policy maker, because they show him how much of a governmental policy action is needed to bring the economy to the potential GNP level—hopefully representing full employment without inflation.

There are two major discretionary tools at the disposal of the fiscal policy maker: government expenditures and taxation. By changing one or both of these magnitudes, the policy maker can influence the rate of economic activity in the country as a whole.

First, we will be concerned with the role of government expenditures. Let us assume that the economy's aggregate expenditure function is given by the line labeled E_{old} in Figure 13-2. That is, the economy will be in equilibrium at an income level of $800 billion. If full employment is at $1,000 billion, we can now calculate how much of an increase in governmental expenditures is needed to bring the economy to its potential GNP level. Given a multiplier of 4, only a $50 billion increase in government spending is needed to close the gap between equilibrium and full-employment GNP. The initial increase of $50 billion in government spending (equals deflationary gap) will bring forth—as a result of the workings of the multiplier—a $200 billion increase in GNP. See Table 13-2.

To repeat again: *the deflationary (or inflationary) gap measures how much of a change in government spending is needed to close the GNP gap between actual and potential GNP.*

Figure 13-2

The effect of government expenditures *An increase in government expenditures will shift the total expenditure function upward by the amount of the increase. Equilibrium GNP will increase by a multiple of that amount due to the operation of the multiplier:* $M = 1/(1 - MPC)$.

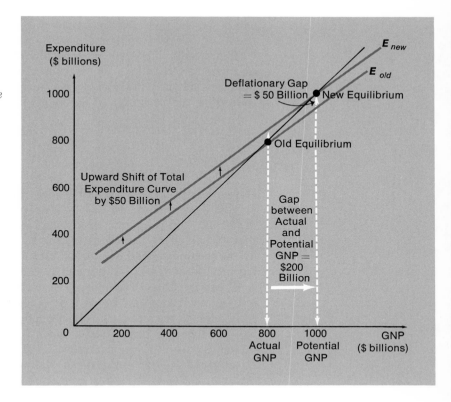

Table 13-2   The multiplier

	Change in income (billions)	Change in consumption (assuming MPC = .75)	Change in saving (assuming MPS = .25)
Initial change in expenditures	$ 50.00	$ 37.50	$12.50
Second round spending change	37.50	28.12	9.38
Third round spending change	28.12	21.09	7.03
Fourth round spending change	21.09	15.81	5.28
All further rounds spending change	63.29	47.48	15.81
Totals	$200.00	$150.00	$50.00

$200.00

This, of course, assumes that the spending habits of the private sector of the economy do not change as a result of the governmental expenditures. If this assumption is not fulfilled, and the governmental expenditures constitute replacements or substitutes for private expenditures, we will experience simultaneous shifts of the private expenditure functions, and the final result, as far as changes in equilibrium are concerned, will be determined by the effect of the combined changes. But for our purposes we will assume that private spending is not directly affected by government outlays.

But just as increases in governmental expenditures will lead to an increase in GNP, so decreases in governmental expenditures will lead to a decrease in GNP—again by a multiple of the initial change caused by the workings of the multiplier.

Government taxation

Governments not only spend money, they also impose *taxes* on the private sector. Here we will deal only with the effects of the most important tax: the personal income tax, which accounts for approximately half of all tax receipts. The personal income tax is imposed on the income earned by individuals and in effect lowers the disposable income of the taxed person by the amount of the tax.

Clearly, if the government imposes taxes of $50 billion on private individuals, their take-home pay is decreased by that amount and consequently the amounts they can spend on consumption and saving will be lowered. But by how much exactly will consumption and saving decrease? For our purposes of national income determination the effect of the tax on the *spending* by consumers is most important.

We remember that the marginal propensity to consume shows the portion of each dollar earned that goes for consumption. If taxes take away part of a person's income, it may be a reasonable assumption that the individual will reduce his consumption expenditures by the amount of the tax times his marginal propensity to consume. Thus, if the marginal propensity to consume is .75 and the government imposes taxes of $50 billion on the citizens, we might expect that consumption will decline by .75 × $50 billion, or $37.5 billion.

If people reduce their consumption by $37.5 billion, but must pay a total of $50 billion in taxes, where do the remaining $12.5 billion come from? The obvious answer is out of lower saving. Saving will fall by $12.5 billion, and this, in conjunction with the $37.5 billion drop in consumption, provides the $50 billion of taxes.

What is the effect of the taxation on national income? Private consumption expenditures drop by $37.5 billion—and hence the aggregate expenditure function in Figure 13-3 shifts *downward* by $37.5 billion. What is the effect of this shift on GNP? Again the

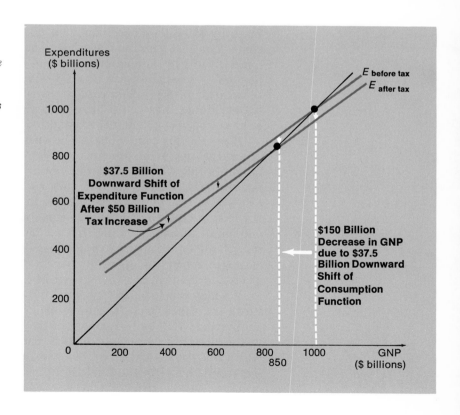

Figure 13-3

The effects of a tax *A tax imposed on personal income will lower aggregate consumption expenditures by the amount of the tax times the marginal propensity to consume.*

multiplier has to be used to determine the effect of this initial change on GNP. Assuming a *MPC* of .75 or a multiplier of 4, the $37.5 billion drop in expenditures caused by the tax will magnify itself to a reduction in GNP of 4 × $37.5 billion, or a $150 billion GNP decrease.

The balanced budget

We are now in a position to determine what happens if the government increases both public spending and taxation by the same amount. If the government does so, it will maintain a *balanced budget*, that is, it will pay for all its current expenditures by taxation. On a first hunch, we might be tempted to argue that the effect of equal increases in expenditures and taxes would exactly offset each other. If the two effects cancel out, equilibrium GNP remains undisturbed. Given our previous analysis of the impact of governmental spending and taxation, this notion is clearly false.

Let us assume that the government increases expenditures and taxes by $50 billion each, and that the marginal propensity to consume equals .75. Our analysis shows that the increase in government expenditures by $50 billion will result (in conjunction with a multiplier of 4) in an increase of $200 billion in GNP. But the increase in taxation of $50 billion results only in a decrease of GNP by $150 billion. Hence there must have been a *net expansion* of GNP by $50 billion—the amount of the expenditure and tax increases.

How did this come about? The answer lies mostly in the role of private saving. While the governmental expenditure increase of $50 billion is fully felt by the economy as additional expenditures, the tax increase by that amount does not reduce private spending by $50 billion, but merely by a *fraction* thereof: $37.5 billion. Hence, *in the first round,* additional governmental spending exceeds the reduction in private spending by $12.5 billion. This amount of the total tax bill comes out of a reduction in saving. Then the $12.5 differential is magnified by the operation of the multiplier, and the end result is a net increase in national income of 4 × $12.5 billion, or $50 billion.

We may conclude that an equal increase of government expenditures and taxes (maintaining a balanced budget) will increase the equilibrium GNP by the amount of the budget increase. Some economists refer to this phenomenon as the *balanced-budget-multiplier*, which is always equal to *one:* the amount of the expenditure and tax increase is equal to the final GNP increase.

Fiscal policy alternatives

Let us assume that the actual (equilibrium) GNP is currently at the $800 billion level, but that a reliable economic analysis shows that the potential (full-employment) level of GNP is at $1,000 billion. The question before us is how to use fiscal policy most effectively to bring the economy up to its potential GNP.

Three main alternatives are open to us: (1) an increase in governmental expenditures, (2) a decrease in taxes, or (3) a balanced-budget policy of an equal increase in governmental expenditures and taxes. Of course, an infinite multitude of various combinations of these main alternatives is possible. For instance, we might increase governmental expenditures just a little, while cutting taxes a lot, or strongly increase expenditures and decrease taxes very little. We will focus attention only on the three main alternatives open to us.

How are we to decide between the three alternatives provided? There are two important aspects in which the policies can be distinguished from each other: in their effect on the relative size of the public and private sectors of the economy, and in their effect on the national debt. Let us analyze how each one of the three alternatives measures up according to these two major criteria.

What determines the optimal size of the private and the public sectors? In Chapter 8 we developed a criterion according to which we could decide whether economic efficiency was increased by changing the relative size of the private and public sector by one dollar. The basic requirement for economic efficiency was that the social benefits of the last dollar spent by the public sector should be equal to the marginal social benefits which could be obtained in the private sector. That is, the marginal social benefits of additional expenditures in the two sectors should be equal to each other. If, for instance, the marginal social benefits of the last dollar of public expenditures exceeds the marginal social benefits of the last dollar of private expenditures, an increase in the relative size of the public sector improves economic efficiency.

An increase in government expenditures designed to bring about an increase in GNP by $200 billion is easily calculated with the help of the multiplier. Given a multiplier of 4, an increase in governmental expenditures of $50 billion will suffice to bring about a $200 billion expansion in GNP.

What happens to the relative size of the private and public sectors? The additional governmental expenditures will increase the *relative* size of the governmental sector, and hence economic efficiency will increase *if* the marginal social benefits of governmental expenditures exceed those of private expenditures: MSB gov. $>$ MSB priv. But if the reverse holds true, i.e., MSB gov. $<$ MSB priv., economic efficiency will be decreased because the relative increase in the size of the government sector will allocate resources to a use where their benefits are lower than in the private sector.

It is clear that, starting with a balanced budget, an increase in governmental expenditures will result in a budget deficit, and hence an increase in the national debt (to be discussed on p. 225).

A decrease in taxes levied upon personal incomes will increase the disposable income of individuals, and hence their consumption. As a result of the tax cut and the consequent increase in private consumption, the private sector will grow in relation to the public sector. This is efficient if the marginal social benefits of private expenditures are greater than those of public expenditures; inefficient if the reverse is true.

But let us remind ourselves that the tax cut will stimulate the economy only through its effect on consumption. Given a MPC of .75, consumption must increase initially by \$50 billion to bring about the \$200 billion GNP increase. Hence, taxes must be cut by \$66.6 billion (Δ Tax $\times MPC = \Delta$ Consumption) to shift the consumption function upwards by \$50 billion.

The effect of the tax cut on the governmental budget—given constant government expenditures—is a deficit and a corresponding increase in the national debt.

A balanced budget policy increases both governmental expenditures and taxes by the same amount. Here, too, the public sector will grow in relation to the private sector. But now the relative change is likely to be much stronger than in the case of a government spending increase alone. The national debt will remain unchanged because the budget will remain in balance. The three alternative policies and their effects are summarized in Table 13-3.

We have discussed the first criterion according to which we can select between the fiscal policy alternatives open to us: the relative size of the private and public sectors. If it is desirable to expand the private sector in relation to the public sector, tax cuts are called for. If the public sector is to play a relatively more important role, increases in government expenditures are called for. But note that if we insist on maintaining a balanced budget, the increase in the size of the public sector required to bring about a desired economic expansion is much larger than it would be with deficit finance.

The second criterion that may be applied to judge the desirability of alternative fiscal policy measures is their effect upon the national debt. To this we will now turn our attention.

Policy	Change required (billions of $)	Effect on relative size of private and public sectors	Effect on government budget
1. *Increase government expenditures*	Increase government expenditures by $50 billion	Private sector: decrease Public sector: increase	Deficit of $50 billion
2. *Decrease taxes*	Decreases taxes by $66.6 billion	Private sector: increase Public sector: decrease	Deficit of $66.6 billion
3. *Increase government expenditures and taxes by equal amounts (balanced budget)*	Increases both government expenditures and taxes by $200 billion	Pricate sector decrease Public sector: increase (but more strongly than under (1) above)	None

The national debt

The national debt represents the net effect of all governmental budget deficits and surpluses of the past. Whenever the government spends more than it raises in taxes, it has two ways of financing the differential: it may print up new money—a method that will be discussed in greater detail in the following chapter—or it may sell bonds to the public. The problems associated with the national debt, which is the sum total of past borrowings that have not yet been repaid, are many and varied. We will concentrate on the main question associated with the national debt. Does its existence impose a burden on the economy?

Three crucial questions have to be asked in order to determine the effect of the national debt. (1) Do we have full employment or unemployment during the period that the deficit-financed governmental expenditures are made? (2) Are the expenditures financed by the bonds for public investment projects or for current operating expenses? (3) Are the bonds sold to domestic residents or to foreigners? Let us consider the relevance of each one of these questions in turn.

Full employment versus underemployment Let us assume that there is a situation of general underemployment of resources in the economy. That is, our actual GNP is below the potential GNP. In such a situation, the private sector alone does not engage in enough spending to fully utilize all available resources. If the government's expenditures start to increase, and this increase in governmental expenditures is financed by the sale of bonds to the public, which uses previously idle funds to purchase these bonds, then there is no reason for *private* resource use to decline. That is, the private sector will not have to cut back on its use of resources, and individual households and firms can continue to consume and invest the same amounts as before. The private sector will be no worse off. No real costs, in terms of opportunities that have to be sacrificed, are borne by the citizens at the time of the governmental expenditures.

Contrast this with a full-employment situation. Now, if the government increases its expenditures, resources will be bid away from the private sector. The private sector will acquire the government bonds, which are sold by the government at attractive interest rates, and because the private sector spends *its* money on the bonds, resources will be set free for the government to use. In this case, total real consumption and investment expenditures of the private sector will decrease, and this decrease represents a real cost to the private sector. But note that this real cost is borne voluntarily, because people are not obliged to purchase the government bonds, but do so out of their own free will.

To sum up: the deficit financing of government expenditures during a period of underemployment will impose no real costs on the private sector, but merely put previously idle resources to work. Hence, no real costs are incurred because of the deficit financing. But the sale of government bonds during a period of full employment will result in the relinquishing of command over resources by the private sector. The private sector bears a real cost in reduced consumption and investment spending, but it does so voluntarily. Clearly, if the governmental expenditures are financed by taxes instead of bonds, the private sector has to give up the same resources, but it will do so only because it is forced to by the tax authorities.

"Current" goods versus investment goods Many economists draw a distinction between governmental expenditures for "current" goods and investment goods. A current good or service provided by the government is defined as one whose benefits are enjoyed immediately. Police protection, protection against fires, and garbage hauling are good examples of this kind of activity. An investment-type governmental expenditure is characterized by the fact that it will benefit not only the current generation but will also increase the welfare of future generations. Dams, freeways, hospitals, and school buildings will all be around for some time to come, and yield benefits also to their future users.

What does all this have to do with the public debt? The reasoning is simple. We may argue that the people who enjoy a governmental service should also be the ones who pay for it. If a governmental expenditure primarily benefits the current generation, the current generation should also bear the burden in the form of taxes. If the expenditure will increase the welfare of future generations, we might want to impose some of the tax burden also on these future generations.

The following principle emerges: finance governmental expenditures whose benefits will accrue mainly to the current generation by taxes; finance governmental expenditures that will also benefit future generations by the selling of bonds. Those who benefit will then bear the burden of taxation.

The term "burden" in the last sentence should be used with caution. It refers only to the burden of having to pay taxes—an involuntary act in most instances. It does not refer to the "real" burden that has to be borne by the present generation if resources have to be shifted to the public sector. Whether there is such a real burden depends on the state of the economy—whether we are in a situation of full employment or underemployment, as discussed in the previous section.

Domestic debt versus foreign debt   All that has been said so far refers to the burden of the *domestic* debt—that is, United States government bonds held by American citizens. In this case the United States government taxes American citizens to pay the interest on the bonds held by other Americans. A domestically held debt involves a gigantic reshuffling of funds between taxpayers and bondholders. The bondholders voluntarily reduce their expenditures at the time when the governmental projects are undertaken—and thereby willingly free the resources to be used in the governmental projects. Clearly, these persons have to be repaid later for their sacrifices. People who abstain from present consumption and buy government bonds to be able to finance the college education of their children or their own retirement are in this category.

If the government wishes to repay these people, plus interest accrued, it must tax future generations. But note that the tax monies raised are merely transferred to other citizens. The welfare of the nation as a whole is not changed—only the distribution of the tax burden is changed over time.

The case is entirely different for a *foreign-held* public debt. If the government sells its bonds to foreigners, it will have to pay interest and principal back to foreigners. At the time when the debt is sold to foreigners, we obtain *real* resources. No sacrifices have to be made by the current generation—neither in the form of reduced consumption or investment, nor in the form of tax payments. But future generations have to bear both kinds of burdens. Future citizens will have to be taxed. The tax proceeds go directly to foreigners, who in return will demand real goods and services from us. Future generations will have to make some sacrifices. If the resources initially obtained from the foreigners are put to good use and yield a high rate of return, future generations may readily bear the burden of having to pay for the benefits they receive. But if the foreign resources are misspent, future generations have to pay while receiving no commensurate benefits.

As we have seen, there is no one easy answer to the question whether there is a burden involved in the public debt. The three main factors to be taken into consideration are (1) whether we are in a full-employment or underemployment situation; (2) whether present or future generations will benefit from the public expenditures to be financed, and (3) whether the debt is held internally or abroad.

Figures 13-4 and 13-5 provide some empirical clues regarding the burden of the United States public debt. In addition, we might point out that the percentage of the total public debt held abroad is very small. In 1969, it amounted to only 5.1 per cent of the total national debt. And here we should consider, too, that Americans owned foreign assets amounting to $140.8 billion dollars, while foreigners only owned $90.7 billion of United States assets, $11.4 billion of which represented public debt and the remainder private liabilities.

Second, the ratio of interest payments to GNP has not changed substantially over the last decades. Hence the tax burden in relation to total income has not increased substantially.

And, finally, we should not forget that the private debt, the total amount owed by households and firms, is almost three times as large as the outstanding public debt.

But mere numbers do not tell the whole story. The important information is in what circumstances the debt was incurred, what was financed with it, and who holds the bonds. Only an answer to these questions can determine whether we as a nation are better or worse off because of the deficit financing of governmental expenditures undertaken in the past, and the consequent emergence of the public debt.

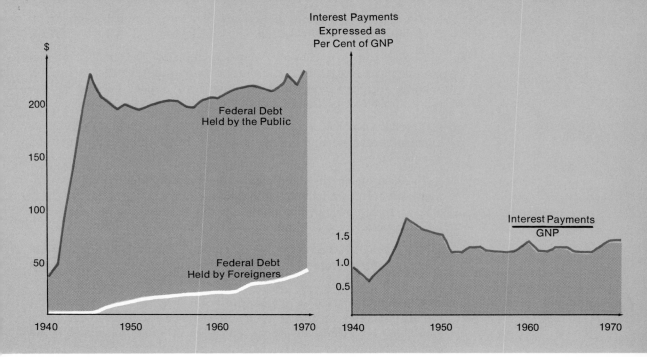

Figure 13-4

The public debt *The figure shows the total amount of the public debt in the hands of the American public and amounts held by foreigners.*

Source: Council of Economic Advisors

Figure 13-5

The interest on the public debt *The ratio of interest paid to the total GNP may be used as a measure of the relative burden of the public debt over time.*

Source: Historical Statistics of the United States and Council of Economic Advisors

Summary

□ The government has assumed a responsibility to help the economy attain the triple *goals* of full employment, price stability, and a high growth rate.

□ *Fiscal policy* consists of the use of government taxation and spending policies to influence economic activity.

□ The *inflationary* and *deflationary gaps*—showing the excess or deficiency of planned expenditures at full employment—are important indicators of governmental policy required to achieve the goals of full employment and price stability.

Summary □ **229**

□ Changes in governmental *expenditures* have a multiple impact on GNP via multiplier effects. The *multiplier* is equal to $1/(1 - MPC)$.

□ Changes in governmental *taxation* influence the amount of disposable income to private economic units, and thereby their spending volume. Again, there will be a magnified impact because of the multiplier effect of the changes in private expenditures.

□ The *balanced-budget* multiplier, resulting from the simultaneous expansion of government spending and taxation by equal amounts, is equal to *one*.

□ In deciding on the appropriate mix between changes in government spending and taxation to achieve a given objective, we may look at the impact of the policy on the *relative size of public and private sectors* and the influence upon the *national debt*.

□ The *optimal size* of the public sector is reached when the marginal social benefits of public expenditures are equal to the marginal social benefits of private expenditures.

□ The *deficit financing* of governmental projects may or may not impose a *burden* on the economy. If there are unutilized resources available, the burden on the present generation is minimized; if the public expenditures will benefit future generations, we may attempt to shift some of the burden of taxation to them; if the debt is financed by the sale of bonds, we will have to pay interest in future years.

14

Monetary policy

Until now, we have said very little about money in our discussion of the functioning of the economic system, but we all know that money plays an extremely important role in all economic activity. The purpose of this chapter is twofold: first, we will answer the questions of what money is and what function it serves, and second, we will analyse how the quantity of money is controlled in the modern United States economy, and what effect monetary policy, that is, the management of monetary magnitudes by governmental authorities, has on the economy.

The functions of money

Money serves as a unit of account, a medium of exchange, and a store of value. Money is the *unit of account* in which most economic transactions are stated. It represents a common denominator that allows us to compare the price of a pizza and a mug of beer. This common denominator permits the aggregation of the values of diverse commodities. Our unit of account is the dollar, but we might as well use francs, marks, or pounds. Other societies have used stones at the bottom of the sea, cows, pig tusks, and cigarettes as units of account. The main requirement that a unit of account has to fulfill is that its own value remains relatively stable in terms of other commodities. Only then can the unit of account selected fulfill its role as a common measuring rod for the value of other commodities. In periods of hyperinflation, where the value of currency drops at extremely fast rates, other commodities, such as cigarettes, have been used as a substitute unit of account.

Money also serves as a *medium of exchange*. It is used to facilitate economic transactions. Without money, we are forced to barter one commodity for another. In a barter economy, a person who wants to buy a sailboat has to find somebody who is willing to take a mountain cabin in exchange. When you want a pair of shoes, you have to find somebody willing to accept some old economics books in return. When you want to go out and have a pizza, you have to find a pizza-maker who is willing to let you earn your pizza by singing for half an hour. Clearly, such a system of barter is not only extremely cumbersome and time-consuming but also very inefficient. Too much time and effort is used up in merely conducting the transactions, in searching for willing buyers and sellers.

Money as a medium of exchange removes the necessity of finding an appropriate buyer *and* seller. Instead, any commodity can be bought or sold for money. Hence transactions are greatly facilitated. The economy as a whole saves on transactions costs and specialization is made much easier. Whatever a person or firm produces can be sold for money.

Money is also a convenient *store of value*. You can accumulate money in order to be able to pay for some expected or unexpected outlay. Should you get sick, you can pay your doctor; should you want to buy a house, you can make the down payment. Of course, the basic requirement that a store of value has to fulfill is that its exchange value is stable in terms of other commodities. Inflationary price increases of other commodities reduce the purchasing power of money. In those circumstances, the usefulness of money as a store of value diminishes because its value in terms of other commodities is no longer stable.

Types of money

In the modern United States economy three types of money are in existence: coins, currency, and demand deposits. Coins constitute only a small fraction of the total money supply. A more important component is currency, issued generally by the Federal Reserve banks, which are the nation's monetary authority. Finally, demand deposits are created when an individual or a firm deposits currency or coin at a commercial bank. To qualify as a demand deposit, the funds must be available "on demand," that is, they can be withdrawn in cash without prior notice or transferred by check to another account. We will have much more to say about the role of commercial banks at a later point in this chapter. For the moment it may suffice to say that along with the Federal Reserve banks, private commercial banks play an important role in determining the total size of the money supply in the economy. At the end of 1970, approximately $6 billion of coins and $49 billion of currency were in circulation. In addition, Americans held $166 billion in their checking accounts, making for a total money supply of $221 billion.

The demand for money

We talked about the various functions that money serves in our society. Now we need to analyze more fully why individuals, households, and businesses hold a certain amount of money. Or, to put it differently, we will look at the *demand for money* by individual economic units.

In Chapter 3 we developed a theory of demand for goods and services. We argued that individuals will—subject to the general income constraint—buy goods and services until the marginal utility of each commodity is equal to its price. Can we apply these concepts also to the "good" money?

Economists distinguish between a transactions demand, a precautionary demand, and a speculative demand for money. Let us look at each one of these concepts in turn. The *transactions demand for money* arises from the use of money as a means of payment. As we pointed out previously, money is able to perform certain services: it eases transactions and does away with the need for finding an appropriate partner for a two-way barter exchange. Money saves both time and effort, and it seems reasonable to assume that the demand for money on behalf of an individual economic unit increases as its volume of transactions increases. Transactions, in turn, go up if the unit's income increases. As a person earns more, he will buy more, i.e., he will engage in more transactions. We may conclude that *income* is one important determinant of the transactions demand for money.

A second determinant of the transactions demand for money is the *rate of interest*. To see why the rate of interest is important, let us remember that the quantity of any commodity demanded depends crucially on its price. But what is the "price" of holding money? The price for holding money is whatever we have to forgo in order to hold the money. For instance, instead of holding cash, we could have put the funds into a savings account, bought government bonds, or lent the money to a businessman. In all these alternative uses of our funds, we would have earned interest or dividends. In order to hold money, we have to forgo these alternatives. We incur *opportunity costs* in holding money. The higher the rate of interest which we could have earned, the greater the opportunity cost of holding money. It follows that with high rates of interest prevailing in the rest of the economy, you have a strong motivation to economize on your money holdings—because every dollar held in cash could have earned so much elsewhere. If interest rates are lower, the opportunity cost of holding

Figure 14-1

The demand for money *The quantity of money demanded by private economic units increases as income goes up and as the rate of interest goes down.*

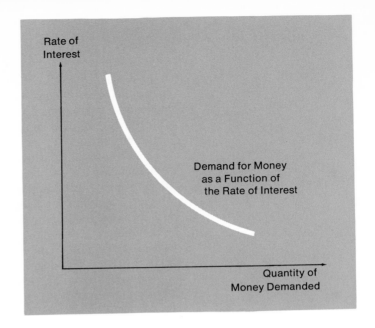

Rate of Interest

Demand for Money as a Function of the Rate of Interest

Quantity of Money Demanded

cash is lower. The motivation to economize on your money holding is not as great. Hence the quantity of money held will vary *inversely* with the rate of interest that can be earned by holding alternative assets. This is shown in Figure 14-1, where we show the quantity of money demanded as a function of the rate of interest.

The *precautionary demand for money* arises from the fact that the future holds many uncertainties. Your car may need repair, you may become sick and need medical attention, the roof of your house may start to leak, and for many other contingencies you may need cash. If you hold no money, these occurrences might be very costly to you. For instance, if you do not have the money to have the roof fixed immediately, the leak might become larger, and the seeping water might damage the carpet and furniture. These additional costs can be avoided if you hold a sufficient cash reserve. People with higher income or greater wealth may want to hold a higher money reserve for these precautionary motives. But the interest rate once more plays an important role, in that it increases the opportunity costs of holding money for precautionary purposes.

Finally, there is the *speculative demand for money*. The speculative demand for money has much to do with expected or anticipated price changes. If you expect that prices of other assets are going to fall, you may do well to wait before purchasing them in order to take advantage of the expected lower prices. If you expect the stock market to plummet, or the price of bonds to fall, you may hold cash in the meantime. Then, after the prices drop, you can move in and buy at the lower prices. Clearly, this is speculative behavior, and money balances held for this reason depend largely on expectations about future prices.

We may sum up by noting that the quantity of money that people will want to hold (1) *increases* with the level of *income*, and (2) varies *inversely* with the rate of *interest* (as shown in Figure 14-1).

The supply of money

Before going more deeply into the way in which money is created in a modern economy, let us simply assume that the monetary authority—like the Federal Reserve in the United States—is able to determine the quantity of money. What will happen if the quantity of money supplied changes?

In Figure 14-2 we graph the hypothetical aggregate demand for money curve, which shows the quantity of money demanded by all private economic units as a function of the rate of interest. We also show the supply curve of money. The supply curve of money is shown

Figure 14-2

The money supply and interest rates *Given a certain demand function for money, an increase in the money supply will lead to a reduction of the rate of interest.*

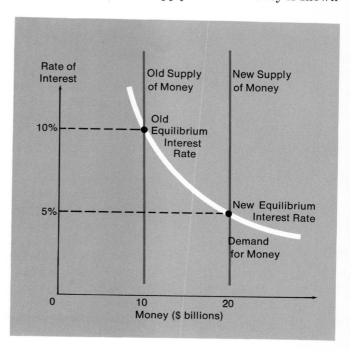

as a vertical straight line, because we assume that the monetary authorities are able to determine the amount of money in circulation at will.

Now that we have both a hypothetical supply and a demand for money curve, we are able to determine the equilibrium rate of interest in the economy. The equilibrium interest rate is determined by the intersection of the demand and supply for money curves. Given a hypothetical money supply of $10 billion, the equilibrium rate of interest in the economy will be 10 per cent.

If the Federal Reserve disturbs the equilibrium by increasing the money supply to $20 billion, money becomes more plentiful in the economy, and the price of money—the rate of interest—will go down. In our hypothetical example, the interest rate drops from 10 per cent to 5 per cent.

Let us note that the interest rate is determined by the demand and supply of money. The Federal Reserve is able to influence the interest rate by changing the supply of money in existence. An increase in the supply of money will—other things being equal—lead to a fall in the interest rate, while a decrease in the supply of money will bring about an increase in the interest rate.

The rate of interest and economic activity

The change in the interest rate in itself would probably not be of major importance, were it not for the effect that the rate of interest has on general economic activity. In Chapter 11 we analyzed the relationship between the rate of interest and new investment. As the rate of interest falls, the amount of investment projects undertaken in the economy will increase. This is because it is cheaper for businessmen to borrow money at the lower interest rate, and therefore more investment projects become profitable. Hence business investment increases if the rate of interest falls.

The same is true about the rate of new housing construction. If interest rates are high, the interest costs associated with a mortgage are high. Most people are not wealthy enough to pay cash for a house, and they must borrow the money to purchase it. But with high interest rates, these borrowing costs go up, and fewer people are able to afford a new house. The reverse holds true if interest rates are low. Then it becomes more attractive for people to borrow funds, and construction activity is likely to increase as interest rates fall.

State and local government units are similarly affected. State and local governments cannot print up their own money like the federal government. All expenditures have to be financed by taxes or by borrowing money from the public by floating bonds. If interest rates are high, legislators are much less likely to ask for, and voters are less likely to approve, any proposed new bond issues. Especially state and local capital investment projects—such as schools, hospitals, and highways—are less likely to be undertaken in times of high interest rates than in times when borrowing costs are low, i.e., when interest rates are low.

We have now established a link between the interest rate and economic activity. When the interest rate is low, economic activity is likely to be stimulated by new expenditures by firms, households, and governments. Conversely, when interest rates are high, economic activity is likely to slow down.

The money supply and economic activity

The relation between the money supply and the rate of economic activity is now well established. There are two important links in the chain of events: the money supply-interest rate link, and the interest rate-economic activity link. Given a certain demand schedule for money (which is determined by the sum of the transactions demand, the precautionary demand, and the speculative demand for money), the money supply set by the Federal Reserve determines the rate of interest. The rate of interest, in turn, influences the rate of economic activity—especially in the sectors of investment, residential construction, and state and local government. An increase in the money supply will lower the rate of interest, and this will increase the rate of economic activity. A decrease of the money supply will raise the rate of interest, and a decrease in economic activity will result. The chain of events runs as follows:

Change in money supply $\longrightarrow$

Change in rate of interest $\longrightarrow$

Change in economic activity

We may also trace these developments graphically in a hypothetical example. Figure 14-3a shows the demand and supply for money

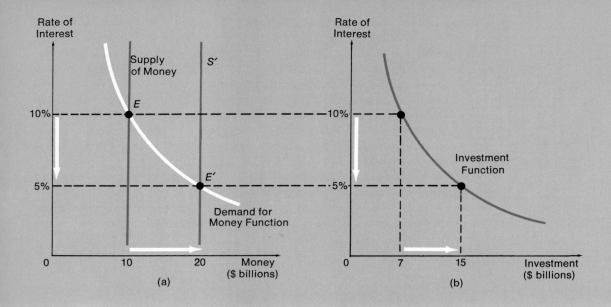

Figure 14-3

Money, interest, and economic activity *An increase in the money supply will tend to depress the rate of interest and the lower interest rate in turn will tend to stimulate economic activity.*

functions. Figure 14-3b depicts the investment function. Let us assume that the initial money supply is $10 billion, and that the economy is in equilibrium with an interest rate of 10 per cent and a rate of investment of $7 billion per annum. Now let the money supply increase from $10 billion to $20 billion. The money supply curve shifts to S', and the equilibrium point in the money market moves from E to E'. Consequently, the rate of interest will drop from 10 to 5 per cent. The effects of this lower interest rate can now be determined in the investment diagram of Figure 14-3b. At the 10 per cent interest rate, only $7 billion of investment projects are worthwhile. But as the interest rate falls to 5 per cent, more investment projects become lucrative and total investment rises to $15 billion.

We should not close this section without noting that the initial changes in spending, brought about by the change in the money supply and transmitted via the interest rate, may be magnified by the workings of the multiplier. The multiplier process was discussed in detail in the previous chapter. We found that any initial change in expenditures (which is not caused by a change in GNP itself) leads to an increase in income for other economic units and consequently their spending in turn increases. Further rounds of income and spending increases follow. The size of the multiplier depends crucially on the marginal propensity to spend—in our simple model the marginal propensity to consume out of additional income. The multiplier is equal to $1/(1 - MPC)$.

As the effects of fiscal policy (changes in government spending and taxation) on the rate of economic activity are magnified by the workings of the multiplier, so are the effects of monetary policy.

The control of the money supply

We have discussed (1) why individual economic units hold money, and (2) the role of the money supply in influencing the level of economic activity. The question that so far has remained unanswered is *how the money supply is controlled.* More precisely, we have to investigate how money is created in the modern United States economy, consider the role of commercial banks in the money-creating process, and show how the Federal Reserve—as the United States monetary authority—is able to control the money supply. To these questions we will turn next.

We stated already that there are three basic types of money in the modern United States economy: coin, paper currency, and demand deposits. Let us turn our attention to the last one of these three categories: demand deposits.

Commercial banks

Banks are in the business of making money in more than one sense: they produce money in the form of demand deposits, and like other private business firms, they are interested in making profits. This is the ultimate goal of the bank's behavior. Let us see how a typical bank will try to achieve this goal.

Commercial banks accept demand deposits from their customers. (They also accept time or savings deposits, but this is of no great importance to us at the moment, because time or savings deposits are not considered as money in our narrow definition. Savings deposits cannot be used to make payments or be transferred instantly by check.) The demand deposits of the customers are the bank's *liabilities.* What does the bank do with the money that it receives from its customers? If it places it all in a vault for safekeeping, the bank is not able to make any profits unless it charges its customers a fee for this safekeeping function. But the bank's customers are not so much interested in knowing that their money is physically present in the bank at all times as in having the assurance that they can withdraw the money if they should need it. This may be next week, or in a month, or in a year.

But the bank provides other services besides the safekeeping of funds to its customers. The main service that every commercial bank performs for its checking account customers is the clearing and collecting of checks. If you have to pay a bill to a merchant in a distant city, you merely send him a check. The recipient deposits this check in his own bank account. The commercial banks will do the rest by assuring that the funds will be properly transferred from your account to his. These services provided by the banks save you time, energy, and money. That's the main reason why you are willing to put your funds in a bank account—rather than placing them in a savings account or buying interest-yielding bonds.

There is no reason why all the funds deposited in checking accounts have to be held in cash by the bank. Few persons ever draw their funds completely out of the bank. Instead, they maintain a certain working balance in their account. And even if some people were to draw their accounts down to zero, chances are that not all people would do so at the same time. This fact is one of the bases of the functioning of the commercial banking system.

Because not all funds are withdrawn from the bank at the same time, the bank can utilize some of the funds deposited by its customers. The two basic uses to which commercial banks can put the funds in their custody are (1) purchases of *securities*, including United States government bonds, and (2) *loans* made to private individuals or firms. The bank lends the funds to these customers in order to earn *interest*. The interest that is earned on the bank's security portfolio and its outstanding loans represents *income* to the bank. The securities that the bank holds as well as the IOU's signed by the persons to whom the bank lends money represent—in conjunction with its reserves in the form of cash deposits at a Federal Reserve Bank—the *assets* of the bank.

Now we are able to look at the bank's operation as a whole. The bank's *liabilities* are the deposits that have been made by the customers. These are the amounts that the bank owes to other people. In addition to the amounts the bank owes to its customers, the capital paid in by the owners of the bank counts as a liability. On the other side of the ledger sheet are the bank's *assets*. Here we find the IOU's that secure the loans made to borrowers, securities that the bank holds, and the bank's reserves held in cash or at the Federal Reserve Bank. Table 14-1 shows the assets and liabilities for all 13,687 commercial banks that were in existence in the United States on December 30, 1970.

Table 14-1 *Consolidated balance sheet of all 13,687 commerical banks at the end of 1970 (in billions of dollars)*

Assets		Liabilities	
Loans	$314	Deposits	$470
Securities	147	Owner's capital	43
Cash assets	87	Other	57
Other	22		
Total	$570	Total	$570

Source: *Federal Reserve Bulletin*

Multiple deposit money creation

Commercial banks are required by law to maintain a certain proportion of "reserves" against their outstanding demand-deposit liabilities. Both cash at hand and amounts that the bank has on deposit with the Federal Reserve count as legal reserves. Typically, these reserve requirements mandate the bank to hold somewhere between 10 and 20 per cent reserves against its demand deposits. The Federal Reserve has the power to set the reserve requirement for all member banks of the system.

The reserve requirements that are imposed upon the banks are important because they limit each bank's ability to lend funds to its customers. Consider the following example. Assume that you open a new checking account with a bank, and that you deposit $1,000 cash in your checking account. Also, let us assume that the bank must maintain a 20 per cent legal reserve against all demand deposits. This means that from the $1,000 deposited by you, $200 must be kept in cash in the bank's vault, or on deposit with a Federal Reserve Bank. The bank is free to do with the remaining $800 as it wishes (only subject to some general requirements imposed on banks, designed to minimize the riskiness of the bank's ventures). The bank may choose to lend the $800 to a customer who is asking for a loan. Typically, after the bank grants the loan, it will give a check for $800 to this borrower.

Now let us consider what happens to the $800 check that the borrower receives. Clearly, he will not just keep the check in his pocket—because he will have to pay interest on the $800 and this would probably be an unwise use of the borrowed money. Let us assume that he deposits the $800 check with some other bank. This second bank will now collect the funds from the first bank, which issued the check, and consequently the second bank will acquire $800 in cash or have its account with the Federal Reserve Bank credited by that amount. In either case, the second bank *gains* $800 in deposits.

What will the second bank do with these new funds? Again, it is obligated to hold 20 per cent in reserves, that is, $160. The other $640 may be lent out. If the bank lends the money out, the cycle will repeat itself. As long as nobody withdraws any *cash* from the banking system, each successive bank may engage in some new lending. In the process, new demand deposits are created, because funds lent out by one bank will be deposited in another bank's checking accounts.

Given a certain legal required reserve ratio, we are able to calculate the maximum amount of new demand deposits that may be created by this process. Table 14-2 shows some of the successive rounds that may take place. The maximum amount of additional demand deposits that can be created through this process is dependent on (1) the amount of the initial new deposit, and (2) the legal reserve requirements imposed on the bank. The smaller the legal reserve requirement, the larger the amount that each bank is able to lend out, and the greater, therefore, the funds that will be re-deposited into the banking system. It follows that each bank in the chain will gain deposits and, in turn, be able to lend out more funds. The multiple deposit creation will be larger, if the legal reserve requirements are smaller.

For instance, the initial new deposit of $1,000 may lead to a maximum of $10,000 in new demand deposits if the reserve requirements are 10 per cent. Only half that amount, i.e., $5,000 in new demand deposits could be created if the reserve requirements were 20 per cent instead. The deposit multiplier showing the maximum

Table 14-2 Multiple demand deposit creation (assuming a 20 percent legal reserve requirement)

Bank	New deposit	Possible loans	Required reserves
First bank	$1,000.00	$ 800.00	$ 200.00
Second bank	800.00	640.00	160.00
Third bank	640.00	512.00	128.00
Fourth bank	512.00	409.60	102.40
Fifth bank	409.60	327.68	81.92
Sixth bank	327.69	262.14	65.54
Seventh bank	262.14	209.71	52.43
Eighth bank	209.71	167.76	41.95
All other banks	838.87	671.11	167.76
Total	$5,000.00	$4,000.00	$1,000.00

multiple (of initial deposits) by which demand deposits can expand is given by the reciprocal of the legal reserve ratio.

We stated that the inverse of the required reserve ratio gives the maximum multiple by which demand deposits may expand after an initial new deposit. For instance, given a 20 per cent legally required reserve ratio, the new deposit will permit a five-fold expansion of the demand deposits at the most. Actually, the expansion may be less than that amount. This is because of the existence of two possible drains or leakages out of the deposits, loans, and redeposits chain. For one, funds may "leak" into cash. There may be some persons who do not redeposit with a bank the total funds borrowed. If some persons hold onto cash, the bank cannot lend out these funds, and the multiplier process described is interrupted. Second, the bank may not lend out all the funds it can legally lend out. For instance, if the bank that receives the initial deposit of $1,000 lends out only $500 instead of the legally permissible $800, it holds $300 in *excess reserves*. The amount held by banks in the form of excess reserves is similar to a leakage into cash in that it interrupts the workings of the multiple demand-deposit expansion process. While a multiple demand-deposit creation is possible if banks are required to hold legal reserves amounting to only a fraction of their demand deposits, there is no necessity for this to happen.

The Federal Reserve System

The Federal Reserve System was created by Congress in 1913 and it serves as the nation's central bank. As such, it is responsible for the nation's monetary policy, serves as a banker to the government, and fulfills several supervisory, regulatory, and banking functions for private commercial banks. In keeping with the federal structure of the United States government, the Federal Reserve System is composed of a network of twelve Federal Reserve Banks, which are headed by a seven-member Board of Governors of the Federal Reserve System appointed by the President. The Federal Reserve Banks are located in Boston, New York, Philadelphia, Cleveland, Richmond, Atlanta, Chicago, St. Louis, Minneapolis, Kansas City, Dallas, and San Francisco, while the Board of Governors meets in Washington, D.C.

Banker to the government The Federal Reserve System serves as banker to the government. The United States Treasury maintains accounts at all the Federal Reserve Banks, and federal funds are channeled through and disbursed by the Federal Reserve Banks. Also, the Federal Reserve System will sometimes purchase bonds issued by the United States Treasury and pay cash to the Treasury. These operations are of little interest to us, because they merely represent borrowing by one federal agency, the Treasury, from another federal agency, the Federal Reserve. This does not affect the money supply in the hands of the public in any direct way.

Banker for commercial banks   There are two main service functions that the Federal Reserve performs for commercial banks. First, the Federal Reserve Banks perform check clearing services for the private commercial banks. The Federal Reserve System acts as a central clearing house through which checks that are deposited with one commercial bank but written on another commercial bank are channeled. By providing one large clearing system, individual banks do not have to submit each check written on another bank to that bank for payment—an operation that would take much time and effort. Instead, the checks are simply turned over to the Federal Reserve Bank nearest the commercial bank and the Federal Reserve will do the collecting for the private bank. These transfers of funds from one commercial bank to another commercial bank are accomplished by crediting or debiting the individual bank's accounts at the Federal Reserve Bank.

Second, the Federal Reserve acts as a "lender of last resort" to commercial banks. If a commercial bank should experience an unexpected and large withdrawal of funds, it may not have enough cash at hand to honor this request. As we learned earlier, commercial banks must maintain certain legal minimum reserves. Any additional funds the bank will try to keep in interest-yielding securities and loans, so as to maximize its own profits. Hence an unexpected demand for a large sum of cash might catch the bank without sufficient cash at hand, or, in more technical terms, *illiquid*. In situations like these, the Federal Reserve Bank stands ready to act as a lender of last resort to the commercial bank. Of course, the Federal Reserve will charge interest for the funds provided. The rate that the Federal Reserve charges for this service is called the *discount rate*, and is changed from time to time. Clearly, the higher the discount rate, and thereby the higher the interest rate that the banks have to pay, the more reluctant will banks be to borrow funds from the Federal Reserve.

Regulator of the money supply   The Federal Reserve is the main regulator of the money supply in the United States. We learned why the money supply is such an important variable in the economic system, and how the quantity of money in circulation will affect the rate of economic activity. Basically, the more money is in circulation, the more people will spend and thereby exercise an expansionary influence on the economy. Whether this expansionary influence will lead to higher prices or an expansion of real output depends mainly on the circumstances in which the money supply is expanded. In times of full employment of all resources, an increase in the money supply may well be inflationary; while in times of underemployment, a similar increase in the quantity may lead to an increase in the rate of resource utilization, and thereby in the volume of output produced by the economy. Let us look at the role of the Federal Reserve as the regulator of the nation's money supply in greater detail.

Controlling the money supply

We stated earlier that there are three main components to the money supply of the nation: coin, currency, and demand deposits. All coins are produced and distributed by the United States Treasury Department. Currency used to be issued partly by the United States Treasury and partly by the Federal Reserve System. But nowadays currency consists almost exclusively out of Federal Reserve Notes. The total amount of currency in circulation is divided between the public at large and the commercial banks. The public holds currency for the transactions, precautionary, and speculative motives we discussed earlier. In addition, commercial banks hold currency as part of their reserves.

The currency held by the public is just what its name implies: money. But the currency held by commercial banks is more than that. It serves—as we have seen—as the base for the multiple expansion of the demand deposits. A cash deposit with a commercial bank will allow the banking system as a whole to expand demand deposits by a multiple of that amount.

How does the Federal Reserve control the total money supply? It has three main control instruments at its disposal: open market operations, reserve requirements, and the discount rate. Let us discuss each one of them in turn.

When the Federal Reserve engages in *open market operations*, it simply buys or sells government securities to the public. If the Federal Reserve sells government securities to private households, firms, or banks, it receives cash from the buyers of these securities. As private economic units pay money to the Federal Reserve, the total money supply in the hands of the public is *reduced*. Conversely, if the Federal Reserve wants to *expand* the money supply, it buys securities from the public, thereby pumping additional cash into the private sector.

The effect of open-market operations on the excess reserves that commercial banks hold above and beyond the legally required reserves is particularly important. By buying up these excess reserves through open-market operations, the Federal Reserve can directly influence the banks' ability to lend funds to its customers and thereby set a multiple demand-deposit creation process in motion.

The Federal Reserve's open-market operations are conducted by the Open Market Committee, which operates on behalf of the whole Federal Reserve system out of the offices of the New York Federal Reserve Bank. The Open Market Committee meets regularly and is composed of twelve members: the seven members of the Board of Governors and five out of the twelve presidents of the various Federal Reserve Banks.

Reserve requirements are imposed by the Federal Reserve on all member banks. These are the percentage of reserves that individual banks must hold in currency or on deposit with a Federal Reserve Bank against that bank's demand-deposit liabilities. The mechanism of multiple deposit expansion was discussed earlier in this chapter. What is important for our current discussion is how a change in reserve requirements will influence the quantity of money. Let us assume that reserve requirements are initially equal to 20 per cent of demand deposits. If banks hold a total of $100 billion in demand deposits, then they must hold $20 billion in reserves. Now let us assume that the Federal Reserve lowers the minimum reserve requirements from 20 per cent to 18 per cent. Immediately, commercial banks have excess reserves of $2 billion, because they now have to hold only $18 billion in reserve against $100 billion in demand deposits. So they are free to lend an additional $2 billion. But this is not where the story ends. The familiar money multiplier will magnify the expansion. Given the new reserve requirements of 18 per cent, the money multiplier is equal to 1/.18, or 5.55. Hence, the money supply can expand by 5.55 times $2 billion, or $11.1 billion. The *total* money supply in the form of demand deposits will then amount to $111.1 billion.

This result could also have been obtained by calculating directly the total amount of demand deposits that can be supported by $20 billion in reserves, given the reserve requirement of 18 per cent. An 18 per cent reserve requirement yields a money multiplier of 5.55, and hence the $20 billion in reserves are sufficient for (5.55 × $20 billion) $111.1 billion in demand deposits.

As the Federal Reserve lowers the reserve requirements, the money supply may *expand.* Conversely, if the Federal Reserve wishes to *contract* the money supply, it can do so by *raising* the reserve requirements.

Finally, the *discount rate* will influence the willingness of commercial banks to borrow funds from the Federal Reserve. The discount rate, or the rate of interest that commercial banks have to pay to the Federal Reserve for funds borrowed, represents a cost to individual commercial banks. If the cost of borrowing funds is high, banks will be more reluctant to borrow. Thus, if the Federal Reserve wants to discourage banks from borrowing, it raises the discount rate. This has a contractionary influence on the money supply. If the Federal Reserve follows the opposite policy, i.e., if it lowers the discount rate, banks will use their borrowing privileges more freely and therefore the lowering of the discount rate will have an expansionary influence on the money supply—and by this on the rate of economic activity.

Summary

☐ Money serves as a *unit of account,* a *medium of exchange,* and a *store of value.*

☐ Individual economic units hold money for *transactions* purposes, *precautionary* motives, and *speculation.*

☐ The demand for money on behalf of individual economic units generally increases as their *income* increases and as the rate of *interest* decreases.

☐ The Federal Reserve Banks and the commercial banks together determine the *money supply* in private nonbank circles.

☐ The demand and supply of money together determine the price of money: the *interest rate.*

☐ The rate of interest influences the *rate of economic activity* by making money "cheaper" or more "expensive" to borrowers.

☐ The money supply is *controlled* by the Federal Reserve Banks, but commercial banks play an important role in the money-creating process.

☐ By lending out part of the funds deposited by a bank's customers, a *multiple* expansion process of demand-deposit balances is possible. The legal reserve requirements set an *upper limit* of the money-creation process by the commercial banks.

□ The Federal Reserve acts as a *banker* for the government and the commercial banks. It is also the *regulator* of the money supply. The main control instruments at the disposal of the Federal Reserve are *open market operations, reserve requirements* imposed on commercial banks, and the *discount rate* (the rate of interest charged to banks for loans made to them by the Federal Reserve).

15

The international balance of payments

In Chapter 9 we looked at the composition of international trade. We analyzed the determinants of comparative advantage, and by this the foundations of the pattern of international trade. But so far we have not talked about the international sector of the economy from the aggregate viewpoint.

The market for foreign exchange

Whenever you buy a good that has been produced abroad, sell a commodity to a resident of a foreign country, send a present of a few dollars to a cousin in Europe, or invest in a foreign enterprise, your action will have repercussions on the foreign exchange market. When you buy a foreign product, say, a Porsche from Germany, you will want to pay for the car with the dollars you have earned here in the United States. But the German manufacturer of the car has to pay *his* workers and raw material suppliers with German marks. Two alternatives exist: either you go to your local bank and exchange your dollars for German marks, so that you can pay for your car in German currency, or you pay dollars to Porsche and the firm will go to the bank and exchange the dollars for German marks. In either case, a bank or foreign exchange dealer will be asked to change the dollars for German marks. Put into more technical language, as a result of your buying the Porsche, there will be a supply of United States dollars and a demand for German marks.

Each time an American buys a foreign product, he will supply dollars and demand foreign currency in exchange. The same is true if you send a money present to a friend in another country. Your friend will want to use his own local currency, and if you send him United States dollars, he will sell these dollars to a foreign exchange dealer or a bank and receive his own country's currency in exchange. Alternatively, you could send him a present in his own currency.

Besides goods, services and gifts, there exists an important third category of international transactions: transactions in foreign assets such as stocks and bonds. When you purchase a foreign stock, giving you partial ownership in a foreign enterprise, you will want to pay for the foreign stock with United States dollars. But the foreigner who sells the stock to you wants to be paid in his own local currency. So there will again be a supply of United States dollars and a demand for foreign currency.

The aggregate supply and demand for foreign currency which results from all international transactions is shown in Figure 15-1. Along the horizontal axis we measure the amount of foreign currency which is supplied or demanded. Along the vertical axis we measure the price of foreign currency. The price of a unit of foreign currency is simply the amount of dollars we have to pay in order to acquire one German mark, one French franc, or a British pound. In previous chapters we used to plot the prices of automobiles or pizza along the vertical axis; now we simply plot the price of a unit of foreign exchange. There is another name for the price of a foreign currency, which is widely used: the *exchange rate*. The exchange rate is nothing but the dollar price you have to pay for one unit of foreign currency.

The supply and demand curves for foreign exchange are *derived* supply and demand curves. They are derived from the underlying supply and demand curves for goods and services and financial assets.

Figure 15-1

The foreign exchange market
The exchange rate shows the dollar price that we have to pay for a unit of foreign currency. It is determined by the supply and demand for foreign exchange.

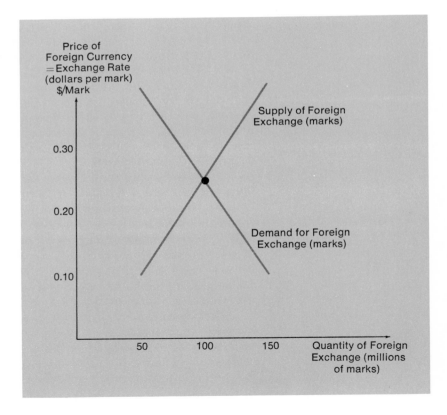

Let us discuss briefly the shape of the supply and demand curves for foreign exchange and see how they relate to the supply of and demand for real goods and services or investments.

The *demand for foreign exchange* is due to our desire to import, give foreign aid or presents, and acquire foreign stocks and bonds. If the exchange rate is very high, that is, if we have to pay a high dollar price for each unit of foreign exchange, the quantity of foreign goods demanded and the attractiveness of foreign investments will be small. This is because the exchange rate has just as much an effect on the dollar price of a foreign good as the price charged by the manufacturer. If, for instance, the price of one German mark is 25 cents, a Porsche that has a price tag in Germany of 12,000 marks will sell in the United States for $3,000. If the exchange rate were to rise, because of an appreciation of the German mark, to 30 cents per mark, the United States price of the Porsche would increase to $4,000. At that higher price you might no longer be interested in buying a Porsche, and therefore the amount of foreign exchange demanded might be *less* at that higher exchange rate.

The same will hold true for foreign investments. An investment will become less and less attractive, the higher the price you have to pay for it. A bargain at a low exchange rate may no longer look profitable if the exchange rate goes up. Hence the demand curve for foreign exchange will slope downward to the right—just like any other demand curve.

The *supply of foreign exchange* is caused by foreigners' purchases of American goods and services, their gifts to us, and foreign investments in the United States. The reasoning is analogous to that used when discussing the demand for foreign exchange, only with the roles reversed.

Foreigners will want to acquire more dollars—and thereby *supply* their own currency in international currency markets—when American goods and investments look cheap to them. American goods are inexpensive in the eyes of foreigners when they receive a large number of dollars (and thereby United States purchasing power) for each unit of foreign exchange. The higher the exchange rate of dollars to marks, the more American goods foreigners will purchase, and the more investments they will want to make. In the process, they will supply foreign exchange. This is why the supply curve of foreign exchange of Figure 15-1 slopes upward to the right.

The balance of payments

All pertinent data on international transactions are recorded in the *balance of payments* accounts. The balance of payments accounts are an extension of the regular national income accounts that we discussed in Chapter 10. All transactions involving domestic residents and foreign economic units are recorded in the balance of payments accounts in the customary double-entry bookkeeping fashion. Because every transaction involves two entries, it is clear that the total of all credit entries must be equal to the total of all debit entries at all times. In an accounting sense, the balance of payments must always be in balance.

Table 15-1 shows the United States balance of payments for the year 1970. All entries that represent a supply of foreign currency

Table 15-1 *United States balance of payments, 1970 (billions of dollars)*

Account	Receipts (supply of foreign currency)	Payments (demand for foreign currency	Balance
Goods and services account			
1. Merchandise trade	+42.0	−39.9	
2. Military transactions	+ 1.5	− 4.9	
3. Travel and transportation	+ 6.0	− 8.0	
4. Investment income	+11.4	− 5.2	
5. Other services	+ 2.1	− 1.5	
BALANCE ON GOODS AND SERVICES			+3.5
Transfer account			
6. Private transfers, net		− .9	
7. U.S. government transfers		− 2.2	
BALANCE ON CURRENT ACCOUNT			+ .4
Capital account			
8. Direct investment	+ 1.0	− 4.4	
9. Other private non-liquid capital	+ 3.8	− 2.3	
10. U.S. government capital flows	+ .2	− 2.3	
11. Allocations of SDR's	+ .9		
12. Errors and omissions		− 1.1	
BALANCE ON LIQUIDITY BASIS			− 3.8
13. Liquid private capital	+ .2	− 6.2	
BALANCE ON OFFICIAL SETTLEMENTS BASIS			− 9.8
14. Liabilities to foreign official agencies	+ 7.3		
Official reserve account			
15. U.S. gold holdings*	+ .8		
16. Foreign exchange holdings*	+ 2.2		
17. International Monetary Fund*	+ .4		
18. Special Drawing Rights		− .9	
ACCOUNTING BALANCE			0.0

* Plus entry denotes decrease in U.S. holdings of reserve assets.
Source: "The U.S. Balance of Payments: Revised Presentation," *Survey of Current Business*, June, 1971.

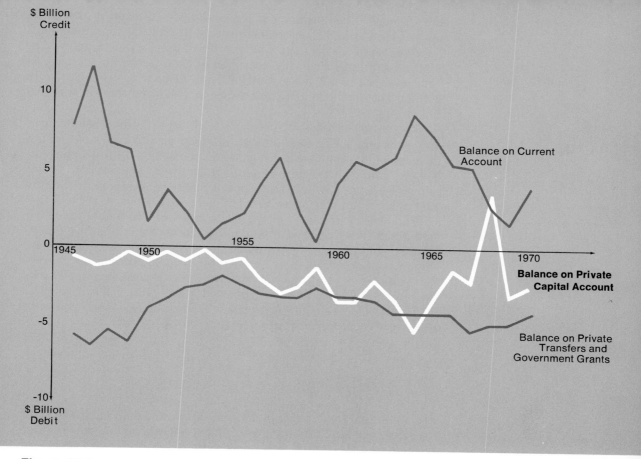

$ Billion
Credit

10

5

0

1945   1950   1955   1960   1965   1970

Balance on Current
Account

**Balance on Private
Capital Account**

-5

Balance on Private
Transfers and
Government Grants

-10
$ Billion
Debit

Figure 15-2

The international accounts
*During most of the post
World War II period the
United States has had a
surplus on current account
and a deficit on the transfer
and capital accounts.*

Source: Council of Economic Advisors

are booked as credits, while all entries that constitute a demand for foreign currency are booked as debits. For instance, a demand for foreign currency (resulting in *debit* entries in the United States balance of payments) will be the result of (1) imports of foreign goods by Americans, as well as travel expenses incurred by Americans abroad; (2) the sending of remittances to friends abroad or the payment of pensions to Americans living abroad; (3) the purchase of foreign property, stocks, and bonds by Americans. Any item that results in a payment to a foreigner will result—sooner or later—in an increase in the demand for foreign currency, simply because we will have to pay to the foreigner in his own currency. Conversely, any action by foreigners that will increase their demand for *our* goods, services, or assets will result in a supply of foreign currency to us and will be booked as a *credit* entry.

For convenience purposes, the international transactions discussed are grouped in the balance of payments presentation in the goods and services account, the transfer account, and the capital account. The *goods and services account* records all transactions in merchandise, all foreign travel, the provision of transportation services, as well as fees and royalties received from or paid to economic units abroad. The net United States balance in goods and services was $3.5 billion in 1970.

The *transfer account* summarizes all international remittances and pensions. Gifts sent abroad, military grants made to foreign governments, economic aid payments, pensions paid to former employees now residing abroad, and similar items are recorded in the transfer account. In 1970, the United States showed a net deficit on this account amounting to $3.1 billion.

The *capital account* records all transactions in assets involving foreigners. The purchase of land abroad, acquisition of a foreign enterprise, and the buying of foreign stocks or securities all involve no shipment of physical assets across international borders, but merely the transfer of titles of ownership.* The capital account (omitting lines 11-12 in Table 15-1) showed a $2.7 billion deficit in 1970.

The development of the various balance of payments accounts since 1946 is shown in Figure 15-2.

Exchange rates and reserves

Let us assume for a moment that the supply and demand for foreign exchange arising from the goods and services account, the transfer account, and the capital account is initially balanced at an exchange rate of 25 cents per German mark. Let us assume further that the German mark is the only foreign currency in which transactions are conducted.

Now consider what happens if Americans want to import more German cars or undertake more investments in Germany because they expect a higher rate of return on their investments there. Clearly, the demand for foreign currency, i.e., German marks, will increase. The whole demand schedule for German marks shifts to the right. Given an unchanged supply schedule, the exchange rate (the price of foreign currency in dollar terms) will tend to increase. In the example provided by Figure 15-3, the new equilibrium exchange will be 30 cents per German mark. This amounts to an *appreciation*

---

*Actually, the use of the term "capital account" in the balance of payments is somewhat unfortunate, because we might easily confuse it with the term "capital," which was used to refer to all man-made resources. It would have been less confusing if the account had been named the "foreign assets" account.

Figure 15-3

Disequilibrium in the international accounts *If the demand for foreign exchange is as shown by D', there exists an excess demand for foreign exchange at the exchange rate of 25¢ per mark. The monetary authorities may eliminate the excess demand by selling foreign exchange—i.e., drawing down their international reserves.*

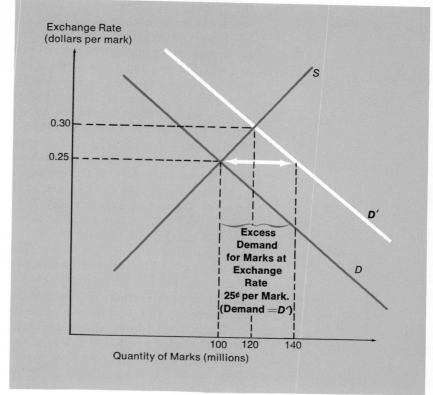

of the value of the German mark—viewed from the United States vantage point—or a *depreciation* of the United States dollar—viewed from the German vantage point. (For Germans the dollar has become cheaper in terms of marks.)

If exchange rates are free to respond to free market forces, this is indeed what will happen. The exchange rate will adjust and at the new equilibrium exchange rate the quantities of foreign currency supplied and demanded will again be equal to each other. The value of a few of the world's currencies is determined in such free markets, and other countries have from time to time experimented with free exchange rates.

Foreign exchange rates are a very important economic variable for a nation in that they determine the competitive position of the whole country vis-à-vis the outside world. Therefore, the policy makers of most countries attempt to control the exchange rate. One argument used to justify government stabilization of the exchange rate is that an exchange rate that fluctuates widely from day to day or month to month introduces additional elements of instability into the economy. By intervening in the foreign exchange markets, governments are able to stabilize the exchange rate and thereby make life easier for exporters, importers, bankers, and others involved in international transactions. Instead of having to adjust on a daily basis to exchange rate fluctuations, these businessmen are now in a position to use one fixed exchange rate for their calculations.

How does the government stabilize the exchange rate? It does so by direct intervention in the foreign exchange market. For instance, in our previous example, which started with an exchange rate of 25 cents per German mark, the increase in the demand for German marks will lead to an excess demand, or a shortage of German marks at that exchange rate. If the exchange rate is left free to respond to market forces, the excess demand will lead to an increase in the price of German marks. But instead of permitting this to happen, the United States monetary authorities can sell an amount of German marks just sufficient to fill the excess-demand gap. Using the example of Figure 15-2, the United States monetary authorities must sell 40 million German marks to eliminate the excess demand that prevails at the old exchange rate. By providing the market with these additional German marks, the excess demand is eliminated, and the exchange rate will remain at 25 cents per German mark.

The United States monetary authorities simply sell 40 million German marks, which they are holding as part of their *international reserves* in the foreign exchange market. International reserves are those funds that are available to the monetary authorities for direct intervention in the foreign exchange markets. At present, international reserves consist of the following four components: gold, foreign exchange holdings, the "Reserve Positions" with the International Monetary Fund (IMF), and any IMF Special Drawing Rights (SDR) that the particular country might own. Let us look in turn at each of these components of international reserves. (See also Table 15-1.)

Gold Gold is the oldest and most traditional component of international reserves. Because of its wide and ready acceptability by private individuals and governments all over the world, gold has for a long time occupied a key position on the international monetary scene. Gold could be bought and sold easily at a predetermined value, and it was therefore valued by central banks as a reserve asset.

However, since August 15, 1971 the United States no longer stands ready to convert dollars against gold at a fixed rate. Consequently, we might expect that the role of gold as an international reserve asset will decline in the years to come.

Foreign exchange Other country's currencies are held—alongside gold—by the monetary authorities for intervention in the foreign exchange market. For instance, if the United States monetary authorities hold German marks, they can sell these German marks in times of United States balance of payments deficits and thereby prevent a change in the exchange rate. Customarily, central banks hold only a few particularly strong *key currencies* because of their wide acceptability in world financial markets. The United States dollar and the British pound have traditionally served this role, but recently also German marks, French francs, and some other selected currencies have been added to the portfolios of the various central banks.

IMF reserve position   The International Monetary Fund (IMF) was formed in 1944 to help central banks to finance temporary balance of payments disequilibria. The IMF is essentially a world-wide credit union for central banks. Upon becoming a member, the country joining the IMF is assigned a quota, which is set according to a formula taking into account the economic importance of the country, its trade volume, and a number of other factors determining its balance of payments position. The country then pays to the IMF an amount equivalent to its quota (25 per cent of which must be paid in gold, the remainder in the country's own currency). In turn, the IMF will lend foreign currency to the country if this should be necessary to maintain a stable exchange rate. The first borrowings by a country are approved automatically, but further borrowings are often "conditional" in that the IMF requires that the country take certain corrective measures. The maximum amount that a country may borrow under any circumstances amounts to twice the amount of the quota assigned to the country. The amount of the country's unused automatic borrowing rights is called its *Reserve Position.*

IMF special drawing rights   Special Drawing Rights (SDR's) were made available by the IMF to all member countries effective January 1, 1970. SDR's are different from the regular quota in that the SDR's are a new international means of payments that has been *created* by the IMF, whereas the funds available to a member country under the regular system are merely re-lent by the IMF. Because countries contribute to the IMF in the form of quota payments upon joining, the IMF is able to re-lend these funds to other member countries. The SDR's are different, because they represent a genuine *new* asset, created by the IMF, which is made available to member countries without forcing them to make any initial payments to the fund.

Together, a country's gold, its foreign exchange holdings, its IMF Reserve Position, and its SDR holdings comprise the nation's international reserves. To hold international reserves is a costly endeavor:

resources that could be invested productively are held in the form of liquid assets that yield little or no interest. These *costs* of holding international reserves have to be balanced—at the margin—against the *benefits* derived from the international reserves. What are those benefits of holding international reserves? They can be found in the *avoidance of adjustment costs* that would otherwise be imposed upon us. We will analyze these later in greater detail.

Deficits and surpluses

Let us return to Figure 15-3, which shows the U.S. economy's supply and demand for foreign exchange. Initially the equilibrium exchange rate is at 25 cents per German mark. After the demand for German marks increases, there will be an excess demand for German marks of $40 million at the old exchange rate. We will refer to this discrepancy as the balance of payments imbalance—here, the balance of payments *deficit*. To repeat: the balance of payments deficit is defined as the excess demand for foreign exchange that prevails at the going exchange rate. Conversely, a balance of payments *surplus* is the excess supply of foreign exchange that exists at the going exchange rate.

In our example, the monetary authorities recognize that there is an excess demand for foreign exchange amounting to $40 million. By supplying $40 million from its own international reserve holdings the excess demand is eliminated and the exchange rate will remain where it is—at 25 cents per German mark.

Now we are in a position to understand the function of the official reserves account in the balance of payments (see Table 15-1). Changes in the official reserves reflect any excess demand or supply for foreign exchange that existed at the going exchange rate and that had to be financed by the monetary authorities. If there is a deficit in the sum of the transactions on the goods and services, transfer, and capital accounts, this means that there exists an excess demand for foreign exchange, and the monetary authorities must meet this demand by selling international reserves if they want to maintain a fixed exchange rate. Consequently, international reserves will fall. If there is a surplus on the first three accounts, there exists an excess supply of foreign exchange. The monetary authority will buy up this excess supply of foreign exchange (to keep the exchange rate constant) and consequently international reserves will decrease. In 1970 our reserves (Table 15, lines 11, 15–18) decreased by $3.4 billion.

There is one additional problem that we have to take into account. We argued that the changes in our own international reserve holdings reflect the excess demand or supply of foreign exchange that exists. Not only our own monetary authorities but also the central banks of other countries may desire to keep their exchange rate constant. Thus there will not only be intervention in the foreign exchange market on behalf of the United States but also by other countries. If, for instance, there exists an excess *demand* for German marks from *our* viewpoint, there will be an excess *supply* of United States dollars from the *German* viewpoint. If the German central bank wants to keep the mark from appreciating, it will attempt to eliminate the excess supply of United States dollars. It can do so by buying up these dollars and adding them to Germany's international reserves. Hence not only changes in the United States international reserves, but also changes in the United States dollar holdings of foreign central banks reflect official intervention in the foreign exchange market. Foreign official holders increased their dollar balances by $7.3 billion in 1970.

The *official settlements balance* gives an indication of the aggregate amount of official market intervention that was required during the period to keep the exchange rate from changing. Hence, if we add up all accounts in the balance of payments (Table 15-1, lines 1–13), except those accounts representing official intervention in the foreign exchange market by foreign (line 14) and United States authorities (lines 15-18), we obtain a measure of the deficit that would have prevailed at the going exchange rate in the absence of official intervention.

But some economists and government officials have argued that the official settlements balance may be unduly influenced by erratic short-term capital flows to which a widely used currency like the U.S. dollar is especially exposed. For instance, the U.S. liquid liabilities account changed from a surplus of $8.6 billion in 1969 to a deficit of $6.2 billion in 1970. To make long-term economic policy on the basis of such erratic shifts is hazardous at best. Hence, a measure which focuses on the long term underlying changes in the balance of payments is called for. Such a measure is the *liquidity balance* (see Table 15-1), which summarizes the goods and services account, the transfer account, and the capital account except private liquid capital and the official reserve transactions.

For countries whose currency is not widely held abroad—either by private persons or by public institutions—there is little difference between the official settlements balance and the liquidity balance. Most of the world's nations are in this category. Only for those countries whose currencies play an important role on the international monetary scene, like the U.S. dollar and the British pound, will there be a significant difference between the two measures.

But even these two balances do not tell the whole story about a

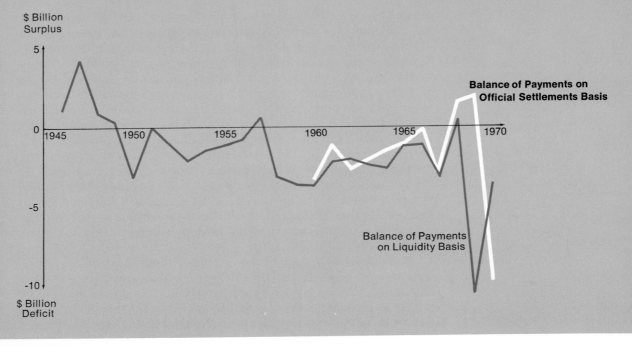

$ Billion
Surplus

5

0

1945   1950   1955   1960   1965   1970

**Balance of Payments on
Official Settlements Basis**

-5

Balance of Payments
on Liquidity Basis

-10

$ Billion
Deficit

Figure 15-4

The balance of payments *The
balance of payments deficit
according to the official
settlements basis is defined
as the change in our
reserves plus the change in
all foreign official dollar
holdings. The liquidity basis
measures the deficit as the
change in our reserves plus
the change in all liquid
dollar holdings (public
and private).*

Source: Council of Economic Advisors

country's international economic position. Other balances are important, too. For instance, if we are interested in the net effect of foreign
transactions on our GNP, we will focus on the *balance on goods and
services* (see Table 15-1). This balance measures the foreign trade
components of the national product and shows the net export of goods
and services to and from the United States.

The *balance on current account* shows, in addition, the effect of
unilateral transfers. All transactions which are recorded "below" the
current account balance represent changes in the international investment position of the United States. To focus attention on one
measure of the balance of payments may be seriously misleading.
All the measures must be taken together to give a true picture of
the international position of a country.

Relative price adjustments

A country that experiences an excess demand for foreign exchange
at the current exchange rate may elect to *adjust* to the imbalance,

instead of *financing* it by the use of reserves. Three main adjustment alternatives open to a country will be discussed here. They are relative price adjustments, exchange rate adjustments, and income adjustments. We will start with relative price adjustments.

Let us assume that there exists an excess demand for foreign exchange. That is, at the going exchange rate domestic residents want to import more goods from abroad than foreigners want to purchase from us. (We will assume in the remainder of this chapter that the goods and services account is the only one that matters. The transfer account and capital account are assumed to be unaffected by the policies undertaken.) One way to make our goods more attractive to foreigners, and thereby boost our exports, is to lower the price that we are charging for our goods. This will not only induce foreigners to purchase more goods from us—thereby boosting the supply of foreign exchange—but also make domestically produced goods more attractive to our own residents. Our own residents will purchase more domestic goods and fewer foreign goods, which will decrease our demand for foreign exchange. Consequently, the supply curve for foreign exchange in Figure 15-5 shifts to the right and the demand curve for foreign exchange shifts to the left, and the balance of payments deficit (excess demand for foreign exchange) that prevailed at the exchange rate r_0 will eventually disappear.

An automatic mechanism that provides for the kind of relative

Figure 15-5

The effect of price changes *A lowering of our domestic price level will decrease the demand for foreign exchange and increase the supply of foreign exchange, thereby eliminating a balance of payments deficit that might have existed at the going exchange rate.*

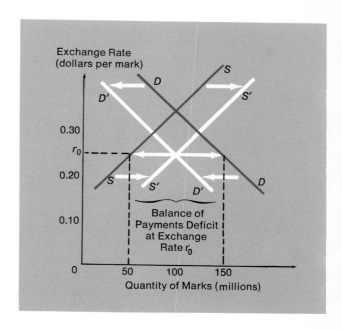

price adjustment discussed here is given by the *classical gold standard*. Balance of payments adjustment operates theoretically in the following manner under the gold standard. First of all, all exchange rates are permanently *fixed*. Second, each country's currency consists of *gold* or gold-backed paper money. Third, prices and wages are assumed to be *flexible* in the upward and downward direction. Now let us assume that the United States experiences a balance of payments deficit. This means that we are buying more goods from abroad than foreigners are purchasing from us. As we pay more to foreigners than they pay to us, a net outflow of gold will take place. The gold outflow, in turn, represents a reduction in our money supply and an increase in the foreign money supply. As our money supply is reduced, people have less money to spend and prices will fall. In the foreign country, the gold inflow means that people's money balances are increased, leading to increased spending and a consequent inflation of the price level. Our prices are falling and foreign prices are rising, and as consumers react to these relative price changes, they will buy more from us and less from foreigners, thereby eliminating the balance of payments deficit.

Preconditions for the functioning of the classical gold standard are (1) that prices and wages are flexible, and (2) that the monetary authorities will sit still while the money supply of the economy changes because of the perhaps fortuitous changes in the international accounts. Neither condition is likely to be satisfied in a modern economy. One reason is that prices and wages are relatively inflexible in a downward direction. Monopoly power exerted on behalf of large industrial firms and unions prevents prices from falling even if there should be an excess supply. Output rather than price is likely to decrease first in response to a reduction in demand. Hence the desired relative price changes may not materialize for quite some time. A second reason is that the monetary authorities will probably be unwilling to let the money supply react exclusively to the developments of the international sector. Instead, central bankers try to tailor the money supply to the overall needs of the economy. The present state of the domestic economy has a powerful influence on the decisions made by the monetary authorities, and it is rare indeed that balance of payments considerations are given priority over domestic needs. Consequently, while the gold standard is a nice theoretical model, its practical importance in modern economies is minimal.

We should also note that there are costs associated with the change in the relative prices. As our domestic prices fall, foreigners are able to acquire our goods more cheaply. At the same time, we have to pay higher prices for the foreign goods we import. Thus our purchas-

ing power in terms of foreign commodities is likely to be reduced.*
We are therefore worse off than we were at the old prices—we have
to bear an adjustment cost.

Exchange rate adjustments

A second way in which the relative attractiveness of foreign and
domestic goods may be changed is by allowing exchange rates to
respond to changes in supply and demand. This case was discussed
earlier in this chapter. By allowing the exchange rate to change the
relative attractiveness of foreign and domestic goods is altered, and
the balance of payments imbalances that would exist at the old
exchange rate are eliminated.

We stated that businessmen and bankers are fearful of the additional uncertainty that is created by the exchange rate changes, but
it is difficult to assess the validity of this claim in the absence of
reliable empirical evidence. It may be that exchange rate changes
are so smooth and gradual that the fluctuations are hardly felt.
Several nations adopted flexible exchange rates in 1971 and their
experience will add to our knowledge about free foreign exchange
markets.

We should also not forget that exchange rate changes will be
accompanied by the same kind of relative price effects as we discussed
in connection with the gold standard. As the relative price of domestic
and foreign commodities changes as a result of changes in the exchange rate, the purchasing power of our currency changes in terms
of foreign goods. If you never buy a foreign product, or a product
produced with foreign raw materials, and if you never take a vacation
abroad, you will probably hardly be affected by a change in the
exchange rate. But if you do, the exchange rate changes have a
powerful influence on your purchasing power. If the dollar's value
declines in relation to foreign currencies, all foreign goods become
more expensive, while we give away our own product at a lower price.
The real exchange ratio of domestic to foreign products is likely to
turn against us. Conversely, if the dollar appreciates in relation to
the foreign currencies, the purchasing power of the dollar abroad is
boosted, and we are likely to be better off.

---

*However, there are some rare circumstances in which this statement does not
hold true. This is the case if the demand curves are all highly inelastic while at the
same time the supply curves are highly elastic. The practical importance of this
theoretical possibility is probably small.

Income adjustments

Finally, there exists a rather drastic adjustment method to external imbalances: income adjustments. Again let us assume that we face a balance of payments deficit, or an excess demand for foreign exchange. One way to eliminate this excess demand is by instituting fiscal and monetary policies that bring about a domestic depression. As soon as income levels drop off at home, Americans are much less likely to buy an expensive Ferrari or go on a leisurely vacation to Europe. As aggregate demand at home is depressed, the demand for foreign goods and services will be reduced too. Consequently, the demand for foreign exchange will decrease and the balance of payments deficit at the going exchange rate will be eliminated. In terms of Figure 15-6, the lowering of the income level at home will bring about a leftward shift of the demand curve for foreign exchange, thereby eliminating the balance of payments deficit at the exchange rate r_0. This is certainly a very drastic and expensive method of eliminating a deficit, and only when compelling reasons force its use will a country be willing to bear the costs associated with this policy.

Figure 15-6

The effect of income changes *A reduction in our income level will decrease the demand for foreign goods and services and thereby decrease the demand for foreign exchange. A deficit existing at the exchange rate r_0 will be eliminated in our example.*

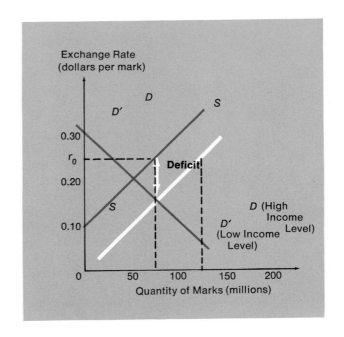

Summary

□ All international transactions are summarized in the nation's *balance of payments* accounts.

□ International transactions in goods and services, international transfers, and purchases or sales of foreign assets will result in a *supply and demand for foreign exchange*.

□ The *demand* for foreign exchange—resulting in *debit* entries in our balance of payments—results from our *purchases* of foreign goods and services, transfer payments *to* foreigners, and the *acquisition* of foreign assets.

□ Foreign exchange will be *supplied*—and booked as *credit* entries in the balance of payments—when we *sell* goods and services to foreigners, receive transfers *from* them, or when there are *foreign* purchases of domestic assets.

□ The aggregate of all desired credit transactions and all desired debit transactions *at a certain exchange rate* may not match. In that case, excess supplies or demands for foreign exchange will tend to change the exchange rate—if the exchange rate is free to respond to market forces.

□ The balance of payments *deficit* (surplus) is measured by the *excess demand for* (supply of) *foreign exchange* prevailing at the *going* exchange rate.

□ The monetary authorities of most countries attempt to *stabilize* the exchange rate by official intervention. This official *intervention* takes the form of sales or purchases of foreign exchange, thereby eliminating the excess demand or supply of foreign currency.

□ In the case of a balance of payments *deficit*, the monetary authorities will make up the excess demand for foreign exchange by *reducing* their own *international reserves*. They will increase their reserves as a consequence of an excess supply of foreign exchange.

□ *International reserves* consist of gold and foreign exchange reserves held by the monetary authorities, as well as the resources available from the International Monetary Fund through the "regular" and "special" drawing rights.

□ Alternatives to the *financing* of international payments imbalances are provided by *adjustment* to the disequilibrium.

□ Adjustment to the disequilibrium may be achieved by *relative price level adjustments*, a system that was provided for by the automatic gold standard mechanism of the last decades of the nineteenth century.

□ Adjustments may take the form of *exchange rate changes*, thereby eliminating any excess supplies or demands that would exist at other exchange rates.

□ Adjustments may be made in the *income level*, in order to influence aggregate demand for commodities, thereby also influencing the demand for foreign commodities.

□ All adjustments to balance of payments deficits are costly. The *costs of adjustment* have to be weighed against the *costs of holding international reserves*.

16

The economic system

We have studied the functioning of the economic system in detail, and this chapter will serve as a convenient summary—designed to pull the many threads together and to show the economic system as one coherent whole.

Scarcity and choice

The basic economic problem of *scarcity* emerges because we do not have enough resources at our disposal to produce all the commodities that people desire to satisfy their wants. While there are perhaps a few items, such as salty ocean water, for which the available supply exceeds the quantity demanded, these examples of free goods are few indeed. Furthermore, given our expanding world population, more and more commodities that used to be in plentiful supply are now becoming scarce: fresh river water and clean air are two obvious examples.

As long as our resources are not sufficient to satisfy all wants, scarcity will be with us, and we will be forced to *choose* between alternatives—not all of which can be attained. The choice process is central to the economic system. Different economic systems may be characterized by the type of choice that is dominating: are choices made in the market place, by some administrator, or are they made in accordance with tradition? In the modern American economy, we find elements of all these choice processes, but among them the market system is dominant. Hence we will be concerned with the market as a central institution of the economy.

The market

Transactions between buyers and sellers are conducted in the market. It is here that commodities are traded. The price acts as a regulator of the quantities that are offered for sale by sellers and that are demanded by buyers.

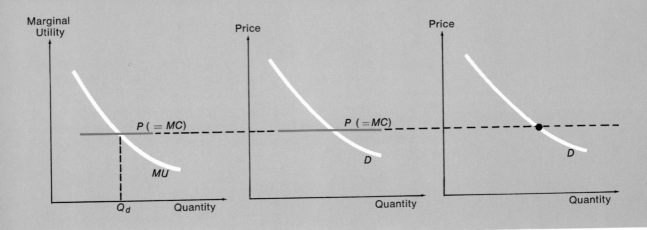

Figure 16-1

Individual utility

Figure 16-2

Individual demand

Figure 16-3

Market demand

From the individual's marginal utility curve we can derive his demand curve for a product. Then we can aggregate all individual demand curves to obtain the market demand curve.

Demand

We assume that consumers maximize their satisfaction or utility subject to an income constraint. If the income constraint does not exist, consumers have essentially unlimited resources to satisfy their wants, and the problem of scarcity does not exist for them. But given the income constraint, consumers will allocate their limited funds in a way that will maximize their satisfaction.

The satisfaction derived from the last additional unit of a commodity purchased is called the marginal utility obtained. In general, the marginal utility decreases as additional units are purchased. The consumer maximizes his satisfaction by purchasing that quantity of a commodity at which the marginal utility is just equal to the price which he has to pay. In Figure 16-1 we show the marginal utility curve for pizza on behalf of one individual consumer. In the same figure we also show the price of pizza. In order to show marginal utility and dollar prices in the same graph, we select the marginal utility units in such a way that one utility unit equals exactly one dollar. Given a certain price for pizza, the consumer will purchase all pizzas for which the marginal utility is greater than the price. That is, he will purchase Q_d pizzas in our example. If he would buy fewer pizzas, he would be able to increase his total satisfaction by purchasing more: the marginal utility of additional pizzas is greater than the price he has to pay. Were he to buy more than Q_d pizzas, the pizzas would yield him less utility than the money he has to pay for them. At Q_d, the additional utility gained is just equal to the price paid. No reshuffling of resources can increase his satisfaction. Given the price P, the consumer will demand Q_d pizzas, where his marginal utility is equal to the marginal cost (= price) paid: $MU = MC(= P)$.

The marginal utility curve can be translated into a *demand curve* for pizzas, which shows the quantity demanded at various prices. Such a demand curve for pizza on behalf of an individual consumer is shown in Figure 16-2.

There remains the task of aggregating all the individual demand curves to form the *market demand curve*. To do this we merely add the quantities of pizza demanded by all the individual consumers at each and every possible price. In this fashion we obtain the aggregate market demand curve for pizza shown in Figure 16-3.

Supply

Turning to the theory of production, we first identify the firm as the basic unit of production. It is the goal of the firm to maximize profits. As a production unit the firm combines various inputs or resources to produce outputs or commodities.

The technological relationship between inputs and outputs is described by the *production function*. The production function shows how many physical units of inputs are required to produce a given number of output units. A typical production function is shown in Figure 16-4.

From the production function we are able to derive a *total cost curve* for the firm that shows the dollar cost of producing any given quantity of output. We must be careful to include in our cost calculations not only the *explicit* dollar costs incurred, but also the *implicit* cost of resources for which no formal payment has to be made. The use of every resource entails opportunity costs—representing the alternatives that have to be forgone. A typical total cost curve for a firm is depicted in Figure 16-5.

From the total cost curve we derive the marginal and average cost curves. The marginal cost curve shows the additional cost incurred by the production of one more unit of output. It shows the additional cost as more output is produced, or, in other words, the incremental costs.

This part of the theory of the firm—describing the relationship

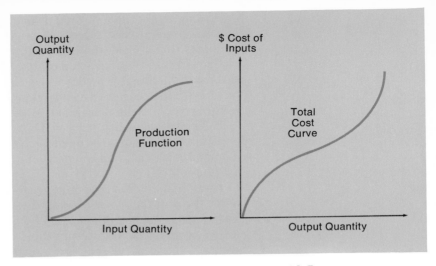

Figure 16-4

The production function

Figure 16-5

The total cost function

The production function shows the technological relationship between physical inputs and outputs. By calculating the costs of all the inputs, we can derive from it a total cost curve. (Note that the axes are reversed.)

between the production function and the various cost curves—is the same for all firms. While the underlying cost curves may be the same, firms differ in the type of market environment in which they have to sell their commodities. We distinguish four main categories of markets: perfectly competitive markets, monopolistically competitive markets, oligopolistic markets, and monopolistic markets.

Perfectly competitive markets

Perfectly competitive markets are characterized by a large number of participants, free entry and exit, independent decision making, and homogeneous products. Because individual economic units have only an insignificant share of the market, and perfect substitutes are available, no individual unit has any control over the market price: all perfect competitors are *price takers*.

A perfectly competitive firm is able to sell all it wants to sell at a given market price: it faces a perfectly elastic demand curve (*D*) in Figure 16-6. In conjunction with the information on its own marginal cost, the firm decides how much to produce. Profits will be

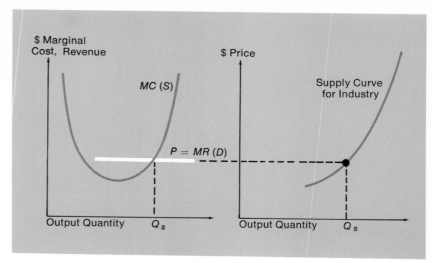

Figure 16-6

The competitive firm's supply curve

Figure 16-7

The industry supply curve

The individual firm's supply curve is given by the marginal cost curve, which is derived from the total cost curve of Figure 16-5. The industry supply curve is obtained by summing the individual firms' supply curves.

maximized at a point where the marginal cost of production is just equal to the price (= marginal revenue in perfect competition) that can be attained: $MC = MR$. To produce more would mean to incur higher costs than the additional revenue that will be received. To produce less means forgoing the additional profits that would result from selling a unit at a price that is higher than the marginal cost of producing it. Equilibrium is attained at the output level where the additional revenues received are just balanced by the additional costs incurred.

Given any market price, the perfectly competitive firm will produce the output at which that price is equal to the firm's marginal cost. Hence the marginal cost curve of the perfectly competitive firm is also its *supply curve* (see Figure 16-6).

Market supply

The short-run market supply curve (or industry supply curve) is obtained by adding the quantities supplied by all firms in the industry at each and every price. It is shown in Figure 16-7.

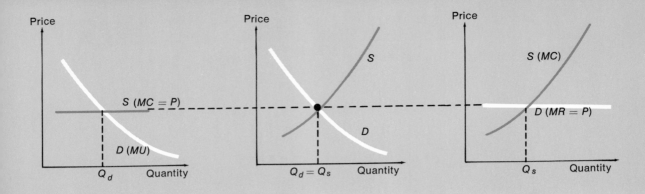

Figure 16-8

The individual buyer

Figure 16-9

The market

Figure 16-10

The individual seller

The individual buyer will purchase the quantity at which his demand and supply curves intersect ($MU = MC$). The individual seller will sell the quantity determined by his supply and demand curves ($MC = MR$). The market supply and demand curves determine the price.

Let us add that in the long run, when all inputs are variable and new firms can enter (or leave) the industry, the supply curve becomes more elastic. The longer the period of adjustment allowed, the more elastic the market supply curve for the whole industry is likely to be.

Perfect competition reviewed

Let us briefly review the model for a perfectly competitive market. We start with an individual consumer's marginal utility curve and derive his demand curve (Figure 16-8). Next, we aggregate the individual demand curves into the market demand curve (Figure 16-9).

From the individual firm's marginal cost curve we obtain its supply curve (Figure 16-10). By aggregating all supply curves of the firm in the industry, we derive the aggregate or market supply curve (Figure 16-9).

In the market, the intersection of the market supply and demand curves determine the market price of the product (Figure 16-9). Then, at this market price, individual consumers can buy *all* they want to buy: the market supply curve facing each individual consumer is perfectly elastic. The intersection of the consumer's demand curve (showing his MU's) and the supply curve (showing also the price and the marginal cost of the product to the consumer) determines the quantity he will purchase: $MU = MC$.

Similarly, the intersection of the individual firm's supply curve (based on its marginal cost curve) and the demand curve (equal to price or marginal revenue) determine the quantity supplied by the firm: $MC = MR$.

The intersection of the market supply and demand curves shows the total quantities of the good that will be supplied and demanded, i.e., exchanged at the market equilibrium price.

Monopolistic competition

Monopolistic competition is distinguished from perfect competition by *product differentiation*. Individual firms sell products that are not homogeneous but slightly different from each other.

The market demand curve is obtained in the usual manner by adding the individual consumers' demand curves (Figure 16-11). But

Figure 16-11

The industry demand curve

Figure 16-12

The individual monopolistic competitor

The individual, monopolistically competitive firm faces a demand curve that is much more elastic than the industry demand curve. The firm sets a price by charging a mark-up over MC at its most profitable output level ($MC = MR$).

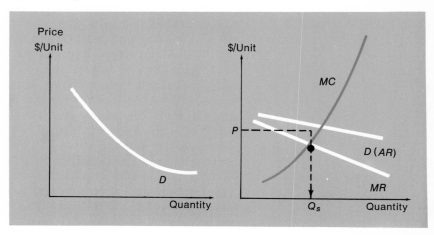

from the viewpoint of the individual firm, the demand curve looks much more elastic—because of the presence of many firms that sell close, but not perfect substitutes. If a firm were to raise the price of its product, the quantity of sales would diminish rapidly.

Due to the fact that the demand curve (AR) facing the firm slopes downward, its marginal revenue curve must lie below the demand curve. The firm determines its profit-maximizing output by equating MC and MR. Then it looks at its demand curve to find the price at which it can sell that output. The monopolistically competitive firm will sell its product at a mark-up above its marginal cost. This case is illustrated in Figure 16-11, which shows the market demand, and Figure 16-12, which shows the demand curve as seen from the viewpoint of the firm as well as its marginal cost curve.

Oligopoly

The distinguishing feature of an oligopolistic firm is its interdependence with the other firms in the industry. The actions of one firm have an influence on the other firms.

The market demand curve (Figure 16-13) is again obtained in the familiar manner by aggregating individual consumers' demand curves. For the individual oligopolist, the demand curve reflects the actions of his competition. If an oligopolist raises his price above the current market price, other firms are not likely to follow suit. Hence the price raiser will experience a sharp drop in sales as customers switch to competitors. The demand curve above the current market price as viewed from one firm's standpoint is likely to be highly elastic. Were an oligopolist to lower his price, his competitors would probably match this price cut. The oligopolist would not greatly increase his sales, and the demand curve is much less elastic than it would be if the competitors did not follow suit.

It follows that the demand curve—as viewed from the standpoint of an individual oligopolist—has a "kink" at the current market price (Figure 16-14). Above the kink, the demand curve is more elastic than below the kink. The kink comes about because of the varying assumptions made about the behavior of the firm's competitors.

Because the demand curve exhibits a kink, the corresponding marginal revenue curve will have a discontinuity where the kink occurs. Marginal revenue makes a discrete jump at that output level. If the firm's marginal cost curve intersects the marginal revenue curve in the region of this discontinuity, small changes in marginal

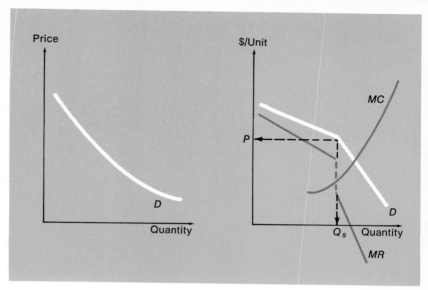

Figure 16-13

The industry demand curve

Figure 16-14

The individual oligopolist

The individual oligopolistic firm faces a demand curve that exhibits a kink at the going price and output quantity.

costs will not lead to a different price and output level. Oligopolistic prices have a tendency to be highly stable, because it is not in the interest of the oligopolist to react to every small cost change.

Monopoly

A monopolist is the only producer of a commodity that has no close substitutes. Hence he faces the total market demand curve for the product. The demand curve for the industry is identical with the one facing the monopolist. (The demand curves in Figures 16-15 and 16-16 are identical.)

The downward-sloping demand curve results in a marginal revenue curve below the demand curve. The monopolist will also follow the profit-maximizing rule of producing that output level at which his marginal costs are just balanced by the marginal revenues obtained. Then he looks at his demand curve and sets a price at which he can just sell the amount produced.

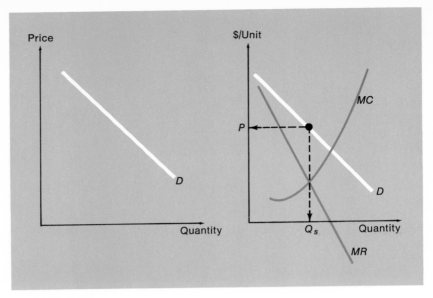

Figure 16-15

The industry demand curve

Figure 16-16

The monopolist

The monopolist faces the whole industry demand curve. His profit-maximizing output level is where MC = MR. Then he applies a mark-up to MC to find his optimal price.

Monopoly regulation

Because monopolists have the power to raise the price over the cost of production, it has been suggested that the government might want to step in and break up the monopoly in order to restore competition. This solution, however, has its drawbacks in declining-cost industries. In a declining-cost industry, the average cost of production declines. Hence one firm can produce a given output level at lower cost than two or three firms might be able to do. It would not be economical to break up such a monopoly. Instead, governmental regulation is often used as a substitute. In that case the government will regulate the prices that the monopolist can charge, determine his output level, or control his profits.

Spillover costs and benefits

Spillover costs occur when one economic unit imposes costs on other economic units. Similarly, spillover benefits present themselves when one economic unit's operation benefits other economic units. Because spillover effects are not accounted for through the operation of the market mechanism, they will lead to a misallocation of resources. Industries with spillover costs produce a larger than optimal output level. If all costs, including the spillover costs, were properly borne by the firm, it would produce less.

Whenever spillover effects occur, the private costs and benefits, which are the basis for the firm's decision making, are different from the social costs and benefits, which represent the costs or benefits to society as a whole. We may eliminate the distortions brought about by the divergence of private and social costs by imposing regulations, taxation of creators of spillover costs, subsidization of spillover benefit producers, or by merging the economic units that are subject to the spillover effects.

Public goods

There is one category of goods that is entirely "spillover." In these circumstances no one can be excluded from the benefits attributed to the good. It is in the self-interest of every individual economic unit to avoid payment for the good, while still being able to enjoy the benefits, from which no one can be excluded. In such circumstances, the government, acting as the agent of all society, has to provide the goods or services. Commodities falling into this category are referred to as *public goods*.

The optimal amount of public goods is provided when the marginal social costs of providing a public good are equal to the marginal social benefits associated with it ($MSC = MSB$). These in turn, should be equal to the marginal benefits that could be realized if the resources were to be used in the private sector instead.

Optimality

In an over-all optimal economic system, we find that each good or service is being produced up to the point at which the marginal social costs are equal to the marginal social benefits. If there are no spill-overs, the free market system will provide just that result, provided that no monopolistic elements are present. If either condition is violated, some regulation may be called for to bring about the socially optimal result. Finally, public goods are not provided by the private sector, and should be provided by the government up to the point at which the social marginal costs and benefits are equal to each other.

International trade

If we look at countries as a whole, we are able to derive a market supply and demand curve for each commodity. This enables us to determine the excess supplies or demands that will prevail for each commodity at various prices. If the country is able to trade with other countries, these excess supply and demand curves show the quantities that the country is willing to export and import at the various prices. The intersection of the export supply (demand) curve of one country and the excess demand (supply) curve for the other country determines the international market price of the commodity and the amount traded.

Among the governmental interferences with free international trade, *tariffs* are among the most important policy instruments. Countries that have a certain degree of monopoly power in international trade may exploit this monopoly power by levying a tariff. The price of the commodity in home markets (including the tariff) will generally increase, while the price paid to the foreign producer will decrease. It is this latter price that is important from the viewpoint of the country as a whole. The tariffs collected go first to the government and may be either redistributed as lump-sum payments to the population or used to reduce taxes. The optimal tariff is similar to the mark-up charged by a monopolist.

Tariffs are sometimes advocated for newly established, so-called infant industries. In that case, the tariffs should be imposed for a limited time period only, so that the newly established industry is able to grow up and become competitive in world markets.

The aggregate system

We have looked at the operation of the individual components of the economic system. Now it is time to analyze the economic system as a whole. We can differentiate four main sectors: households, firms, the government, and the foreign sector.

The total output produced by all four sectors together is the national product. The total income derived from this productive activity is the national income. If all resources are fully employed in their best possible use, the economy attains the *maximum potential income and product.*

The maximum output level or potential national product is determined by (a) the volume of available resources and (b) the available technology. Increases in the available resources, such as land, labor, and capital, shift the potential output level upwards. But for actual output to keep in step with the increases in potential output, aggregate expenditures must expand simultaneously.

Aggregate expenditures are composed of consumption, investment, governmental purchases, and net foreign demand as shown in Figure 16-17. Together, they determine the equilibrium level of national income and product. If equilibrium GNP is just equal to the potential GNP of which the economy is capable, the economy will experience full employment without inflation.

If equilibrium national income is below full-employment national income, underutilization of resources will result. If equilibrium na-

Figure 16-17

Aggregate equilibrium *The economy as a whole is in equilibrium where aggregate expenditures are equal to national income. Aggregate expenditures are composed of consumption (C), investment (I), governmental (G), and net foreign (X) expenditures.*

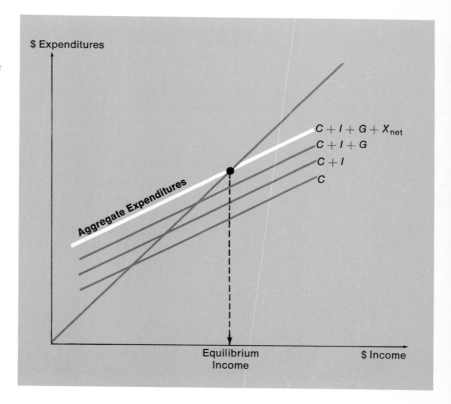

tional income exceeds the potential the economy is capable of producing, inflation will result. Because of the likelihood that different sectors of the economy will not reach the full-employment level at the same moment, inflationary pressures may make themselves felt already at a time when other sectors are still experiencing underemployment of resources. This is the case of the so-called bottleneck inflation.

Aggregate consumption

Turning to the individual sectors, we find that aggregate consumption is mainly a function of personal income. As income increases, so do personal consumption expenditures. The change in consumption that accompanies a change in income is called the marginal propensity to consume. Amounts not consumed are saved, and hence the marginal propensity to consume plus the marginal propensity to save must always add up to one. Historically, aggregate consumption has been a very stable function of income.

Investment

Investment in new plants, equipment, buildings, and the like has been a much more unstable component of national income. Investment increases rapidly when the business outlook is good and quick profits are expected. When new innovations occur, the rate of investment activity is likely to increase sharply. Also, when interest rates and therefore borrowing costs are down, investments become more attractive to businessmen. Consequently, investment tends to be a rather volatile component of national income and product.

Because the private sector of the domestic economy may generate ups and downs in the level of economic activity, it is up to the government to act as a stabilizer. It does this by engaging in fiscal and monetary policy.

Fiscal policy

The government may use its expenditures and powers of taxation to achieve the triple goals of full resource utilization, a stable price level, and a high growth rate.

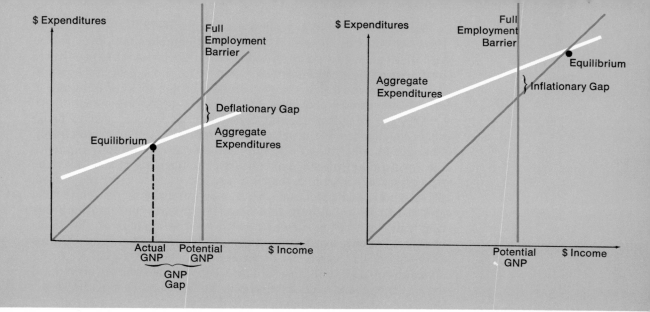

Figure 16-18

An unemployment situation

*If equilibrium GNP is below
potential full-employment
GNP, a GNP gap exists.
The GNP gap may be closed
by increasing aggregate
expenditures by the amount
of the deflationary gap in
Figure 16-18. Conversely,
if equilibrium GNP is
above the potential GNP, a
decrease in aggregate
expenditures equal to the
inflationary gap will
eliminate the inflationary
pressures.*

Figure 16-19

An inflationary situation

We stated that the difference between the actual and the potential
national income is a measure for the extent to which resources are
underutilized in the economy, or of the inflationary pressures that
make themselves felt. If the government wishes to remedy the
deflationary or inflationary situation, it has to decide by how much
to increase or decrease government spending—if it is decided that
a change in governmental spending is the proper way of eliminating
the discrepancy. Figure 16-18 shows a situation where the actual
national income is below the potential national income. Hence there
exists a GNP gap. How much of an increase in governmental expenditures is required to fill this GNP gap depends on the economy's
marginal propensity to engage in new expenditures, or the slope of
the aggregate expenditure curve. The deflationary gap is measured
at the full-employment level of income and it shows by how much
the nation's expenditures at the full-employment level (if it were
attained) fall short of the potential GNP. If the government engages
in additional expenditures equal to that amount, the deflationary gap
will be closed. Successive spending rounds will lead to a total national
income increase which is a multiple of the increase in government
spending. The size of the deflationary gap—measured at full employment—gives the required change in government expenditures
to bring about full employment.

Fiscal policy □ **287**

The reverse situation is shown in Figure 16-19. Here the equilibrium national income level is above the full-employment level. Hence an inflationary gap exists. A reduction of government expenditures by the amount of the inflationary gap shifts the aggregate expenditure curve downward by that amount and brings about an elimination of the inflationary pressures due to excess aggregate demand.

Changes in governmental taxation may also be used to bring about an equality of the actual and potential national income levels. Changes in government taxation, however, do not directly influence the level of aggregate expenditures. Instead, they will shift the private sector's aggregate expenditure curves. If taxes are increased, private individuals will have less money left from any given income and will therefore also consume less. The private consumption function will not shift downward by the whole amount of the taxes imposed, but only by the amount by which consumption expenditures are reduced. The remainder of the tax comes out of savings. To bring about an equal shift of the aggregate demand curve via governmental expenditure changes or tax changes, the tax changes must be larger than the expenditure changes.

Finally, we should note that the way in which the governmental stabilization program is undertaken has effects on the size of the public sector and the size of the national debt. Increases in governmental expenditures (other things being equal) will increase the size of the public sector and also the national debt. Whether an increase in the size of the public sector is beneficial or not depends largely on whether the marginal social benefits of public expenditures are greater or smaller than those of private expenditures. Whether a change in the size of the national debt imposes a burden on present and/or future generations depends on the state of the economy at the time of the debt-increasing expenditures, the rate of return realized on the public investment project, and the time pattern of the expected benefit streams.

Monetary policy

The monetary authorities of a country—in the United States the Board of Governors of the Federal Reserve System—can control certain monetary magnitudes that have an influence on the rate of economic activity in a country.

Individual economic units have a demand for money for transaction, precautionary, and speculative motives. Money increases the ease with which transactions can be conducted, it can be used as a highly liquid store of value for use in case of unexpected payments, and it may serve as a convenient hedge against loss in value assets whose prices fluctuate.

The nation's money supply is regulated by the Federal Reserve, which has three main control instruments at its disposal. (1) The Federal Reserve may engage in *open-market operations*, i.e., purchases and sales of securities. By buying or selling these securities for cash, the quantity of money is altered. (2) The Federal Reserve may change the *legal reserves* that commercial banks must hold against outstanding demand-deposit liabilities, thereby influencing the amount the commercial banks are able to lend out, and the amount of additional money creation that the commercial banks as a group are able to engage in. (3) The Federal Reserve sets the discount rate, that is, the rate that banks have to pay for the privilege of borrowing funds from the Federal Reserve. At a high discount rate, banks are presumably more reluctant to borrow funds from the Federal Reserve, and again the money supply will be influenced.

Changes in the nation's money supply have an influence on the prevailing rate of interest. The interest rate is the "price" that lenders charge borrowers for the use of their funds. Both changes in the demand for and the supply of money have repercussions on the interest rate. The interest rate, in turn, has an influence on the rate of economic activity—especially new investment, and if the interest rate is low, more investments are profitable than is the case at a high interest rate. Also, consumers who purchase houses, cars, TV sets, and other durables on credit will be influenced by the rate of interest in their purchase decision. The same is true for state and local governments, which rely upon bond issues to finance their expenditures. The lower the rate of interest, the more of an expansionary stimulus is given to the rate of economic activity. Conversely, a high rate of interest generally represents a retarding influence on the rate of economic activity.

The balance of payments

All international transactions are recorded in the balance of payments. International transactions give rise to a supply of and demand for foreign currency. When we pay a foreigner, we have to make payment in foreign currency or the recipient has to go to his own bank and exchange the United States dollars for his own currency. In both cases a demand for foreign currency results. Conversely, foreign purchases in this country lead to a supply of foreign currency.

The supply and demand for foreign currency determines its dollar price—generally called the exchange rate.

If the exchange rate is left free to adjust to market forces, the quantity of foreign currency demanded will always be equal to the quantity of foreign currency supplied. The balance of payments will always be in balance in these circumstances. Surpluses or shortages of foreign exchange cannot develop.

But in many economies, the government has taken on the obligation to keep the exchange rate stable, in order to facilitate international trade and finance. If the exchange rate is fixed as a matter of policy, other means of adjustment have to be found. One alternative is to let prices and wages fluctuate in response to changes in the international sector. But given the fact that most prices are relatively inflexible in the downward direction, this method of adjustment is no viable alternative for deficit countries.

Another alternative consists in the deliberate creation of *income changes* at home in order to eliminate excess demand for foreign exchange at the going exchange rate. Clearly, this may be a very costly and probably unpopular policy to pursue.

Finally, the government may elect to finance the excess demand for foreign exchange by supplying the amount of the shortage out of its own international reserves. Most governments hold a stock of international reserves precisely for this purpose. International reserves consist of gold, foreign exchange reserves, and resources available through the International Monetary Fund. All these resources are readily available to the government in case an excess demand for foreign currency occurs, and if its international reserves are sufficient, the government can avoid the costs of price or income adjustments for a certain time period.

A final word

We have studied the operation of the economic system in some detail, but obviously it has only been a first glimpse of some of the economic problems that exist. Many economic problems have hardly been touched upon, but we have provided a basic framework within which most economic problems may be analyzed. Once we understand the basic framework, the mastery of more complicated problems is not all that difficult.

The basic economic system developed here has four sectors: households, firms, the government, and the foreign sector. We have studied the operations of each on the micro level of individual economic units. We also looked at the aggregate implications of the individual economic actions—i.e., the economic system as a whole.

While the basic economic problem is caused by the relative scarcity of resources that are available to satisfy our economic wants, we have paid much attention to the role of an efficient and full use of all the resources at our disposal.

As the title of the book implies, we have dealt only with the *economic* aspects of human behavior. To get a full understanding of all human behavior, we must widen our scope and include other social sciences such as psychology, sociology, and political science. And to understand the whole world we live in, the circle must be drawn wider still so as to encompass the biological and physical sciences. But the times in which one man could hope to know all about everything that was known to science are long gone, and specialization among scientists has led to a fragmentation of human knowledge. Hence we should never forget the fact that the economic system is only a small subsystem that deals with a limited—although important—part of the whole world we live in.

Index

THE ECONOMIC SYSTEM

By H. Robert Heller, University of Hawaii

"This book provides the student with a basic tool kit for the analysis of economic problems. Leaving aside institutional, historical, and descriptive detail, the emphasis is on analysis. The tools of economic analysis, which are often scattered and fragmented throughout voluminous textbooks, are presented in a succinct, clear, and comprehensive fashion. In the first half, the text studies the basic components of the economic system from a micro-economic viewpoint. In the second half, the interaction between these components and the aggregate implications of economic behavior are developed."

—from the *Preface*

THE MACMILLAN COMPANY, 866 Third Avenue, New York 10022

72 220M P 70 I 3173

35345

Cover design: Don Crews

3 5282 00355 4725